Study Skills for Town and Country Planning

Study Skills for Town and Country Planning

Adam Sheppard and Nick Smith

Los Angeles | London | New Delhi
Singapore | Washington DC

Los Angeles | London | New Delhi
Singapore | Washington DC

SAGE Publications Ltd
1 Oliver's Yard
55 City Road
London EC1Y 1SP

SAGE Publications Inc.
2455 Teller Road
Thousand Oaks, California 91320

SAGE Publications India Pvt Ltd
B 1/I 1 Mohan Cooperative Industrial Area
Mathura Road
New Delhi 110 044

SAGE Publications Asia-Pacific Pte Ltd
3 Church Street
#10-04 Samsung Hub
Singapore 049483

Editor: Robert Rojek
Editorial assistant: Keri Dickens
Production editor: Katherine Haw
Copyeditor: Kate Harrison
Proofreader: Avril Ehrlich
Marketing manager: Michael Ainsley
Cover design: Lisa Harper
Typeset by: C&M Digitals (P) Ltd, Chennai, India
Printed by: Replika Press Pvt. Ltd, India

© Adam Sheppard and Nick Smith 2014

First published 2014

Library of Congress Control Number: 2013931186

British Library Cataloguing in Publication data

A catalogue record for this book is available from
the British Library

ISBN 978-1-4462-4968-0
ISBN 978-1-4462-4969-7 (pbk)

Contents

Preface

Numerous books exist that consider town and country planning from an academic and/or practice perspective, but few consider how it is studied. The aim of this text is to provide an effective introduction to the essential university study skills associated with town and country planning. The text is interspersed with activities, tips, definitions and further reading to help the reader develop their skills and understanding, and to support onward learning. The book will support those intending to study, or already studying for, a degree or high qualification in town and country planning and associated built environment fields such as architecture, geography, urban studies, housing, property development, construction and surveying.

Acknowledgements

For our family, friends and colleagues, whose love and support have been, and continue to be, invaluable.

List of Boxes

List of Figures

List of Tables

About the Authors

Adam Sheppard Adam joined the University of the West of England, Bristol as a lecturer in 2007 from planning practice. Adam previously worked in Essex, South Gloucestershire and the Bristol urban fringe, and Herefordshire as a Local Planning Authority development management officer. He has been involved in a diverse range of planning projects at varying scales and degrees of complexity. Adam has worked in both the rural and urban context and has experience across the planning spectrum, from green belt areas and open countryside to city centre redevelopment projects. Adam has research interests in planning implementation, history, law and the decision-making process, and teaches to undergraduate and postgraduate students, and on professional practice short courses.

Nick Smith Nick joined the University of the West of England, Bristol in 2007 following six years in private practice. During this time he was involved with a variety of projects for both public and private clients. He now leads the department's undergraduate programme in town and country planning and has research and teaching interests in strategic planning, the planning and delivery of infrastructure, planning history and regeneration. He is a chartered member of the Royal Town Planning Institute and a member of the Town and Country Planning Association. He chairs the RTPI South West in 2013.

Part one

Studying in Higher Education

1

Town Planning and Society

Aims

To explore the historical evolution of town and country planning in the UK and to identify the role of planners in shaping the places we live in.

Learning outcomes

After reading this chapter you will:

- understand the origins and development of town and country planning in the UK
- recognise the importance of planning to the management of the built and natural environment
- appreciate the role and importance of planners in society.

Introduction

The Royal Town Planning Institute (RTPI), the organisation which represents the planning profession, state that "planning involves twin activities – the management of the competing uses for space, and the making of places that are valued and have identity" (RTPI, 2012a). This goes some way to identifying the breadth of 'planning' and it is of note that unlike many other subjects, the content of your course will have both theoretical elements and practice orientated aspects. Studying town and country planning at university therefore means engaging with both an academic subject and a professional discipline.

tip

Although we have used the term 'town and country planning' and 'planning' interchangeably throughout this book, the reality is that a range of terms are used to explain the activity. University courses are labelled in a variety of ways but their content is typically quite similar as we explain later on. With regards to those practising planning, we use the general term 'planner' but again a variety of titles are used in reality.

Planning is a dynamic, challenging and fast-changing subject area, and the profession involves a diverse range of interesting and challenging careers. In your studies you will not just learn about planning and the profession today; to truly understand planning demands an appreciation of the past and the evolution of the art and science of the activity into its current form.

Origins and history

It is easy to think of town and country planning as a relatively modern phenomenon. The modern planning *system* that now operates in the UK can trace its origins directly to the early 1900s and the emergence of public health-focused planning legislation, but regulations which existed to manage places and spaces can be traced back to the Medieval period, and the idea of planned places can be traced back to the ancient world.

The earliest settlements were not planned in the same manner that urban areas are planned today, but that does not mean that planning did not take place when they were created. Important factors like the need to have access to clean water and land suitable for farming would have been foremost in the minds of the community group, as would the need to consider defence, flooding risk and the availability of potential building materials, food supplies and so forth. Where a town was positioned would therefore have been a considered and thought-out matter. Similarly, the layout of the actual settlement would have been undertaken with regards to uses, religion and societal hierarchies and relationships.

The extent to which the earliest settlements were consciously 'planned' will have varied considerably, but there is evidence of 'town planning' dating back to the Egyptians and we can certainly see planned settlements from the classical Greek period. Many ideas and philosophies can trace their origins to the Greeks, and this includes theories and concepts for town planning. Greek settlement plans can be found which are clearly laid out having regard to the physical geography of the area, and most demonstrate elements of the grid pattern arrangements many people now associate with the United States of America. An important point here is the difference between *planning*, and the *planning system*. The *planning system* is a fairly recent phenomenon, but humankind has *planned* since the earliest settlements were created. This history is important and as a planner understanding settlement patterns, morphology, growth, systems and networks and the historical evolution of a place is hugely important.

Activity

Take the opportunity to learn about the town or city where you live, or near where you live. Consider:

1. How the settlement has changed over time; where is the oldest part? How has it grown? Is much of the history still visible from the buildings and layout?
2. What type of settlement is it? Is it an important retail centre for the wider area? Are there a lot of industrial uses? Or office buildings? Is there a dominant employer like the military? Or a large factory?
3. Can you find out why the settlement is where it is? Was it an important river crossing? Or a port? Did it grow because of a particular industry like coal mining? Or has it grown as a 'commuter town' because of the influence of a nearby major city or access to good transport links like the railways?
4. Can you map out the key periods of growth? Did it grow quickly during the industrial revolution? Was there a period of growth following a particular event, such as the end of the Second World War? Has there been recent growth? And is more growth planned?

Understanding the history and change that has taken place in an area is vitally important to the art and science of town planning. This understanding, together with an appreciation of the current pressures and demands facing the area and its population, helps us to create plans for the future; to help protect what needs to be protected and support growth and change where this is appropriate.

The idea of regulatory control is also not a new one. Although legislation requiring the creation of *plans* to guide development in a given area is relatively new, the use of legal controls to manage the built and natural environment can trace its origins back almost as far as the early evidence of planning activity through very simple laws relating to construction. In the UK, evidence can be found of construction laws dating back to medieval times. Although evidence suggests that even earlier controls existed in London, the Assize of Nuisance in 1275 can certainly be highlighted as one of the earliest forms of control over buildings. This introduced various controls that are akin to basic building regulations and arguably all modern systems of control over the built environment, from planning through building regulations to environmental health legislation, can trace its history back to this point (Booth, 2003).

From the Assize of Nuisance we can see the evolution of control, with further mechanisms introduced to regulate construction standards, layouts, fire prevention, public health and neighbour nuisance. This was not just a case of strengthening control though; some important changes took place to which planning today owes much. For example, Elizabeth I introduced systems to manage the growth of London, while James I and Charles I both created controls that influenced the use of resources, material and appearance. From these origins we can draw parallels to modern planning and its policies to deliver well-designed, sustainable development (Booth, 2003).

In the nineteenth century, public health acts and local government legislation, and then the creation of bylaws, developed. These changes were in response to the challenges associated with the massive growth and change seen during the industrial revolution and by the early 1900s legislation required the preparation and approval of plans for new housing growth, and stricter standards in construction, design and layout of new development. The culmination of this period of evolution in the system of development management effectively occurred immediately after the Second World War.

Before and during the Second World War, even while the bombs were still falling on London, research was being undertaken into how the UK would emerge from the war. Evidence highlighted the need for large scale reconstruction, but also a change in the way spaces and places were managed to respond to the social and economic changes occurring across the country. In 1947 a Town and Country Planning Act was published and the system we have today still works in the same basic way. From this point forward *control* (not ownership) of land was nationalised plans were required to manage town and country, and permission was required to undertake all new development.

Globally, the development of systems to enable town and country planning have evolved at different rates and the legal systems that have emerged do vary, but the fundamental principles, approaches and theories transcend borders across the UK and the wider world.

 **tip**

From the very start of your studies you should familiarise yourself with the historical evolution of the modern planning system. It is only by understanding the past that we can truly understand how things work in the present, and plan for the future. There is a grouped list of further reading at the back of this book.

Town planning today

As you undertake your studies at university you will learn about the theories and principles behind town and country planning. The skills of good planning are international, but if you pursue a career in planning, or work within a related field, you will find yourself working within an organised system of regulations and legislation, processes and procedures. The world of planning is also occupied by a hugely varied and complex network of organisations and groups from the private, public and voluntary sectors. It is through these systems, networks, people and organisations that planning is facilitated and, although it may all seem a little overwhelming at first glance, few other subject areas and professions offers the range of opportunities that planning does. Understanding this intricate environment is therefore important whether you intend to work as a planner, with planners, or in a related field.

Town and country planning and the planning system

An important point to first emphasise is the difference between planning and the planning system. When 'planning' is discussed in the media it is often in relation to the systems that exist to enable the practise of planning. For example, the process that people go through to get permission to undertake development, or the procedure involved in producing a plan for a given area. At university you will be studying the practise of planning, the art and science of the activity; this is the dynamic, exciting and challenging world of places and spaces, urban and rural landscapes, regeneration, growth, heritage and environmental protection, sustainability and, above all, managing change. This field area requires people and organisations, but it also requires systems. A legal framework, a process, a system; these are all things that are required to *facilitate* and *enable* planning. They are not the essence of planning, but they are the mechanisms that allow planning to take place.

Town planning people

Town planning as a profession, as opposed to an activity, is a relatively recent phenomenon in the sense that it is only really since the early 1900s that planners have been recognised as a distinct group of professionals, distinct from architects, surveyors and engineers. As you will have realised from the earlier sections of this chapter, individuals have participated in town planning for centuries, but the evolution of the art and science of the act of planning

7

into a profession occurred in parallel with the emergence of the *systems* of planning from their health and building regulation origins.

Today, planners operate in multiple arenas and can be found in the private, public and third sectors working in a range of areas from housing to retail, transport to heritage and conservation, and regeneration to law. Some planners will work in the various tiers of government; others will operate in the private sector for planning or multi-disciplinary consultancies. Career opportunities are therefore wide ranging and diverse. Importantly, it should also be remembered that planning as an activity is also undertaken by 'non-professionals', with politicians, interest groups and community organisations either interacting with the system, or undertaking planning activities directly. Some will employ professionals to support them with their interactions with the system. Finally, there are academic planners such as those you will encounter at university. Some of these will have come from practice, others through an educational routeway via a Doctorate. You will find in your university, as in practice, that the staff will have diverse backgrounds, specialisms and interests.

The term 'town planner' is therefore something of a dynamic term since, unlike architects who can only refer to themselves as such if recognised by their professional body, an individual can call themselves a 'town planner'

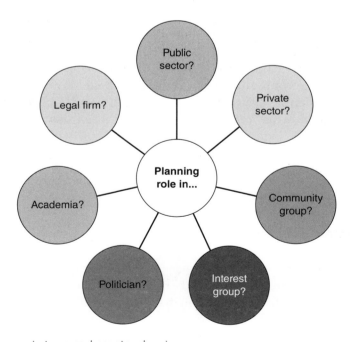

FIGURE 1.1   Careers in town and country planning

but not be an accredited professional recognised by the RTPI. Moreover, a person may be involved in town planning, but not be a town planner.

The variety of roles and the range of opportunities that exist within the field of town planning can be considered in the section below, but is also explored more fully in the final chapter of this book.

The organisations

Individuals and organisations operate at various different levels and in various different sectors. All of these interact throughout the development process.

A prominent feature of all planning systems across the world is that of a role for government. Although the extent of involvement and the manner in which it is executed will vary considerably, almost all nations operate on the basis of state management of space to some degree.

Globally, a number of different approaches to managing development and property rights exist. As a student you will explore many of these. You will learn about the differences between zoned systems of planning, where legally binding plans are created against which development must comply, to the discretionary systems where plans provide a framework to inform individual decisions. Each approach has advantages and challenges, and there is no right way to do it. At university you will begin to understand these different approaches and what we can learn from them.

To give an example of the complexity of the approaches that can be found, this book will briefly present the system in the UK. If you are studying in the UK you will likely find that much of your work at university will be presented and discussed having regard to the systems and approaches found in England, Scotland, Wales and Northern Ireland. That said, comparative planning on a global scale will be a key feature throughout your studies.

In the UK, the state functions at different levels and at each level a number of organisations operate. Planning functions similarly operate and exist at different levels of government, with a diverse range of people and organisations all working together to plan and manage change.

The most strategic level of government is the national government of the UK, based in Westminster. In relation to planning however, most of the national level power is found at the 'home nation' level, i.e. England, Scotland, Wales and Northern Ireland. To ensure effective and efficient operations, the national governments across the UK (and internationally) have departments which look after different areas of work, one of which will include planning. This department will set the guiding policies to manage change, protect and conserve, and encourage economic and physical growth. The national government will also set the legislation and regulation that provide the framework for the creation of plans with which change is managed, and specify the legal requirements and definitions in relation to development proposals. It is worth bearing in mind at this point that more than one department will be involved in some way in planning matters. For example the historic and natural environment, highways and economic growth will all be managed to varying degrees by departments other than the one primarily responsible for planning; as you will discover later in this book, effective working relationships between people and organisations are extremely important in planning because most matters will involve individuals and permissions from different departments or organisations.

In addition to the government departments, a range of national level executive agencies and QUANGOs (quasi-autonomous non-governmental organisations) exist to deliver functions and services. These are organisations which have varying degrees of separation from government departments and operate with some degree of independence. They all ultimately remain answerable to government however to some degree. These organisations normally exist to deliver certain management responsibilities for the government, examples of which would include the Environment Agency and the Highways Agency. A number of these organisations have a role in planning and often employ planners in specialist roles. Some will play more significant roles in planning than others, for example the Planning Inspectorate has a significant involvement in policy guidance and decision-making in England and Wales and only works in the field of planning, whereas the Ministry of Defence clearly has other areas of focus, but will nevertheless engage with the planning system in various ways as a consultee, developer, or land owner/manager.

Below this national level things become a little complicated in England and a greater degree of variation exists between the 'home nations'. Between the national and the local level there is a regional or sub-regional approach to governance and strategic organisation and delivery, but the precise nature of these varies. In Wales, for example, there is a regional approach to coordinate waste planning and the idea of city regions is gaining traction too. In Scotland, a regional approach is used for matters such as transport planning. In addition, sub-regions exist in Scotland around the major urban areas for strategic planning activities. Northern Ireland takes a similar approach, with strategic matters such as waste and transport planning being managed through a regional system. This activity is not, however, undertaken through regional government; rather there is a collaborative approach between the local authorities within the identified area in partnership with the national government. England used to have a complex system of regional bodies, with three different organisations responsible for different areas of regional planning and development. This system was dismantled however with the formation of the Conservative Party and Liberal Democrat Party coalition government in 2010. Now organisations called 'Local Enterprise Partnerships' exist as the sub-regional level, focusing on economic development. In addition, many areas have sub-regional bodies for other forms of partnership working – including economic growth, waste and transport planning – and strategic spatial planning activities are managed through organisations formed of groups of local authorities, as is found in the home nations. This mainly occurs around major urban areas, conurbations, or the old traditional 'counties' where there is arguably an increased need for strategic planning and delivery.

The regional tier demonstrates the diverse range of approaches that can be taken in relation to the organisational arrangements for government, and this is further highlighted at the local level. Wales and Scotland have a relatively simple system with a single tier of local authority, and Northern Ireland has parallels with this approach in some respects, although the scale and history of this area makes for some notable differences. England, however, is again somewhat troublesome having a single tier of local authority in some areas, but two tiers in others. The single-tier authorities manage all local council services, whereas the two-tier areas split responsibility between them based upon whether the service area is more strategic (i.e. minerals, waste and transport planning) or local (wider planning functions to manage development).

Below the local level, a further tier of public authority exists consisting of Community Councils in Wales and Scotland, or Parish Councils in England. This tier of sub-local authority is important, but it has relatively limited powers compared to the local authority. The powers also vary based upon history, population numbers and so forth, sometimes even between neighbouring areas. The coverage of Parish Councils in England is not universal, with large urban centres often not having such a tier. In some cases, for some planning purposes, a Neighbourhood Forum will exist in the areas without a Parish Council, but these are somewhat different in relation to their structure, roles and responsibilities.

The public sector is only one part of planning though. In addition, the private and third (or voluntary) sectors are hugely important.

Private sector planning consultancies represent their clients' interests, effectively acting on their behalf within the systems of planning. In the private sector you may find yourself working as a town planner within the organisation of a house-builder or national retailer. However, you may also work as a planning consultant, effectively working for a range of clients to ensure their interests and intentions are suitably addressed through the planning system. The private sector often provides support to the public sector, particularly in the delivery of specialised services. Consultancies vary significantly in size, from very small local businesses to huge international organisations that operate around the world. The nature of the organisations varies considerably too, with some being very specialised in certain areas of planning work. The private sector also includes universities, and planning lawyers who play an important role in shaping and informing decisions.

The third sector is a diverse group of organisation which range from charities to voluntary groups. These organisations play a hugely important role in planning, representing planning professionals (the Royal Town Planning Institute), interests (such as the Town and Country Planning Association, Campaign to Protect Rural England, the National Trust, the Royal Society for the Protection of Birds), or frontline community organisations (such as community transport services, support for the elderly, church groups, youth groups). All of these organisations play a significant role within planning and, although they will interact with the systems of planning in different ways and at different points, they all have a key part to play. Significantly

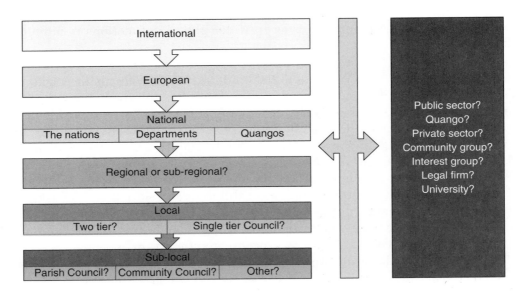

FIGURE 1.2   The hierarchy and organisation of town and country planning

these organisations often represent the views of local communities and groups of society.

Internationally, organisational approaches do vary significantly. Some countries will have stronger and more influential tiers of government; others operate in a manner which provides for a greater role for the private sector. During your studies you will not only learn about planning in the UK, you will also explore other systems from around the world. This is important for academic reasons because it will allow you to consider theories of planning and the different approaches that exist and the basis and merits of this, but it will also be important for your professional future. You may find yourself working overseas, or you could be working for a company that has operations in a number of countries. Of course, you may be an international student studying in the UK; in this case you may not study the system of your own country, but you will develop an understanding of the different approaches that exist internationally, allowing you and everyone else on your course to practice the art of planning anywhere in the world, albeit you may need to read up a little on the precise details of your system!

It is important for you to understand this complex web of public, private and third sector organisations, for it is these bodies which manage the systems for planning.

Activity

For the area that you live or study in the UK, try to identify the structure of government:

1. Can you find evidence of national organisations operating in your local area?
2. Is there a regional or sub-regional organisation you can identify? What is their role?
3. Do you live in an area with a single-tier local authority? Or two tiers?
4. Do you live in an area with a Parish or Community Council? Or is there a Neighbourhood Forum instead? Perhaps there is no sub-local tier at all?
5. Can you find any evidence of planning consultancies in your area?
6. What is your community organisational infrastructure like? Is there a 'Community/ Voluntary Action' group for example?

Understanding the network of organisations is important to your understanding of how the planning system works in the sense of who is doing what. You could find yourself working in any of these areas, or indeed for an organisation which needs to interact and engage with planning. How well these organisations work together is essential to the effectiveness and success of the planning outcomes locally and nationally

The law

The law plays an important part in town and country planning. Across the world, system variations do exist but legislation, regulation and court decisions provide the legal framework with which the planning system operates. It is through this framework that planning is enabled.

The ability to create and implement plans is enshrined in law, as are the processes and mechanisms involved in their creation and adoption. The purpose, scope and implementation of plans are all guided by legislation and policy, and the decisions made on the nature of these plans, and the subsequent decisions made having regard to these plans and other factors, are all influenced by planning law. The system of plans has evolved over the course of the last century, but the approach today remains based around the principles of planning for, and managing, change and balancing competing interests in land.

A further important consideration to identify is the fact that it is through the law that we establish what falls under the control of the planning application system, and what falls beyond its influence. The manner in which this is defined will vary between nations but in the UK, legislation specifies that planning permission is required for the 'development' of land. Development is subsequently defined as building, mining, engineering and other operations in, on, over or under the land, or a material change of use of land or buildings. Each element of this definition has been further defined through legislation and the decision made in the courts. Through this we are able to identify what requires planning permission and therefore what may be managed through the planning system. During your course you will study the law and its importance. You will also learn about its complexity and, importantly, its limitations.

Although planning law provides the parameters and framework to facilitate a functioning planning system, it is essential that the art and science of planning is not limited to the scope of this structural concept. Town and country planning actually goes beyond this framework because of the inter-relationship of planning with other areas, such as health and economic development. Planning therefore operates outside of its structured framework in a conceptual sense, with the system then attempting to respond to the desire to create a holistic approach to physical, environmental and social sustainable development.

The system

The planning 'system' is a term applied to the activitie of planning. These can broadly be divided into two identifiable, but inter-related areas. The first of these is plan-making and policy, the second is development management.

In different parts of the world, different system approaches exist in relation to town and country planning. The most common family of approaches is often referred to as the 'zoned' system of planning. This system operates on the basis of detailed and binding plans and policies which, once adopted, must be adhered to. This is a rigid system in some respects, but the nature of the plans is such that they can provide certainty and flexibility within set parameters. The other main system in operation is the 'discretionary' system. The discretionary system also starts with the creation and adoption of a plan, but it is not completely binding upon subsequent decisions. Instead, a planning application decision may be taken contrary to the plan where entirely justifiable in the context of other policy or external factors. The UK has a discretionary system; in part this is because the legal system is not based upon the codified legal system as is found in much of Europe, but on common law. That said, the two do not automatically sit together; a zoned system can exist in a country with a predominantly common law legal system, such as would be found in part in the US. The discretionary approach offers the benefit of greater flexibility on core matters, but it can reduce certainty and can involve more extensive controls and, arguably, bureaucracy. You will explore both systems of law and planning approaches in your studies at university.

In the UK, plans are informed by, and their creation supported by, planning policies and legislation. As with the organisational structures, the framework of plans and policies varies between the home nations. There is, however, a common theme in that all of the home nations provide national level policy statements and guidance which provide national direction and inform the creation of plans and policies at the lower levels. The arrangement of this documentation is based around themes, so for example, policy guidance is provided to cover areas such as housing, economic development, heritage management, telecommunications, transport and so forth.

The form of this guidance changes with time. While policy in England has traditionally been presented in separate statements since the late 1980s, guidance has recently been consolidated into a single document. This is known as the *National Planning Policy Framework* (NPPF) (CLG, 2012). The equivalent in Wales is *Planning Policy Wales* (WAG, 2012), in Scotland Planning Policy (Scottish Government, 2010), and in Northern Ireland Planning Policy Statements (various dates). These policy statements are also backed up by a range of documents that may be called advice notes, supplementary planning document or similar.

In some instances, the power to influence and take decisions on planning matters is also held at the national level. For example, in England and Wales specific policy exists to direct major infrastructure proposals. Decisions on such proposals are then also taken by a governmental organisation at the national level.

It is important to mention at this point that national governments are not actually the highest level of responsible authority when it comes to planning. Internationally, United Nations designated World Heritage Sites (such as Stonehenge and Bath) and the RAMSAR wetlands areas are examples of supranational activity that impacts upon planning. Similarly, a considerable amount of activity with a planning focus occurs at the European level. Strategic planning in relation to transport and the environment is common, and a number of wildlife protection tools are based upon European legislation. The planning activity in the UK, however, takes place at the national level and below.

One significant difference between England, Northern Ireland, Wales and Scotland is the presence of a 'national plan'. Wales and Scotland both have what could be considered to be 'national plans' where the strategic direction of the nation is presented. England, by contrast, has no such plan, instead relying upon legislation and policy to guide planning activity in all matters beyond major infrastructure. In Northern Ireland, a Regional Development Strategy exists to provide a strategic and long-term direction for the future of Northern Ireland.

As discussed in the 'organisations' section of this chapter, the regional and sub-regional structure in the UK is somewhat complex and this was also the case for the systems of planning in England prior to the abolition of the regional tier of government. Today, regional and sub-regional planning activity is broadly focused around organisational partnerships, policies and plans to manage strategic matters such as housing, waste, minerals and transport, as well as, in the case of England, strategic partnerships between the public and private sectors in the area of economic development. This is still a relatively complex web of relationships and interactions and the nature and existence of regional planning in England particularly remains an area of much academic and professional debate and research. During your studies you will undoubtedly consider this debate, and the strong regional systems of government found in countries elsewhere, such as in Germany, provide for an interesting comparison.

Although planning legislation and strategic policy/plan guidance in the UK is created in London, Edinburgh, Belfast and Cardiff, it is at the local level where much, if not the majority, of planning activity occurs. Regardless of the structure of local government in the area in question, or the name given to the planning documentation created, a 'development plan' of some form will exist. This development plan represents the key document for the guidance and management of change in a given authority area, representing as it does the first and primary consideration in any planning decision. At the heart of the planning system in the UK is the idea of development being guided by this plan, with planning application decisions being taken in accordance with the development plan unless other material considerations are such that a different decision should be taken.

As noted in the 'People' section of this chapter however, planning activity is not limited to national and local government. Planning is a community-focused activity which increasingly operates in a collaborative and partnership model between organisations. Recently, the sub-local level of government (Parish or Community Councils) has gained more responsibility within the planning system, with more responsibility for decision-making and plan-making. This has been an evolutionary process which was most recently highlighted and changed though the system and approach changes introduced by the UK coalition government elected in 2010. The planning system therefore operates from the international level down to the sub-local level, with multiple governmental and non-governmental organisations involved, and all in association with local communities.

When considering the planning system, rather than planning itself, a significant focus is upon the policy-action relationship, that is to say, the creation and implementation of planning policy through activities such as the determination of planning applications or the use of planning powers to stimulate growth or provide protection to buildings or areas. As you pursue your studies you will explore the full extent of the planning system, learning about how the policies, process, mechanisms and activities that form the framework facilitate and enable planning to occur.

 **tip**

During your first few weeks at university you should try to explore the fundamentals of the art and science of planning and start to investigate the organisations and systems associated with town and country planning in the UK. This will help underpin your studies through your time at university. Some useful texts are included at the end of this chapter.

Conclusions

In this first chapter we have explored the history and nature of town and country planning, its importance to society, the environment and the economy, and considered the people and organisations involved. We have also touched very briefly on the planning system and the role of law in planning.

University is an intensive and demanding educational experience and understanding the basics about planning as both an academic subject and a profession will be very important to your studies from the very first week.

Further reading

Many books provide interesting and informative introductions to town planning. The following are particularly useful:

- Hall, P. and Tewdwr-Jones, M. (2010) *Urban and regional planning*. Fifth ed. London:
  Routledge.
- Healey, P. (2010) *Making better places: The planning project in the twenty-first century*.
  Basingstoke: Palgrave Macmillan.
- Rydin, Y. (2011) *The purpose of planning: Creating sustainable towns and cities*. Bristol: The
  Policy Press.
- Ward, C. (2004) *Planning and urban change*. Second ed. London: Sage.

You should be aware that there continue to be many changes in and around
planning which mean no book will be entirely up-to-date. To get a good understanding of the planning *system* today you should take the time to explore the
following government supported website, which is relevant to England and
Wales:

- http://www.planningportal.gov.uk

To explore other nations, try to identify the government department responsible for planning and explore their website, most will have user-friendly
'plain English' guides for non-professionals.

Review points

When reflecting on this chapter you might consider the following:

- there is more to town and country planning than first appears
- the art and science of town planning is different to the planning system, which is what
  facilitates and enables this activity to occur
- town and country planning is a multifaceted and complex subject area which is interesting, dynamic and exciting
- town and country planning influences all aspects of society, the built and natural environment, and the economy
- you have already started to learn about planning and how you will study the subject at
  university.

2

Studying Town and Country Planning at University

Aims

To help appraise your confidence in relation to a number of skills and competencies and to introduce what university study will entail. It defines some of the terms you will come across through your studies and will set out the broad knowledge sets that your course will cover.

Learning outcomes

After reading this chapter you will:

- reflect upon your current abilities to perform certain skills
- begin to understand how your course is arranged
- become familiar with some of the terms you are likely to hear in your studies
- appreciate the type of knowledge and skills that a planning degree has to deliver.

Introduction

Taking the decision to study at university is an important one as it will represent an exciting new chapter in your life. While you will need to work hard and apply constant dedication and enthusiasm to your studies, the experience will be highly rewarding to you in your personal and academic development. You are likely to be excited about what lies ahead but you may also have certain anxieties about how your university life will develop. These concerns will vary from person to person but tend to focus around the fact that you are studying something new, at a different institution, with a whole new group of staff and classmates. You may also be missing your family and friends if you are studying away from home. If you are studying on a part-time basis then your anxieties may centre around concerns about how study, work and life can be successfully balanced.

You may also feel worried about your ability to succeed and achieve your end-goal of receiving a degree. These concerns are likely to be ill-founded since you have already done well to secure a place on your course. However, it is true that your nerves are only likely to subside once you attend your first lecture, write your first essay, and receive some positive feedback in response.

It is important to see your university life as a journey; a long-term project that requires engagement from the very start. Assessment will help to gauge your development but it is important not to become too disheartened if your results are lower than what you expected or are different to the type you received at school or college. It is very likely that your marks will increase as your confidence grows and the skills and knowledge underpinning your degree are developed. Support will be available from a variety of sources along the way, and this book is also intended as a useful source of reference to help strengthen and underpin your learning and development. To make the most of these various sources it is useful to know where your strengths and weaknesses may lie. This type of reflection is encouraged through the activity set out in Table 2.1.

TABLE 2.1   Assessing and developing your study skills

Assess your level of confidence for each of the skills outlined below. Put one tick in the box if you are not confident, five if you are very confident. Try and be as honest as you can.

Skill	Level of confidence (from one tick to five ticks)
I can explain to others what town planning is about.	
I can refer to the type of knowledge and skills that my programme is likely to develop.	
I can search for information relating to town planning via the library, online databases and the internet.	
I can identify the information that I am likely to need to complete a task and find appropriate information if there are gaps in my understanding.	
I can summarise and synthesise a lecture or a text by writing effective notes.	
I am able to read a book or article critically, for instance by assessing its relevance and authenticity.	

Skill	Level of confidence (from one tick to five ticks)
I understand scale and can read plans and drawings.	
I can produce documents that are well-presented and visually engaging.	
I can undertake research around a question or hypothesis and use appropriate techniques to collect and analyse data.	
I can produce essays and reports that are clear, well-written and logically structured.	
I know how my work is likely to be assessed.	
I can write a list of references, and cite sources within the text, using the Harvard system.	
I am able to organise my time effectively and make judgements as to where my priorities should be.	
I can take the initiative and work by myself.	
I can meet deadlines.	
I can work effectively in groups by helping to identify key tasks and activities and ensuring that the work of the team is properly coordinated.	
I can make a valuable contribution to a group debate or discussion.	
I feel able to lead a team and take responsibility for its actions.	
I feel able to solve a problem and explain how a solution might be achieved.	
I can deliver a presentation that is logical, well-timed and engaging.	
I can develop effective arguments and feel able to negotiate with others.	
I know about the type of work that town planners do and how I might go about finding possible opportunities for work.	
I can write a good CV and feel able to complete a job application form.	
I can set future goals for my career and identify the steps that I need to take to achieve them.	

Now identify the skills that you feel weakest at. You will see that the ordering of these skills broadly reflects the structure of the book. We hope that your confidence levels can be improved once you have read through, and completed the activities, of each chapter.

Reflect on why you feel your confidence is lacking in these areas and provide some explanation in the boxes provided. Also list some actions as to how your confidence can be improved.

My top four skills that I need to improve on are:	As a result of the following questions and concerns...	Action points include:
One:		
Two:		
Three:		
Four:		

Getting to know your new home

Although you may have visited your university before as part of an open day or some other kind of event, you are likely to feel rather daunted when you arrive on campus for the very first time. You will soon be able to familiarise yourself with your new setting and make sure you spend some time looking around. Take a note of where key facilities or services are located, and do not be afraid to ask someone if you get lost; remember, they would have been in the same situation as you at some point in their university life!

 **tip**

In addition to exploring the campus, also take time to get to know the city or town in which your university is located if you are moving from elsewhere. You may be provided with this information in your course induction pack but if not, you might want to find a relevant guide about the history, development and attractions of your new home. One or two maps of the area would also be a good investment. Remember, you will probably be undertaking some kind of project work across the local area; familiarising yourself with this background will hopefully prove useful and may save you time at a later date. A good place to start could be a visitor centre, a museum or a bookshop with a local history section. Architectural guides are also worth a look, such as those that build upon the work of Sir Nikolaus Pevsner who wrote the comprehensive Buildings of England series between 1951 and 1974.

Studying at a university

There is a temptation to see university life as a simple continuation to the educational experiences you have accumulated to date. However, you will soon see that studying for a degree is very different:

- You are now one of a much larger group of students in your university, faculty, department and programme. As compared to a previous school or college your presence might be quite anonymous. While this may appeal, it is also likely that staff will leave you to get on with your studies; do not expect to be reminded about where a lecture is to take place or when coursework is due.
- You are expected to take responsibility for your learning, identifying areas in which you think you might need to work on and devising your own reading strategy to plug the holes in your personal knowledge and understanding.
- You are expected to think for yourself. You will need to critically appraise what you hear in a lecture or read in a book and take a creative and innovative approach to assessment.

A piece of work that simply regurgitates the 'facts' of a lecture or a book, with little critical reflection, is unlikely to do well.

- You are likely to encounter ideas, theories or concepts that are new to you and, in the first instance, possibly quite challenging. You will come across a whole range of new words which you will be expected to embrace, understand and competently use through your planning studies and beyond.

The university year summarised

For the majority of institutions the academic year is broken down into two half-year semesters. Semester one usually starts in late September/early October and continues through to December. Assessment tends to take place either before or immediately after the Christmas break. Semester two typically starts in late January/early February, with activities scheduled through to, and often following, the Easter break.

A further block of assessment then takes place through the months of May and June. Alongside these core dates you may also have some kind of reading or field trip week; you should ask about the timing of these at the start of your academic year. The bulk of the summer, between years, is typically left free but as we will explain later, this provides a useful block of time to secure some kind of work placement or to get ahead with some of the reading and assessment in the following year.

Activities week by week will obviously depend upon your own programme and institution but it is important to note that your study time should exceed the formal contact time you have scheduled as lectures and seminars. We will cover this in Chapter 13 but the commitment you show as a full-time student should be equal to the kind of expectations you have for a full-time job.

Key activities

Every week you will need to take part in a variety of activities, with lectures and seminars being the most common.

A lecture, which originates from the Latin word for a reading, is perhaps the most common form of learning you will engage with. Although some academics may choose to read aspects of their material 'off the page', it is more common for lecturers to simply refer to their notes when necessary to help deliver a session that is more engaging. It is fair to say that lectures will vary depending on the topic being covered, the size of the group, and the style of the presenter. In some cases the audience may have a passive role in simply listening to what is being said. However, in other sessions,

23

the atmosphere might be quite different with the audience being involved throughout.

You may have the same lecturer each week or have someone different. It could be somebody from within your department or from the wider university or a guest speaker who has been invited to share their knowledge and professional experience. You should attend lectures as fully as possible; even if your absence is not noticed it is always polite to apologise and provide an explanation to the lecturer involved if you are unable to attend.

tip

Rather than just going with the flow of a standard university day, and attending lectures as and when they occur, it is useful to undertake some basic preparation beforehand. Try and find out what topic is to be covered, who will be delivering it, and the type of reading that will be necessary to galvanise your understanding. Think about the topic yourself. How would you structure the session? What sources would you use? What case studies would you want to include? Having these thoughts beforehand will help with your engagement through the session and will ensure that you assimilate the lecture's content more efficiently.

It is impossible for a lecture to cover everything you need to know given the time available; it can only provide a basic overview of the topic. However, a lecturer's job is also to encourage and inspire, thereby helping to provide the motivation and encouragement that you need to undertake your own research and reading once the lecture comes to an end.

In order to make the most of the session it is important to listen and take appropriate notes. Emphasis should be given to the former rather than the latter as you are unlikely to keep up with the key messages of the lecture if you are writing copious notes. Bulleted text will suffice and plenty of space should be left on the page in order that your notes can be added to. This editing should happen as soon as possible after the event and should incorporate the notes arising from your further reading. You may decide to re-write your notes but this may not represent the best use of your time. All you really need to ensure is that your notes are legible and sufficiently accurate. You might want to use a highlighter pen to identify particular points or words, especially if their meaning is rather unclear and you need to undertake further study in order to ensure they become clear.

tip

During the course of a lecture you may come across a word that is new to you. This may be a word linked to the theory or practise of planning, or something more general. In addition to researching their meaning at the time, you may also find it useful to keep a permanent record for future reference. You could produce this type of record in your normal word processing package by creating a new page for each letter of the alphabet; words can then be added and defined as you go. If you prefer something more tangible then you could buy a cheap address book that will have letters printed throughout.

It is important to file your notes as soon as possible in a folder that is clearly labelled and logically structured. The first page of your notes should include the title of the lecture, the date on which it was delivered, and the name of the lecturer making the presentation.

Whereas a lecture can often have more than 100 students at a time, a seminar typically has a much smaller audience (usually up to 30). A seminar may be programmed immediately after a lecture or at some other time in the week. Formats vary but they are generally intended to extend or deepen knowledge in a particular area or skill, or encourage debate and discussion around a certain issue or case study. For example, you may have a lecture that looks at the various factors behind population growth. The accompanying seminar might look, for example, at the relevance of these factors in the context of population growth in the south west of England. Such a seminar might also provide an opportunity for you to have a go at preparing your own projections by interrogating relevant data.

Studio teaching is designed to be even more engaging and further develop the idea of 'learning by doing'. Sessions tend to be longer, with students having to complete one or a number of tasks during the course of a morning or afternoon. These tasks will be sandwiched with discussion which the lecturer will help to facilitate; at other times the teaching team will stand back, intervening only to deal with questions and to provide support and encouragement. Material that would have otherwise been delivered as a lecture is inserted at appropriate times of the session.

A modular system

The activities that you will undertake each week contribute to a series of modules that form the heart of your planning programme. Most universities now operate a modular system which essentially allows programmes to select certain modules for delivering particular learning outcomes. This obviously leads to certain modules being shared with a range of different programmes, particularly in year one, which offers a great opportunity to meet new friends away from your own particular cohort.

Modules are rated by the level of credit that they provide, with figures of 10, 15, 20 and 30 being the most common. The figure denotes the amount of study time that you are expected to give with each unit corresponding to some ten hours of study over the period in which the module runs (in a broad sense, rather than just the time spent in 'class'). So, if you are enrolled on a 20-credit module you will need to study for approximately 200 hours.

It is usual to study 120 credits each year, with eligibility for a bachelor's degree coming after the completion of 360 credits. You are likely to become eligible for some interim awards as you progress; a Certificate in Higher Education can usually be awarded after 120 credits and a Diploma in Higher Education can be awarded after 240 credits. If you are studying on a postgraduate programme the same basic structural approach is taken, with a postgraduate diploma consisting of 120 credits and a master's award consisting of a total of 180 credits.

Each module has a unique code which denotes the level of credit that can be awarded, and the university level at which the module is delivered, i.e. 0 (foundation), 1, 2, 3 or M (masters). You do not need to remember these codes but you will need to ensure you are using the right one when you are seeking to enrol on your course or are submitting work for assessment.

Your programme may include a set range of modules or elements where you can exercise some choice. This flexibility is great if you want to pursue a particular aspect of study; in some institutions these options are often quite wide-ranging and can enable you to study something this is not instantly connected to planning.

Many universities offer the choice to study a language which provides a helpful foundation if you are thinking about living or working overseas once you have completed your studies. Learning a language is also important if you are keen to study part of your degree at another European or international institution. Opportunities for this will vary with each university so it is something to ask your programme team about if you are interested.

An opportunity to undertake some kind of placement may also exist. This could involve being with an employer for a whole year or a segment of it (i.e. a semester). Some courses prefer to include a work-based placement that everyone is required to do; sometimes this is arranged for you but you are often encouraged to search for vacancies yourself which will prove invaluable once you start looking for a permanent position.

Assessment

To gain the module's credit you will need to successfully pass the assessment that is attached to it. You usually need to complete all of the assessment in any one year before you can progress to the next, but you should refer to the academic regulations of your own institution to ensure you know what is required.

tip

The academic regulations of your university are likely to be very different from those that you had at your school or college. You are likely to receive a briefing of the main points during your induction to the course but it is worth identifying where further information can be found. It may be useful to bookmark the relevant pages of the university's website or download any guide that is made available to you. Reading this information should help to answer possible questions such as:

- Will my work be penalised if I submit my work late?
- How many times can I re-sit a module if I fail it at the first attempt?
- What will happen if I fail to sit an exam or fail to submit a piece of coursework?
- Who do I tell, and what information might I need, if I become ill on the day of an exam?
- Can I appeal my mark and, if so, what grounds can I use to do so?

Assessment dates may be spread across a semester or be concentrated at the very end. Chapter 4 emphasises the importance of keeping these commitments sufficiently monitored by keeping some kind of calendar that can be updated as and when work is completed. Assessment will vary module by module but is likely to comprise a mix of the following:

- A written examination, of varying length and format.
- An essay, report or some other kind of written work, such as a research paper, a reflective diary or log, a letter or a blog.
- A verbal presentation.
- A contribution to a seminar debate or some kind of role-play exercise.
- Project work, that will typically require you to produce sheets where text is combined with visual material such as maps, sketches and photographs.
- Modelling or design work, such as an interpretation (in card or wood) of a particular street or building or a set of drawings depicting the type of improvements you envisage for an area.

You may be required to complete this work individually or with others from either your programme or elsewhere.

Examinations may be provided on a seen or unseen basis depending on whether the question is made available to you in advance. An examination may also be described as being 'open book'; in these circumstances you may be allowed to take some 'approved' materials into the exam. This might be a relevant piece of reading or some draft work that you might have produced in class. The requirements per exam will also differ. While one exam may require you to complete a number of short-answered questions, another might require you to complete a single essay over a two- or three-hour period.

Controlled and uncontrolled assessment

A distinction is often made between 'controlled' and 'uncontrolled' forms of assessment. Controlled assessment typically equates to some kind of exam or presentation which is undertaken in front of lecturing staff or university invigilators. Such a format can help to guarantee that the assessment you complete is your own. Conversely, 'uncontrolled' assessment relates to the work you are likely to undertake outside of your lectures in your own time, such as writing a report or an essay. This form of assessment allows you to create a piece of work over a period of time, allowing for more research, depth and detail. However, it is also the case that with uncontrolled assessments there is less certainty that this work is your own. It must be acknowledged that universities impose strict penalties on students who present work that appears to have arisen from plagiarism or some other dishonest act.

Formative and summative assessment

A similar distinction can also be made between summative and formative forms of assessment. Summative assessments are graded and contribute towards the classification of your degree. In contrast, formative work is usually ungraded and is designed to provide advice and guidance in advance of the formal assessment taking place. For example, a formative task might involve you preparing an essay plan for an assignment due at a later date. Feedback arising from such a request might be able to help you improve the structure of your essay, or identify texts that you may have missed when you started your background reading. Opportunities for formative feedback vary but where such an opportunity exists you should seek to do what is asked of you since it is likely to help enhance your final grade for the module.

Grading

You will receive a grade for every piece of summative work you complete and you should expect to receive some kind of feedback sheet that identifies what you did well, and what you might need to work on in the future. Grades should be considered against the context at which your final degree is calculated, usually based upon the following approach:

- A first (or distinction) is awarded where a mark exceeds 70%.
- An upper second (2:1) (or merit) is awarded where a mark falls between 60 and 69%.
- A lower second (2:2) is awarded where a mark falls between 50 and 59%.
- A third is awarded where a mark falls between 40 and 49%.
- It is likely that your work will have failed if it receives a mark of less than 40%.

Studying town and country planning at university

It is possible to study planning across the world, with a variety of undergraduate and postgraduate opportunities being available. The majority tend to be delivered as full-time courses but it is also possible to study on a part-time basis as well, particularly if the course is postgraduate. It is typical for these courses to be delivered through attendance (i.e. you physically participate in class) although a growing number of courses are providing opportunities for either distance (such as online) or blended (a mix between taught and distance) learning.

There are around 30 planning schools across the UK and Ireland, each with their own distinctive offer. This variety extends to the naming of each planning programme, with a range of terms often being used around the core word of 'planning'. Some of these relate to a particular scale or setting (such as town, country, urban, rural, city or regional planning), a particular theme (such as environmental or transport planning), or a particular approach (such as spatial planning).

Some courses blend planning with other related disciplines such as architecture, geography and property development. The split will vary, with different courses offering varying proportions of the identified subject.

Professional accreditation

If you are keen to become a professional planner in the UK then it is important to follow a programme of study that is accredited by the professional institute, the Royal Town Planning Institute (RTPI). Indeed, even if you are considering working overseas, it is still worth following such a programme given the international reputation that the RTPI has. Courses are accredited on the basis of whether their aims and objectives are felt to be appropriate, and if the respective planning school is judged to be effective in ensuring that these goals can be achieved. In examining the effectiveness of each school, the RTPI takes into account such factors as the prominence of the planning school within the university, its resource base, and the quality of its teaching and research base.

A list of UK planning schools can be found on the website of the RTPI. In addition to providing a short summary of the school, the text also outlines the various courses that are offered with a distinction being made as to whether the institute recognises each as a spatial, specialist or combined programme of study.

To satisfy the educational requirements of the institute, thereby enabling you to take the first step towards professional membership, it is necessary for you to complete both 'spatial' and 'specialist' elements of study. Neither a spatial nor a specialist qualification by itself is enough.

The spatial element is intended to provide a broad understanding of planning by facilitating *"integrated understanding of broad matters of principle that reveal and connect:*

- *social science existing as a key analytical framework;*
- *the interplay between land use and transportation;*
- *design and the realisation of place;*
- *economic issues relating to development;*
- *environmental challenges, and;*
- *legal and institutional frameworks"*
  (RTPI, 2012b: para. 6.3)

In contrast to this emphasis on the general, specialist programmes are intended to explore the 'ideas, perspectives and debates' of one particular area of planning in a greater level of depth. The institute does not restrict the type of specialism that can be pursued but current examples include those that centre on the following:

- Heritage and conservation
- Transport
- Economic development
- Tourism
- Regeneration
- Environmental management
- International planning
- Property development
- Urban design.

As an undergraduate student it is typical for you to complete a three-year spatial planning degree, followed by a specialist course at either the same or another planning school. This additional study can often be pursued on a part-time basis or, in some cases, by using some kind of distance or blended learning model.

An alternative to this is to study both the spatial and specialist elements together in the form of a combined programme which typically lasts for four academic years.

As a postgraduate it is possible to study both the spatial and specialist elements together in a combined programme that extends to one (full-time) or two (part-time) calendar years of education.

What will I study on a town and country planning degree?

This is an important question, especially if you have had little contact with either planners or the planning system prior to making your application to study on your course. The reality is that you probably have some knowledge, perhaps as a result of some kind of school or college project, or following a period of work experience. You might also have a friend or family member who works in planning, or have simply come across planning as a result of having an interest in a local development project. Even if you are working in planning at the moment, and have a good working knowledge of the relevant legislation, you may still be unsure as to what an academic course in town planning will actually entail.

Of course you will find out as your studies progress, but there is real merit in trying to understand the big picture now so that you are clear as to the areas of knowledge and the types of skills that you will be expected to acquire.

In reality, syllabuses are shaped by a range of factors, including the teaching and research interests of staff, and the history, culture, and organisational position of the planning school within the university. The RTPI does not set out a particular syllabus for planning schools to follow but it does set out some guiding principles through the New Vision for Planning that was published in 2001. Through this, the institute defines 'spatial planning' as its basic discipline, as witnessed by the corporate strap-line, 'the making of place and the mediation of space' (RTPI, 2001).

By using this as an organising idea, planning schools have been encouraged to *"promote critical thinking about space and place as the basis for action or intervention"* (RTPI, 2012b: 2). The RTPI also has a list of learning outcomes that schools are expected to adhere to when designing and delivering their respective programmes. Specifically, accredited courses must be able to demonstrate how a student exiting from their programme is able to satisfy the learning outcomes set. The outcomes are applicable to all RTPI-accredited courses, although the institute recognises that each outcome is likely to be addressed in different ways.

There are 14 objectives for spatial planning programmes and six for specialist programmes (although schools can identify a further four objectives if they want to add further definition to their specialism). Boxes 2.1 and 2.2 list these in full.

Box 2.1   Learning outcomes for an RTPI-accredited spatial planning qualification

Typical graduates from **spatial planning programmes** should be able to:

1. explain and demonstrate how spatial planning operates within the context of institutional and legal frameworks
2. generate integrated and well substantiated responses to spatial planning challenges
3. reflect on the arguments for and against spatial planning and particular theoretical approaches, and assess what can be learnt from experience of spatial planning in different contexts and spatial scales
4. demonstrate how efficient resource management helps to deliver effective spatial planning
5. explain the political and ethical nature of spatial planning and reflect on how planners work effectively within democratic decision-making structures
6. explain the contribution that planning can make to the built and natural environment and in particular recognise the implications of climate change
7. debate the concept of rights and the legal and practical implications of representing these rights in decision-making processes
8. evaluate different development strategies and the practical application of development finance
9. assess the implications for generating added value for the community
10. explain the principles of equality and equality of opportunity in relation to spatial planning in order to positively promote the involvement of different communities, and evaluate the importance and effectiveness of community engagement in the planning process
11. evaluate the principles and processes of design for creating high quality places and enhancing the public realm for the benefit of all in society
12. demonstrate effective research, analytical, evaluative and appraisal skills and the ability to reach appropriate, evidence-based decisions
13. recognise the role of communication skills in the planning process and the importance of working in an interdisciplinary context, and be able to demonstrate negotiation, mediation, advocacy and leadership skills
14. distinguish the characteristics of a professional, including the importance of upholding the highest standards of ethical behaviour and a commitment to lifelong learning and critical reflection so as to maintain and develop professional competence.

Royal Town Planning Institute (2012b: 11)

Box 2.2 Learning outcomes for an RTPI-accredited specialist qualification

Typical graduates from **specialist planning programmes** should be able to:

1. engage in theoretical, practical and ethical debate at the forefront of the area of the specialism in the context of spatial planning
2. evaluate the social, economic, environmental and political context for the area of specialism
3. evaluate the distinctive contribution of the specialism to the making of place and the mediation of space
4. demonstrate the relationship within a spatial planning context of the particular area of specialism to other specialist areas of expertise
5. demonstrate the type and quality of skills that would be expected of a graduate from this specialism undertaking the practice experience period of the assessment of professional competence [as explained later]
6. assess the contribution of the specialism to the mitigation of, and adaptation to, climate change plus up to four bespoke learning outcomes reflecting the nature of the specialism.

Royal Town Planning Institute (2012b: 13)

Another influence on course design is also provided by the Quality Assurance Agency (QAA) for Higher Education. This body publishes Subject Benchmark Standards for nearly 60 honours degree subjects, including 'town and country planning' (QAA, 2008). Each statement provides a summary of the respective discipline, the defining principles that a course in this field should seek to deliver, and a summary of the knowledge and skills that a graduating student should be expected to achieve.

In describing planning, the QAA statement explains how planning:

…is the study of the way societies plan, design, manage and regulate change in the built and natural environment. It therefore includes the study of why and how (and with what consequences) societies intervene, shape, organise and change natural and built environments in order to secure an agreed range of social, economic and environmental objectives. (QAA, 2008: 6)

The statement also acknowledges the need for students to 'appreciate the rationale for planning and how it is practised' which is elaborated to involve:

…understanding not only the processes of spatial change in the built and natural environments, but also studying the arguments for intervening in these processes. It requires an understanding of the operation and outcomes of land, property and development markets from a variety of perspectives, including the economic, financial and legal aspects. It also requires an understanding of design and the development of sustainable built and natural environments. (QAA, 2008: 6)

In terms of skills, the statement makes a distinction between students acquiring three types of skills:

1. Subject skills, such as the ability to identify and formulate problems and to collect, analyse, evaluate and synthesise planning data and trends.
2. Generic skills, such as preparing and presenting arguments and working efficiently in and with groups.
3. Specialist skills, relating to an area of the profession that a student chooses to study in greater detail (see above).

In addition to setting out these various skills, which are explored in greater depth through Table 2.2, the statement also includes a set of benchmark standards that undergraduate and postgraduate students can be assessed against. Box 2.3 outlines the relevant expectations for threshold (e.g. lower second) students, typical (e.g. upper second) students and excellent (e.g. first class) students.

If you are studying planning alongside another subject, your course may need to satisfy the learning outcomes of other professional bodies (such as the Royal Institution of Chartered Surveyors) or other QAA statements (such as geography).

TABLE 2.2   Understanding the role of your modules

The QAA Subject Benchmark Statement for town and country planning makes a distinction between three types of skill: subject, generic and specialist. In considering the first two categories only, have a go at predicting where they might be delivered across your own planning programme by outlining the relevant name(s) or code(s) of the module(s) that you feel have a role. It is acknowledged that some skills may be developed across nearly all of your modules. Where this is the case you can write 'throughout' in the right-hand column.

In completing this exercise you will need to review the information you hold about your course. It may also be useful to speak to your programme leader; where do they think the skills are tested?

Skill	Likely to be targeted in module(s)...
Subject skills	
Academic research and professional investigation in the planning field	
Collecting, analysing, evaluating and synthesising planning data and trends	
Identification and formulation of planning problems	

Skill	Likely to be targeted in module(s)...
Translation of theory and knowledge into practical planning policies and actions, including the writing of clear aims and objectives, the formulation, articulation, and evaluation/appraisal of strategies, plans and designs	
Creative problem-solving skills and propositions for action	
Practical design skills	
Monitoring and evaluation of planning interventions and outcomes	

Created using the skills outlined in The Quality Assurance Agency (2008: 8–9)

Skill	Likely to be targeted in module(s)...
Generic skills	
Preparing and presenting arguments and illustrative materials in a variety of presentational formats - written, graphic and oral	
Numeracy and use of statistical and quantitative data	
Information sourcing and literacy	
Using information technology in work preparation and presentation	
Critical reflection with an understanding of the need for lifelong learning	
Managing and producing work to time on an individual basis	
Working effectively in and with groups	
Being aware of, listening to and evaluating the opinions and values of others	
Demonstrating an ability to exercise initiative, original thought and independence, within a system of personal values	
Negotiating, facilitating, leadership and networking skills	
The ability to work in a multi-professional working environment	

Created using the skills outlined in The Quality Assurance Agency (2008: 9)

Finding information about your own course

Details concerning your course are likely to be set out in some kind of course or programme booklet which you are likely to receive as you begin your studies. It may also be made available online, perhaps through a dedicated web-page or intranet site. Whatever its form, details are likely to include the following:

- Specific learning outcomes, which are likely to be designed by the programme team who will want to combine their own thinking with the learning outcomes of the RTPI and the standards of the QAA (as discussed above).
- Biographies and contact details for your programme team.

Box 2.3   The Quality Assurance Agency standards for threshold, typical and excellent undergraduate town planning students

All undergraduate students (i.e. **threshold** and above) should be able to:

- demonstrate understanding in the treatment and exposition of the subject matter, making connections between the different areas of the curriculum
- evaluate arguments for planning as a form of action within processes of change
- evaluate political, legal, institutional and administrative frameworks and procedures in planning
- exhibit an understanding of the complexities of planning issues and problems
- demonstrate an understanding of theory and make appropriate connections between theory and practice
- demonstrate an understanding of the place of values and ethics in planning
- define and analyse planning problems effectively and appropriately
- make effective use of evidence and information sources
- use and evaluate a variety of plan and policy-making methods and processes
- formulate and propose policies, strategies, design proposals and other courses of action as responses to planning problems
- effectively communicate planning information, ideas, principles, arguments and proposals through written, graphic, oral and electronic means and demonstrate effectively, written, numeracy, oral, information technology and information literacy skills
- work effectively individually and in groups.

In addition to these standards, **typical** students should be able to demonstrate:

- understanding and application of the majority of the knowledge components listed above to a good level and with appropriate critical discernment
- effective and appropriate application and execution of the majority of the skills listed above showing insight, some initiative, creativity and autonomy.

Excellent students should also be able to demonstrate:

- understanding and application of the majority of the knowledge components listed above with a high level of originality, insight and critical discernment
- effective, fluent and appropriate application and execution of the majority of the skills listed above, showing high levels of insight, initiative, creativity, autonomy and leadership.

Source: The Quality Assurance Agency (2008: 11)

- Summaries of the assessment that you are likely to encounter.
- An overview of the different learning and teaching styles you will be exposed to, with indicative figures for the amount of study you will need to undertake.
- Overviews of the modules forming your programme, with details about the awards you are likely to be eligible for as you progress your studies.

It is likely that individual modules will have their own guides which will 'plug-into' this contextual background. Each guide is likely to provide details of:

- the aims and objectives of the module that will fit with the wider goals of the programme
- the module team, such as the location of their room, email address and phone number
- the syllabus, highlighting the general theme for each week and the name of the person who will be responsible for delivering it
- how the module will be assessed, and when this will be scheduled. It will tell you such things as how long your assignment should be, the format that it needs to be submitted in, and whether opportunities for any kind of formative feedback exist
- the type of assessment you will need to take if you fail, or do not sit or submit, an exam or assignment at the first attempt (if appropriate)
- relevant texts that you will be expected to engage with during the run of the module. This aspect will be covered in the next chapter but it is typical that a distinction is made between 'essential' reading (which you will need to do to support your reading) and 'recommended' reading which may include details of a much larger pool of texts that you can draw from depending on your particular interest.

Disability support

When you start your course it is important to tell your programme team and/or any specific unit about any disability or issue that may affect your studies. Examples might include deafness or being hard of hearing, blindness or having some kind of visual impairment, or having restrictions on personal mobility. Your ability to study may also be affected by mental health issues or by a specific learning difficulty such as dyslexia, dyspraxia and dyscalculia and ADHD/ADD. Your university will have procedures in place for dealing with such issues as and when they are identified. Support will vary depending on individual needs but could include:

- providing enlargements of books and journal articles in a range of forms, including Braille
- adjustment to exams and other assessments, for example by giving longer completion times or by giving the student a personal scribe or reader
- access to note-takers and support workers.

Conclusions

This chapter has hopefully achieved two objectives. It has first sought to develop your knowledge of university life by outlining such things as how learning will be achieved and how you might be taught and assessed. It then provides an introduction to what a town and country planning degree is expected to cover which should help to provide some useful context going forward.

Review points

When reflecting on this chapter you might consider the following:

- studying at university will be different to what you have done in the past
- university life is supported by a new vocabulary which you will need to get accustomed to
- planning courses differ in name and structure but each has to respond to the outcomes set by the RTPI and the QAA
- your studies will be demanding but they will help to develop you in an academic and personal sense.

Further reading

The further chapters of this book will touch upon many of the topics covered by this chapter; relevant texts will be identified at that stage. It is worth reviewing the many documents that you have probably been passed in relation to your course but it is worth supplementing these with the material provided by the RTPI and the QAA. In particular, have a look at:

- The Quality Assurance Agency for Higher Education (2008) *Subject Benchmark Standards: Town and Country Planning*. QAA: Mansfield
- Royal Town Planning Institute (2012b) *Policy statement on initial planning education*. London: RTPI.

The following book is a useful resource for those students with dyslexia:

- Hargreaves, S. (2012) *Study skills for students with dyslexia*. London: Sage.

3

Finding and Using Information

Aims

To help you consider the type of information you are likely to need to support your study and where this can be found. It emphasises the importance of reading critically and how any resources you draw from should be appropriately referenced.

Learning outcomes

After reading this chapter you will:

- begin to think about the type of information you might need to reinforce your learning
- appreciate the many sources of information that exist and be able to make a distinction as to whether they represent a primary or secondary source
- acknowledge the systems that are typically used to classify and sort material relevant to town and country planning
- identify the type of questions you will need pose to critically review a text
- gain an understanding of how information sources should be cited and referred to in your work.

Introduction

The last chapter raised a number of important points about studying town and country planning at university. In reflecting upon this you might have been struck as to how wide the discipline actually is, with a wide range of themes being identified for study. Lectures and seminars will play a role in developing the skills and knowledge that you need but you must also supplement this with your own study. Reading forms an important part of this and you will need to read a variety of sources before, during and after the sessions that you have scheduled. It provides a way for supplementing your lecture and seminar notes and for developing the kind of understanding that you need to demonstrate through assessment.

While the thought of this reading should not be overly off-putting, it is common for a range of questions to be raised:

- How much reading do I need to do?
- What type of material should I be reading?
- When should this reading be taking place?
- How many sources do I need to use for a first year essay or a final year research project?
- Where can I find appropriate resources?
- How do I show that I have used these sources in my work?
- Are certain resources better than others?
- How can I appraise the value or usefulness of a text?

Answers to these will begin to become clear during the course of your year, with assessment providing an important tool for appraising whether you are suitably engaged in undertaking the type of reading that you need to do. Indeed, if you are unfortunate enough to get a poor mark in your first exam or essay then it is likely that a fault has occurred somewhere in your reading strategy. This may be down to you using too few resources, making it difficult for you to present and critically assess the literature relating to the question set. Equally a low mark may arise from a failure to properly record what you have read. Consequently, while you may be impressed by the sources that you managed to get together by way of background research, your assessor is likely to take an alternative view if you decide to mention just one or two sources during the course of an answer.

What information do I need?

It may sound rather obvious but the first thing you should do is to think about the information that you actually require. Your requirements may be quite general (i.e. contextual reading or you want to read for the sake of curiosity) but they may also be quite specific. You may have been asked to find something out, such as an example or a date, or perhaps you want to look at a range of sources to develop your understanding in an area of a recent lecture that you might have found confusing. Your requirements may also be defined by assessment; you may need to find sources to complete an essay question. To help with this first step it is useful to write down a list of questions that you want, or will need to, answer. Box 3.1 provides an example of the type of questions you might pose in response to an exam question you have been set.

Although it is tempting to stop looking for resources as and when you feel you might have an 'answer' to the type of questions listed in Box 3.1, it is important to keep going in order that you have a number of possible 'answers'. For some of your questions these separate answers may be the same, but for others the answers you are able to find might be quite different or, at the very least, add something to your understanding. So, while there may be consensus about what plan-making across the UK entails, you may uncover a spectrum of thought concerning the type of mitigation that might be possible for countering the effects of climate change.

Box 3.1 Thinking about your information requirements

Second-year undergraduate students were required to develop a comprehensive response to the following question during the course of a two-hour 'seen' exam.

As Burton and Piper explain, "spatial planning has an important role to play in responding to the urgent need to address both the causes of climate change and the impacts of unavoidable climate change" (2010: 3). In drawing from your wider reading, and by using examples throughout, critically consider the type of interventions that planners can make through both plan-making and development management activities in the UK.

While the basics of the topic were covered in class, further reading was identified as being necessary. The group was encouraged to think about the areas which their reading and investigation would need to embrace – an exercise that led them to develop a series of sub-questions:

- Who are Burton and Piper? Are they experts in this field?
- What did text surrounding the quote say? What were the principal themes of the book and chapter within which the quote appeared?
- What is meant by the term 'spatial planning'?
- What does climate change involve and why are its impacts described as being 'unavoidable'?
- What is known about the causes and impacts of climate change? Is there consensus on these points?
- What examples exist? Where can examples be drawn from?
- What is meant by 'plan-making'? Is there a particular type of plan I should be referring to? Do plan-making activities vary across the UK?
- What does 'development management' involve? How can this be best described? Again, does practice vary across the UK?
- What impact can planners really have? Are their powers to intervene affected by other factors?
- Have there been any significant changes or notable publications on this subject since the work was published in 2010?

In short, the more sources (and perspectives) you find and use the better your understanding, or your notes or assessment, will be. Only once you are clear about the range of information that exists can you offer a view with any authority. Defining a term by looking at the work of ten authors is clearly safer than just looking at the work of one; just imagine if this single author had misunderstood the term in some way.

Activity

Using the example included in Box 3.1 as a guide, develop relevant sub-questions for the following question:

How do the goals for promoting the future competitiveness of Liverpool respond to the changing socio-economic conditions that the city has experienced over the last 30 years?

Primary and secondary sources

It is typical, when considering the type of information that exists, to make a distinction between primary and secondary sources:

- A primary source typically relates to raw data, such as that arising from some kind of research or census. A good example would be information concerning local income levels, or details concerning car ownership. A primary source can also be the first-hand account of an event or incident.
- A secondary source is something that draws from these primary sources and uses the information in a particular way. For example, data concerning car ownership could be used to highlight two different perspectives. One author could write an article that links low rates of ownership to incidences of deprivation in an area while somebody else could refer to the same low rates as being indicative of a successful programme to promote green and active travel. Secondary sources need to be clear as to the information they have used in order that the reader can look at them independently and make similar or possibly different conclusions.

Box 3.2 gives some examples of typical primary and secondary sources.

Where can the information I am looking for be found?

Beyond this distinction there is a wide range of sources that can be used. Examples include:

- books and e-books
- company reports

- dictionaries and encyclopaedias
- film and television programmes
- government publications (e.g. strategy and policy documents)
- images and photographs
- journals and e-journals
- maps and plans
- newspapers and magazines
- legislation
- statistical data
- student work (e.g. research papers)
- websites.

Box 3.2   Types of primary and secondary sources

Primary sources include:

- autobiographies
- data and statistics, such as that found within a census
- diaries
- interviews, surveys and fieldwork
- government documents
- letters and emails
- newspaper articles (depending on content)
- original documents (such as property deeds)
- photographs and works of art
- proceedings of meetings and conferences
- speeches
- technical reports
- works of literature (such as poems and fiction).

Secondary sources include:

- biographical works (depending on content)
- commentaries
- dictionaries and encyclopaedias
- dissertations or theses (depending on content)
- essays
- handbooks and data compilations (depending on content)
- history
- journal articles (content depending)
- newspaper and popular magazine articles (again depending on content)
- review articles and literature reviews
- textbooks (depending on content)
- works of criticism and interpretation.

Of these, books and journals are the most commonly used in academic study.

Books vary from the general to the specific and exist as both physical and electronic resources. Some students often choose to begin their reading with a general text which tends to offer a brief summary of the topic and introduce some of the terms and concepts that the more detailed literature refers to. They can also help to signpost other resources or identify the names of key people who might be experts in the field. A book may be written in its entirety by a single writing team but you will also find edited volumes where individual chapters have been written by a wide selection of contributors. It is typical for a book to be peer reviewed to ensure that its content is sufficiently robust and appropriate to its intended audience. In some areas, such as in planning law and practice, books are produced on a regular basis to keep up with changes in policy and legislation; for these titles it is important to check that you are referring to the latest edition.

tip

A selection of relevant books is included in Appendix one in this book. The majority of these will be held in your university's library but you may wish to purchase either a new or second-hand copy of some of these titles to create your own personal library. Remember to check that you are purchasing the latest copy if you are buying from new.

Journals encompass both academic and professional titles. Academic journals benefit from being peer reviewed. This means that an article submitted for print is vetted by an editorial board before a decision is taken as to whether it should, or indeed can, be published. Journals cover a range of themes, and each title typically supports a variety of articles from a wide range of contributors. The articles themselves may present the findings of recent research or use reasoned debate to add weight, or challenge, existing ideas, concepts or practices. Journals typically support such things as book or conference reviews, while certain editions are often framed around a particular theme. Journals are published at a variety of frequencies throughout the year. It is likely that your library will hold physical and/or online versions of the journal titles outlined in Appendix two.

Professional journals tend to be published more frequently. Although titles usually have an editorial team who write the majority of the articles, contributions from elsewhere are often included but tend not to be subject to rigorous peer reviews. Professional journals tend to focus on news, be it a new policy development or a company takeover. Jobs and tender opportunities tend to feature as well. The readership of such a journal tends to be pitched towards practitioners and in the context of town planning this would be planners working in the public, private or voluntary sectors. Haymarket's *Planning* magazine is probably the best example which is published each fortnight. Other examples include *Building Design*, *Estates Gazette*, *Inside Housing*, *Property Week* and *Regeneration and Renewal*. Again most titles are now being offered in either hardcopy or electronic formats.

Finding material via your university library

The majority of the sources listed above will be found in your university's library. Certain items can be found relatively easy but others will require an element of searching. Before we turn to this, it is important to get to know how your library works and the facilities it has to offer. You may have been given basic details via some kind of induction tour but it is useful to add to this through your own investigation of the library's physical and online resources. Answering the questions of the activity included in Table 3.1 might be helpful in this.

tip

In addition to familiarising yourself with the university's library it is also useful to know where other libraries are located across your town and city. Joining these will enable you to access a further pool of resources (and particularly those relating to local history) and will provide another environment where you can read and study.

Searching for material in your university's library

Two further questions could have been added to those included in Table 3.1:

- How is material arranged and displayed through my university library?
- How can I see what information my particular library holds?

TABLE 3.1 Familiarising yourself with your library

By visiting your university library and referring to any online advice, have a go at completing these questions:

Question	Answer
How are books and journals organised? Where can those relevant to town planning be found?	
Over what times and days is the library open?	
Do I need to use a swipe card to get in at certain times?	
How many books can I take out at any one time?	
How do I renew material if I am unable to return it?	
What are the penalties if I return a book late?	
Can I reserve a book so that I can collect it once it is returned?	
How long can I take a resource out for? Is there a standard limit or does it vary with the type of information involved?	
Is there a subject-specific librarian?	
Who do I need to contact if I have specific needs, such as large print books?	
Are there areas of the library designed for group work or personal study?	
How can I suggest that the library purchases a new book?	
What can I do if a book I am looking for is out on loan? Can I request a copy from another university?	
Does the library offer any guides or workshops that might be useful to you (e.g. on referencing)?	

The majority of information that a library holds will be classified by using some kind of system. The following are the most common:

- The Library of Congress Classification (LCC) system that identifies each book by giving it an alphanumeric code. Each code begins with a series of letters to denote the subject area, and a series of numbers to identify a specific subject division (Library of Congress, 2012a). For example, subclass HT relates to the social sciences, with HT 161-165 referring to garden cities. Similarly, subclass JS relates to local and municipal government, with JS221-227 referring to the conduct of elections (Library of Congress, 2012b). A letter to denote the author's surname follows a forward slash to complete the code. For the example, the following text:

Dühr, S., Colomb, C. and Nadin, V. (2010) *European spatial planning and territorial cooperation*. London: Routledge.
is given a code of HT 395.E85/D

- The Dewey Decimal Classification (DDC) system, which organises knowledge into ten main categories, such as 300 for the social sciences, 700 for the arts, 800 for literature and 900 for geography and history (OCLC, 2011). Each of these categories is then divided into ten sub-categories, with each sub-category then being broken down into ten specific topic areas. These topics can be broken down even further to cover particular areas of interest. Under this system, the same text by Dühr *et al.* is classified as 307.12094 DUH.

Libraries all manage their resources using these systems. For example, at the University of the West of England, the DDC system is used so that as an item enters the library it is automatically given a DDC number which is typically called its 'class mark'. Publishers tend to provide these class marks themselves, with codes often appearing alongside copyright material. However, for others, the coding is determined by library staff. Minor differences therefore exist for some titles but a summary of some of the main DDC codes relevant to town planning is given in Box 3.3. It is useful to know where these categories are located within your library so you can automatically go to them as you search for material. While such things as books, company reports and government publications will probably be kept together, you are likely to find that there are separate areas for storing journals, DVDs, encyclopaedias and legislation. It is worth investigating this.

Class marks may be given to you by your lecturer via some kind of module or programme guide, or possibly during the course of a lecture or seminar. However, it is probably more likely that you will need to obtain it yourself. This can be done via your library's cataloguing system which you can either access online (usually via a link from the library's home-page) or in the library itself by using some kind of terminal. A code will be provided to you once basic details of the book or resource are entered. Clearly the more details you have the easier this search will be but you should be able to track the resource down if you have the author's surname and some elements of the resource's title.

Increasingly your search via a catalogue will actually enable you to see the item online, with the returned class mark often being accompanied by a link that will allow you to connect to an e-book, e-journal or web-page.

If you have no particular item in mind then the catalogue will also enable you to look for resources around a particular theme. To ensure this search is effective you will need to identify a number of keywords or phrases that relate to the areas of knowledge you are trying to get information on. Keywords from the essay question set out in Table 3.1 might include such terms as 'plan-making', 'development management', 'climate change' and 'the UK'. However, it is worth playing around with these words since different terms may lead to more or less (or possibly more relevant) sources being identified. Some catalogues are able to search for everything that a library holds or has access to but you might find your own library offers different options for searching just books, e-books, journals or e-journals.

Box 3.3 Useful Dewey Decimal Classification (DDC) codes associated with town planning (as used in the University of the West of England, Bristol)

300.72	Research methods	350	Public administration
303.4	Social change	352	Local government
304.2	Human geography	363.5	Housing policy
304.6	Population and population change	371.425	Careers' guidance
		378.170281	Study skills
305	Social structures	380.5	Transport
307.14	Community development	384	Telecommunications
307.72	Rural communities	387.7	Air transport
307.76	Urban communities	388	Sustainable travel
330	Economics	711.3	Rural planning
330.91724	Economic development	711.342	Local/town plan
330.91732	Urban economics	711.409	Urban/town planning
330.941	British economy	711.5	Area planning
333	Land economics	711.7	Transport planning
333.337	Property markets	712	Landscape design
333.71	Environmental impact assessment	720.9	History of architecture
		720.942	History of architecture (Britain)
333.72	Environmental conservation		
333.79	Energy	720.95	History of architecture (rest of the world)
333.917	Coastline		
333.95	Biodiversity	745	Design
337.142	European Union	910	Geography (general)
338.19	Food supply	910.285	Geographic Information Systems
338.4791	Leisure and tourism		
338.941	Economic policies of the UK	911	Historical geography
346.044	National infrastructure	942	English history

It is usually possible to undertake a more detailed search by using the Boolean operators of AND, NOT and OR:

AND   Can allow words to be searched together, e.g. 'climate change' AND 'planning'

NOT   Can allow for certain words to be excluded from your search, e.g. 'United Kingdom' NOT 'United States'

OR   Can allow you to link two words that have similar meaning, e.g. 'development control' OR 'development management'.

Most systems will also allow you to use so-called wild-cards which can enable you to retrieve words with similar stems but alternative endings. They can also be used to search for words with different spellings. A wild-card is often denoted by inserting some kind of symbol such as an asterisk or percentage sign. So:

- 'develop*' will retrieve develop, developing and development
- 'analy*e' will retrieve both analyse (British English) and analyze (American English).

tip

Most e-journals will typically have a home-page where you can search the title for a particular topic. While such a search will yield far fewer results than a much broader search of your library's catalogue, the results you get might be more relevant to your needs.

You may find that your library subscribes to other databases that will also allow you to find a range of resources. It is worth investigating some of these, including:

- The British Humanities Index
- Building Design Online
- DCP Online (Development Control Practice)
- EGI (Estates Gazette Interactive)
- iSurv
- Lexis Library
- Planex
- RUDI
- Science Direct
- Urbadoc

In addition to identifying articles that might be of relevance, it is likely that the platforms will also give access to the resource itself. Copyright rules sometimes prohibit this when a search is made off-campus but access may be possible if it is repeated on site.

Searching for material on the internet

While your library is no doubt a fantastic resource, you may prefer to start your search for information via the internet. Typing the same keywords associated with the exam question outlined in Table 3.1 into a search engine such as Google or Bing will provide a range of sources. Although your search can often be narrowed by applying certain filters, such as 'pages from the UK', the type of information you can find, and the range of organisations and people providing it, will be vast. Some hits will provide pages of text and graphics while others will enable you to download key documents. Websites are particularly useful for capturing the latest information since updating a web-page can take minutes compared to the much longer process of writing a book or journal article.

Appendix three provides a directory of useful websites relevant to town planning. It is worth exploring what exists as you start your course; you might want to add particularly useful sites to your 'Favourites' bar, which most internet browsers have.

Apart from these traditional web resources, information can also be found online through other means, such as blogs, discussion forums and social networking sites such as Twitter.

Developing professional links

Box 3.4   Key membership groups associated with town and country planning

Royal Town Planning Institute (RTPI)

The RTPI is the largest planning institute in Europe with over 23,000 members. It was founded in September 1914 with three principal objectives, namely to:

- advance the study of town planning, civic design and kindred subjects, and of the arts and sciences as applied to those subjects
- promote the artistic and scientific development of towns and cities; and
- secure the association, and to promote the general interests of those engaged or interested in the practice of town planning.

Today the RTPI, as a charity, a learned society and a membership organisation, seeks to:

- promote spatial planning and what it can do for people
- campaign for better planning
- lead, develop and support the planning profession
- champion Institute membership and its value to society
- set professional and ethical standards

- build public awareness, understanding and support for planning with access to the system for everyone
- influence the development of planning policy and legislation
- advance the theory of spatial planning
- link spatial planning theory with practice
- work in partnership with others.

The RTPI offers a number of routes to membership, including a dedicated option for students. Further details are available via: www.rtpi.org.uk

Town and Country Planning Association (TCPA)

The TCPA campaigns for the reform of the UK's planning system to make it more responsive to people's needs and aspirations. The Association prides itself on leading-edge radical thinking and problem solving. Current objectives include the need to:

- secure a decent, well-designed home for everyone, in a human-scale environment combining the best features of town and country
- empower people and communities to influence decisions that affect them
- improve the planning system in accordance with the principles of sustainable development.

The Association offers a dedicated package for students. Members receive a monthly journal that contains a range of articles and news stories written by a variety of practitioners and academics. They also receive discounts on conferences and training as well as a range of TCPA publications. There are also regular bulletins sent by email. Further details are available via: http://www.tcpa.org.uk/

Urban Design Group (UDG)

The Urban Design Group is a campaigning membership organisation with over 1,000 members who care about the quality of life in cities, towns and villages, and believe that raising standards of urban design is central to their improvement. Members receive copies of the 'Urban Design' journal and are given access to the Urban Design Directory which offers information on urban design practices and courses. Reduced rates are offered for student members.

The UDG website contains a wealth of information for anyone interested in urban design and offers details of publications and job vacancies. The website, which is supported by a regular e-bulletin, also provides information on future urban design events. Further details are available via: http://www.udg.org.uk/

(Continued)

(Continued)

Transport Planning Society (TPS)

The Transport Planning Society provides professional development and a meeting place for all those working in the transport sector and leads the response to emerging policy challenges. The society is actively involved in:

- improving education and training to create skilled professionals
- identifying and promoting good practice
- connecting with the regions and nations
- engaging with younger professionals
- promoting working in the sector as an attractive career option
- developing links with other organisations and professions.

A dedicated membership package for students is available which allows, amongst other things, for free attendance at Society meetings and events throughout the country, a bi-annual newsletter, and discounts on a range of related books and publications. Further details are available via: http://www.tps.org.uk/

Other organisations and professional associations

Joining other groups and organisations may also be worthwhile; their relevance may depend on the actual structure of your course. Examples include:

- **Chartered Institute of Logistics and Transport:** http://www.cilt.ie/home.html
- **Institute of Environmental Management and Assessment (IEMA):** http://www.iema.net/student-membership
- **International Planning History Society (IPHS):** http://planninghistory.org/membership.html
- **Regional Studies Association:** http://regionalstudies.org/
- **Royal Geographical Society:** http://www.rgs.org/HomePage.htm
- **Royal Institution of Chartered Surveyors:** http://www.rics.org/uk/
- **Royal Institute of British Architects:** http://www.architecture.com/

Reviewing your material

Once you have brought together the resources you were looking for it is necessary to see whether they fulfil their intended purpose, i.e. will it help you respond to the type of questions that you might have asked yourself when developing your lecture notes or completing an assignment. Although you can assess the resource by reading the article in full, it is often useful to skim or scan the text beforehand to see if a more detailed read would be useful.

Scanning may simply involve you flicking through the document to see if the type of words or headings you expected to see are present. Skimming requires greater interrogation and involves reading certain sections of the text such as the introduction and conclusion.

The abstract of a journal is particularly helpful in this – it is a front-page statement highlighting the general aims of the paper, the relevant context, the approach that the author has taken in preparing the work, and the results or observations that have been made. The notes on the back of a book offer something similar.

Taking a critical approach

Once you have a shortlist of articles to read it is time to start looking through them in detail. To do this justice it is important that you choose the time of the day when you feel most awake, and are in an environment where you can think or concentrate. Before you start reading the article, it is useful to remind yourself of the type of information or perspectives that you are trying to find out; as you see these 'answers' appear it is worth taking some appropriate notes.

As you read an academic text it is important to appreciate and evaluate what is being said. In other words, you need to take a critical stance to your reading. The kind of questions you should be asking are:

- What is the purpose of the article? Why has it been written?
- Who is the paper authored by? Is the author, or authors, similar in their background? Has the author or writing team produced work in this field before? Has the work been cited by others in the field?
- Is there an intended audience?
- When was the article published?
- If the paper refers to some kind of research activity, does it give an indication as to how and when this was undertaken? Do the methods described appear appropriate?
- Do the results of any research activity appear logical?
- Is it possible to see any of the data that the author might have used? Do you agree with the conclusions that the author may have come up with following their analysis of the data?
- Does the article go into a sufficient amount of detail? Have any omissions in content been made and if so, are they significant?
- How has the work and thoughts of others been represented in the text? Is the approach to referencing appropriate?
- Is the article adding something new? Is it advancing a theoretical debate or providing up-to-date reactions to some kind of policy initiative?
- Does the paper appear to be biased in any way?
- Are the results or conclusions appropriate given the research or analysis undertaken?

These questions will certainly help you to engage with the text but it also useful to think about the general narrative of the article. Imagine that you have been asked to give a one-minute summary; what you would say?

Writing your thoughts alongside the type of questions above will certainly be useful and will provide obvious support as and when you develop your lecture notes or progress with your coursework. Apart from writing notes per article, also think about the connections that might exist between different papers. Can some form of common ground be identified? Where do the differences in opinion fall? Do the articles raise similar issues or concerns? Some kind of diagram might be useful to show this. For example, you could use some kind of spider diagram where the titles of each article you have read are positioned around the keywords you used to undertake your initial search.

Further advice about how to make the most of your reading in your dissertation, essay and report writing is included in Chapters 11 and 12. However, to conclude this section it is useful to introduce the importance of referencing.

Referencing

This is a key requirement for university work and is something that might take a while to get used to. In essence, if you draw from the work of others then the sources must be properly attributed. Referencing is an important part to assessment since:

- it allows a reader to appreciate the effort you have put in your work; the more sources you use, the higher the mark you are likely to receive;
- it provides the relevant details for a reader to go about finding the sources themselves; and
- it provides a safeguard against being accused of plagiarism. Plagiarism is an academic offence that is applied when it is felt that a student has presented somebody else's work as their own. Identifying the sources you have used obviously helps to counter this but there are clearly limits. Copying two whole pages of text and including it in your essay unchanged will still constitute an offence even if you attempt to offer a cursory acknowledgement to the author.

Different approaches to referencing exist so it is important that you are clear about the particular system your university uses. The Harvard system is perhaps the most common but variations exist around certain aspects of the code. For example, the University of the West of England has developed what it calls the UWE Harvard standard which sets out in detail the approach that the institution expects its staff and students to follow. The guidance explains how different sources should be acknowledged or cited in the text as you write and how they should be listed at the end of your work. Box 3.5 provides an overview of the entries and editing that is likely to be necessary through using a book. Appendix four offers a more comprehensive guide for how other sources are typically cited and referenced but you should check the guidelines published by your own institution. However, key points include:

- if the point you are making in your essay or report originates from a particular source then you need to cite the author's surname and the year in which the work was published in brackets at the end of the sentence, e.g. (Sheppard and Smith, 2013). An alternative to this, and typical if you want to identify the significance of the author, is to state the author's surname in the main body of the sentence with the year of publication in brackets. It is typical for some kind of reporting word to be used when doing this, e.g. Sheppard and Smith (2013) allege or consider or contend or demonstrate or explain or find or propose or report or show or suggest that referencing is an important skill to develop. However, as this example shows, care is needed over the type of reporting word used since each option can have a significant impact on the direction of the sentence;
- every time you cite a source in the body of your text you will need to provide full details of the resource in a list of references. This list should follow the conclusion to you work;
- references are listed alphabetically by author in ascending order. Where you use the same author more than once it is common to include the most recent publication first;
- if a source has been written by three or more authors it usual for the words 'et al.' (meaning 'and others') to be inserted in the text after the name of the first author;
- give the edition number of the book where appropriate (e.g. Fifth ed.);
- where a book is an edited volume it is important to add (ed.) or (eds) after their name(s);
- in those instances where the same author publishes a number of pieces in a single year it is usual practice to include suffixes after the date, such as Sheppard and Smith (2013a), Sheppard and Smith (2013b) and Sheppard and Smith (2013c) and so on;
- if you want to include a quote from a piece of work, and it is less than 30 words, it is usual for this to be included within quotation marks ("..."). Inverted commas ('...'), often known as single quotation marks, should be used for a quote within a quote. The page number must be included in addition to the author's surname and publication date. The format by which page numbers are represented can vary. Sometimes they are inserted after a colon, such as Sheppard and Smith (2013: 23). However, it is also common to include page numbers after a comma following the date of publication, with 'p' being inserted for a single page and 'pp' for multiple pages, such as (Sheppard and Smith, 2013, pp. 26–34). When you include a quote it is important that the selected text is not presented out of context;
- if you want to use an extract of text that exceeds 30 words it is typical for this quote to be presented below the sentence as indented text (there is some variation as to whether this quoted text is denoted by using quotation marks);
- if you want to remove certain words from a quote then use an ellipsis ("..." three dots). Such a device is often useful to remove the first or last words of a sentence, but it is obviously important that this type of editing does not alter the meaning of the text forming the quote;

- it is important to highlight the title of a book or journal (rather than the title of the chapter or article) in some way; italicising the text is the most common;
- some students choose to produce a separate and much broader bibliography to cover everything they have considered, irrespective of whether they have proceeded to actually cite the reference in their work. Practice on this varies though and having a single list of references is usually the standard.

It is important to take a consistent approach as you acknowledge and list your reference material. Do not mix styles. While a robust approach to referencing takes time to develop, it will serve you well; marks will be lost if sources are missing from your references list, or references are inconsistently cited through the text.

Box 3.5 Referring to a book in your work

Conventions vary as we have already identified but the examples below show how a book can be used as a source in the text and be listed as a reference in your work.

As a citation:

Some cities have pursued growth by trying to capture the command and control functions of the global economy (Newman and Thorney, 2011).

or

Newman and Thornley (2011) explain how some cities have pursued growth by trying to capture the command and control functions of the global economy.

A direct quote (with less than 30 words):

In considering the growth of world cities, Newman and Thornley (2011: 278) describe how "cities have been orientating their strategies towards capturing the 'command and control' functions of the global economy".

A direct quote (with more than 30 words):

In considering the growth of world cities, Newman and Thornley (2011: 278) describe how:

In recent years cities have been orientating their strategies towards capturing the "command and control" functions of the global economy. Tokyo has positioned itself as a leading world city containing the headquarters of top transnational firms and banks.

Or

In recent years:

> Cities have been orientating their strategies towards capturing the "command and control" functions of the global economy. Tokyo has positioned itself as a leading world city containing the headquarters of top transnational firms and banks. (Newman and Thornley, 2011: 278)

As listed in your references:

Newman, P. and Thornley, A. (2011) *Planning world cities: Globalization and urban politics.* Second ed. London: Palgrave Macmillan.

 **tip**

A variety of online tools now exist to help with your referencing; some will be useful as you compile a references list while others are useful for citing material. Examples include EndNote, ProCite, Reference Manager and RefWorks. All of these programmes are chargeable but it is likely that your institution will have chosen a package which you can use for free. Check with your library for information.

Conclusions

While this chapter has outlined the importance of using information to support your study, its key messages have relevance to your post-university life as a planner. For example, if you are preparing a plan for your town, current practice refers to the importance of developing a comprehensive, up-to-date and sufficiently robust evidence base. You will therefore need to explore what exists, critically review it, and draw out the key messages that will ultimately underpin the policy and proposals that you may feel are necessary.

As you communicate these ideas people will want to know (and test for themselves) the links with the relevant literature and evidence. To do this justice you will clearly need to provide accurate information as to the sources you have looked at and the particular pages or paragraphs that you saw as being significant. Failure to provide such an audit trail will undermine your professionalism and could ultimately cost you your job!

Review points

When reflecting on this chapter you might consider the following:

- there are a variety of sources from which information and ideas can be obtained
- in order to find relevant information it is important that you are clear about the reasons for seeking the material (i.e. what questions do you want or need to answer?)
- university libraries have established systems for cataloguing material – understanding these will save you time
- it is important to read texts critically by asking such things as to why the document was produced
- all material must be properly cited and referenced as you begin to develop your work.

Further reading

Some of themes raised through this chapter will be developed in further detail over the proceeding chapters with specific texts being identified. Nevertheless some useful titles include:

- Dochartaigh, N. (2012) *Internet research skills*. Third ed. London: Sage.
- Hargreaves, S. (2012) *Study skills for students with dyslexia*. London: Sage.
- Shon, P. (2012) *How to read journal articles in the social sciences: A very practical guide for research students*. London: Sage.
- Wallace, M. And Wray, A. (2011) *Critical reading and writing for postgraduates*. Second ed. London: Sage.
- Williams, K. And Carroll, J. (2009) *Referencing and understanding plagiarism (pocket study skills)*. Basingstoke: Palgrave Macmillan.

Part two

Study Skills for Town and
Country Planning

4

Time Management

Aims

To identify the importance of being well-managed and clear about the tasks you need to complete. The chapter suggests ways in which your time can be efficiently used, ensuring that timescales are met and commitments fulfilled.

Learning outcomes

After reading this chapter you will:

- recognise the importance of managing your time
- identify the need to identity and map key commitments
- appreciate how project-work can be managed
- consider the steps that can be taken to ensure that you work as efficiently as possible.

Introduction

One of the most important skills that you will develop during your time at university is effective time management. This is something that students often find difficult to grasp at first but, with appropriate thought and action, the ability to manage your time and to respond to competing pressures can be successfully developed.

A common question that many students ask is how many hours they need to devote to their course each week. The answer, for some, is often quite surprising since many fail to take account of the time that needs to be devoted alongside the more formal lectures, seminars and workshops that are scheduled in any one week. While this formal contact could be in the order of 12 to 15 hours each week, the reality is that you will need to at least double this figure if you are to do well and engage with your studies.

In contrast to school, college or work, where your activities per day may be strictly timetabled with clear start and finish times, a standard university day is often very different with commitments being concentrated at certain times of the day or week.

Although some students initially talk about having 'free' time around their core activities, this time will need to be actively used for reading, completing coursework, group work and other activities to support learning. Your lecturers may help to provide some direction as to how your time should be used, for instance by directing you to certain pages of a book, but you will need to take key decisions yourself. For instance, should you develop your lecture notes, should you go to the library, or should you start an essay? It is these types of decision that you will need to make from the first few weeks of your course.

You may need to balance study around other key commitments, such as looking after members of your family or undertaking paid work. You should also make time for yourself; studying is hard work both mentally and physically so achieving a good life—work balance is really important.

Organising your time

The key to being a successful and independent learner is to know what you have to do and by when. Having some kind of organiser is perhaps the easiest way of ensuring that you are clear and prepared in terms of what you have to do. A paper-based organiser could be just a standard diary with pages being used to record commitments over the course of a day or week. Dedicated academic diaries are likely to represent the best option and include other useful features such as blank timetables and schedules for programming your work. Alternatively, you may prefer to purchase a blank notebook which you can begin to personalise and shape to fit your own particular tastes.

Rather than use a paper-based resource you may prefer to use an application on either your phone or computer. Various programmes exist and offer the benefit that information can be updated in real-time and be configured to provide appropriate reminders.

tip

You might find that your university has its own diary which you can purchase on campus at a discounted rate. These in-house organisers often have relevant dates already included which might save you some time in transferring information across.

Activity

As you start or return to university, try and answer the following questions. Mark the dates on your wall-planner and in your physical or electronic organiser.

- How is the university year structured? When are your main teaching blocks?
- Are there particular weeks in the year when exams are likely to be scheduled? Are there key dates for submitting coursework?
- When can you re-sit an exam or re-submit a piece of coursework if you are unsuccessful at passing at the first attempt?
- Have any field trips been arranged during the academic year? How much will these trips cost? When will balances need to be settled by and when will key forms or confirmations be required to be submitted?
- Do you have any work-based placements during the year? When do you need to choose an employer or agree a project brief? Are there any career events scheduled?
- Do you need to attend other programme-centred events, such as computer workshops or staff-student liaison meetings?
- Have you booked a holiday? Have you promised to visit friends and family on certain weekends?
- Are there any other commitments that could interfere with your studies (such as medical treatments or jury service)?

Once you have answered these questions, and key dates entered, you can begin to add further detail by noting more regular and finer commitments such as when lectures, seminars and workshops are organised each week. In doing so you should seek to ensure that details concerning time and location are appropriately recorded.

Your organiser can also keep a track of any meetings you have with members of staff (such as a personal or module tutor) or with fellow students.

 **tip**

Time-keeping is an area that referees typically have to comment on once you apply for a job. So, if you do happen to be running late, or miss an appointment in some way, then be sure to pass on your apologies as soon as possible to the relevant member of staff. To help minimise this issue you might also want to try and organise meetings and appointments at certain blocks each week (for instance, each Thursday morning).

You will also need to enter the hand-in dates of key pieces of coursework, or the days that exams or in-class tests have been arranged. It is typical for your assessments to be set at the start of each term and for hand-in dates to be grouped together; you might even have to submit your work on one set day. Work is typically penalised if it is submitted late so it is important that you plan ahead to ensure that your work is handed in on time and in the correct format. The activity set out in Table 4.1 encourages you to develop a template which should help you keep everything on track.

TABLE 4.1   Assessment tracker

To ensure that certain tasks are not overlooked it is useful to develop some kind of table or template where key details concerning the assessment can be entered. The design of this can suit your own needs and be either physical or electronic in form but the example below suggests the type of columns that might be useful to begin with. Additional columns could get you thinking about the resources that might be needed, or whether particular instructions have been given concerning how the work is to be submitted. Importantly the template makes a distinction between both formative and summative forms of assessment (these terms were introduced in Chapter two).

Module title	Module leader (email address)	F=Formative S= Summative	Nature of submission/ assessment	Length (e.g. words or pages or length of presentation)	Weight of assessment to the module	**Deadline**
Example one						
Example two						
Example three and so on						

Once you are clear about how your academic year will run, and the assignments and examinations you will have to complete, it is worth planning your activities in and around your regular commitments. This kind of 'to-do' list can be produced on either a weekly or daily basis; a commitment to both might be useful during particularly busy periods. In preparing these lists you should seek to:

- identify your general focus for the day or week and seek to prioritise the tasks or activities you have identified. In order that these are sufficiently clear, you might want to rank them according to their urgency from 1 (high) to 4 (low). You could also differentiate by colour or by using some kind of symbol;
- consider the times of the day during which you are at your best. Some people feel fresher at the start of the day while others the reverse. You may also find that certain tasks are better suited to specific times of the day than others;
- identify the periods during which study is likely to be impossible or, at the very least, difficult. For instance, there is no point in scheduling study when you know you will be out with friends, taking part in sport, or working. Try and be realistic with respect to your goals;
- break tasks down into bite-sized portions. However daunting the final project may be, its contributing elements will be much more manageable;
- be clear as to what you are intending to study through each designated session. For instance, if you intend to do some background reading, you might find it useful to set a target for reading so many chapters or a certain number of pages. If you are working on an essay, then you might find it useful to set a target relating to the number of pages or words to draft. If you are successful in meeting your target then think of a way to reward yourself. Conversely, if you failed to achieve your target, or were distracted by something, then try and understand the reasons for this and consider how they might be resolved to ensure successful study next time;
- take regular breaks. Although you should seek to achieve your targets it is important that you know your limits. If you feel that you are becoming tired or disengaged with the activity then take a break. Continuing when you feel drained is counter-productive; it is better for you to put your mind to something else;
- identify the resources that are likely to be necessary for successful study. This could include reading material, your lecture notes or just items of stationery.

It is also worth thinking about where you should study. There are clearly many options, including on-site facilities at the university, your own room or house, a local library, or even a nearby café or bar. Some may be more suitable to a particular task. For instance proof-reading your work might be difficult in a busy or noisy environment whereas browsing the internet looking for resources may be fine.

You may also want to think about whether you want to work alone or with others. Working with a friend or two might be a positive experience if you bounce ideas around and motivate each other. However, having somebody else with you might cause an unnecessary distraction, especially if they are less committed to work than you are or are on a different programme where the assessment profile is different.

In addition to choosing the best location for study it is also important for you to keep your workspace neat and inviting. Think about possible distractions to study and remove them; a good example would be switching off your mobile phone or placing it away from your desk. You may also find it useful to disconnect from a network or WiFi connection while you work; being online is clearly helpful to study but could cause a distraction if you are alerted to incoming emails or those wishing to chat.

Designating a single ring binder for each of the modules you are taking might be useful, with different colours being used to denote different subjects. You should seek to file your lecture notes, relevant readings, and information about relevant assessment at the end of each week or session. Rather than storing this information physically, you may choose to create a folder on your hard disk, portable hard drive or USB memory stick. The portability of the latter may be useful if you decide to choose a variety of places to study.

Creating a library, by means of folders on your computer, may be useful for storing documents. Folders can be labelled to match your own interests but could include key themes such as plan-making, development management, energy, transport, housing and so on. Having such a resource will be extremely useful and will save you looking for the same documents in those circumstances where the document link becomes broken or is removed from the host website or where your internet connection is down (which often happens just at the time when you need it most). You may also want to collect together other bits of information, perhaps a really good design and access statement you have come across or maybe a company brochure which you might be interested in exploring at greater depth in the future. Given the size of a typical disk drive you can probably download and store as much as you like.

When times feel pressured

An effective approach to time management should help you improve your use of time but there are periods when you are likely to feel pressured. This may coincide with the week during which coursework needs to be submitted or when exams have been scheduled. Feeling slightly stressed is often helpful as it can focus your mind but it can also be very damaging and lead to such things as sleep loss, irritability and general poor health.

Stress associated with study may be accentuated by other factors too, such as financial concerns, health-related issues, or a breakdown in a relationship. Some first year undergraduate students often feel down during the first weeks of their university term as a result of concerns over meeting new friends or from being somewhere new. Part-time students may find it particularly stressful when combining certain elements of their study with other family or work-based commitments.

 **tip**

In those situations where you feel are you becoming overwhelmed it is important that you tell somebody about it. Your friends and family will certainly want to help you but you may also want to contact your personal or module tutor if you feel your stress is work related. If immediate members of staff find it difficult to give advice then most, if not all, universities will have specialist advice centres where counselling and direct help can be offered.

Conclusions

In this chapter we have focused on the importance of managing time. Effective study places many different demands on you and key decisions about how you learn, and the activities you undertake day to day, are determined by you. Knowing what you have to do and by when is critical and it is something that lecturing staff (and future employers) will want to ensure that you master during your time at university. The chapter encouraged you to think about how you can work more efficiently to ensure that deadlines are met and achieve a good life–work balance.

Further reading

While effective time management is an element that a number of books on study skills cover, some equally useful publications are also available for the more general business market. Example titles include:

- Allen, D. (2002) *Getting things done: How to achieve stress-free productivity.* London: Piatkus.
- Clayton, M. (2010) *Brilliant time management: What the most productive people know, do and say.* London: Pearson Business.

A useful source for dealing with study-related stress is provided by the following source:

- Rugg, G., Gerrard, S. and Hooper, S. (2008) *The stress-free guide to studying at university (Sage study skills series)*. London: Sage.

Review points

When reflecting on this chapter you might consider the following:

- the need to schedule key dates and commitments
- the importance of having some kind of organiser which you keep up-to-date
- the times of the day and week during which you seem to perform better
- the most appropriate place to study given the tasks you need to complete
- how distractions to study can be minimised.

5

Leadership and Team-Working

Aims

To explore the importance of effective leadership and team-working when studying town planning, and to support the development of personal skills in this area.

Learning outcomes

After reading this chapter you will:

- understand the role and importance of leadership and team-working within the town planning profession
- understand the role and importance of leadership and team working to the study of town planning at university
- develop skills to improve your ability to function effectively within a team, and take a leadership role with success.

Introduction

In the previous chapter you explored time management and how to manage your studies on your own. This is extremely important to your effectiveness and success at university, but it is also the case that much of what you do at university, and outside of your studies, involves you working with a team of some sort. Regardless of your background, you will, throughout your life, have found yourself in a situation where you are either part of a team, or indeed leading a team. This can range from the obvious, like being part of a football, rugby, hockey or netball team, to the less overt, such as your role within a family unit or when going out with friends.

Teams are extremely important to many of the things we all do, whether in the home, at work, or in our social lives. Bringing people together, using the skills, knowledge and abilities of the team members to best effect, means that the outputs are maximised, performance is enhanced and the outcome is the best it can be.

Teams function in different ways, and do not always have a leader, but in most cases someone will take a leading role to coordinate and manage the team. This may occur through a natural process of selection, or may be the result of a conscious selection of the most suitable person to lead the team.

Whilst at university you will find yourself regularly formed into teams, and in most cases there will be a need for someone to lead that team. Preparing yourself for this will enable you to improve your performance in whatever role you have, and in turn help the team be as successful as possible.

Teams and you

Teams are all about a group of people working together towards a common goal. At university you will find that you will have numerous activities and assessments that are based around a team producing an output, such as a report or presentation. You will be responsible for, or contributing to, one element of the output, but will also have to contribute to the workings of the team.

The reason we have teams is that they are considered to bring multiple advantages over individual working. The crux of the argument is that by combining the abilities of the individuals within the group, and through the effective management of the group and the way in which it works, and by focusing upon a common goal, the goal can be achieved more effectively.

John Adair, a noted writer in the field of leadership and team-working, presents the difference between an *effective* team working towards a goal, and a group of individuals working without interactions and relationships such that it is unable to act as a single unit and secure the goal. When the individuals in the 'team' are all doing their own thing, pointing in their own direction, and acting/operating independently of one another, they are not effective and the goal cannot be achieved successfully because not everyone is pulling in the same direction. A successful team is one where all of the individuals are acting towards a common goal through working together effectively. Through such an approach we can achieve success as a team (Adair, 2009).

Effective teams are not an inevitable certainty, however. Some teams prove entirely unsuccessful. The effectiveness of the team comes down to the people who are in the team and the manner in which it is managed and functions.

Activity

Think of a team you were part of, perhaps from when you were at school or college. Write down what you think you brought to the team; your positive and negative attributes.

Consider how you can make the most of your advantages and address your negatives. Being self-aware can help us to be a better team player. By identifying our own strengths and weaknesses we can be more conscious of how we are working within a team, and how we can perform to the best of our ability in the interests of supporting the team to achieve the goal.

R. Meredith Belbin is a noted contributor to thinking about teams, what makes them successful, and how we can form and manage teams more effectively. Everyone has different strengths and weaknesses, the key is identifying these and maximising the potential of the team by working with the strengths of each individual. This will certainly be the case when you are both studying at university and when you begin your career in planning. Belbin (2010) has identified nine team roles which we can map team members against, allowing us to better understand our own strengths and weaknesses. The nine roles can be summarised as follows:

1. Plant – a highly creative problem solver who will use less conventional methods of dealing with issues.
2. Resource Investigator – the link between the team and what is taking place outside the team. Makes sure the team remains relevant and competitive.
3. Coordinator – someone who ensures that the people within the team are playing to their strengths, doing the most appropriate tasks, and that the team is working in a coordinated and effective manner.
4. Shaper – ensures the team is motivated, focused and driven to deliver.
5. Monitor Evaluator – an individual who can weigh up the options in a dispassionate and logical manner.
6. Team Worker – provides the glue that binds the team together and makes sure the internal dynamics are effective.
7. Implementer – a very practical individual who gets things done in an efficient and effective manner.
8. Completer – acts as quality controller. Provides the finishing touches and refines the output.
9. Specialist – provides in-depth knowledge within a given area.
   Belbin, M. (2010a: 22)

Activity

Go back to the notes you made in response to the first activity in this chapter. Consider the attributes you listed and think about which of Belbin's team roles you most closely conformed to in the scenario you were looking at. Look at Belbin's website (http://www.belbin.com/rte.asp?id=1) for assistance with this.

If a group can map out the team roles present, they can ensure people are playing to their strengths and that the team is shaped in such a manner that allows it to produce the best output possible.

Belbin also identifies allowable weaknesses assigned to each of the roles, and this is an important consideration. Take a look at the website identified in the last activity and reflect upon the suggested weakness for the role you have identified for yourself. Knowing our limitations is just as important as knowing our strengths. Identifying both our strengths and our weaknesses allows us to maximise, compensate and mitigate as required to take full advantage of our abilities.

It is important to remember that teams are of differing sizes, that different roles will be present in each circumstance, and the choice of who is in the team may not be in your hands. You cannot always form the team you ideally want and unfortunately you might find yourself working in a team that is unbalanced and under-performing. Notwithstanding this, any team can perform to the best of its ability if it is conscious of its strengths and weaknesses. By doing this you can create an approach within your team to compensate for the areas of weakness. The key is to know what you have, and think about how you can make the most of it.

Teams at university

From your first week at university you will likely find yourself in teams. Team-working is very important to town and country planning because although you will be given your own work and given a degree of independence to complete it, you will also find yourself working within a team on regular occasions; indeed you may find yourself acting as the lynchpin in a team. To take the example of a planner working in local government or for a private sector consultancy, the planner will find themselves in a team of some form, but they might also be acting as the lead officer or consultant. Acting as a team means that the leader will, or should, be supported by a team of individuals providing technical, specialist and support roles. Being team leader is a little bit like being in the centre of a cartwheel, acting as the hub, with the spokes representing all of the vital people who work together to become the wheel:

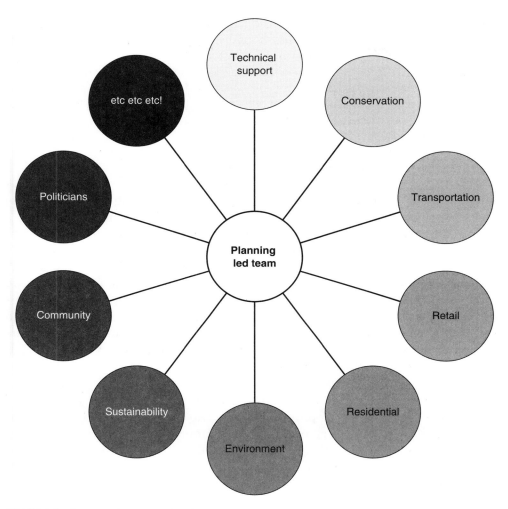

FIGURE 5.1   Town and country planning teams

The multi-disciplinary and inter-disciplinary nature of planning means that team-working will be embedded within your studies. Knowing yourself, as discussed in the previous section, is important to your ability to perform within a team. But you are, of course, just part of the team. Teams are not always successful. You will find that some of the teams you are in do not perform well. There can be conflict within the team, or a team can struggle to gel. At university you may also find some people are more willing than others to contribute, and indeed sometimes people will not engage at all. With this in mind it is important to consider how teams develop. Tuckman and Jenson (1977), cited in Hargie, O (2011), identify the particular stages a team moves through in its development:

- Forming – this is where the individuals come together to form a team, roles are established, tasks are identified, and relationships are worked out. Sometimes teams fail at this point because the team is unable to form effectively.
- Storming – conflict occurs as the team attempts to find the best way of working and each team member finds their position within the team and in relation to the task. This can be a positive stage in development if managed properly because it is during this phase that issues are normally resolved and conflicts dealt with.
- Norming – the team settles and finds an equilibrium.
- Performing – the team begins to perform.
- Adjourning – the work is completed and the team dissolved.

Being aware of these stages is important because recognising how this process works helps the team to move through the stages and perform as required.

Your planning course will, as has previously been noted, include a significant number of situations where you will be placed into teams. This could be for a simple classroom-based activity, or it could be for assessment purposes. The formation of the team might be artificial, that is to say the team is only necessary because of the extent of work involved and the desire of the tutors to include team-working within the skills developed in the module. In other cases however, the team could be necessary because your studies are simulating a practice-based scenario, the kind you could find yourself in once you enter the planning profession. For example, you could be placed in a multi-disciplinary team with architects, surveyors and engineers to simulate how, in the real world, these professions all interact within the process of development; that is, the process from idea and concept through to the delivery of the development on the ground, its subsequent use and the steps taken after the use has ceased. Alternatively, you might be in a group with other planners to simulate how planners work together on major projects, drawing out and maximising the skills of the individuals in the team to create a better outcome.

 **tip**

When you are formed into teams at university it is easy to just dive in and get straight on with the task at hand. Instead of this, start by exploring who is in the team, what strengths they have, and what weaknesses they might possess. With this knowledge you can allocate tasks more appropriately, create a team structure that works well, and develop a team that performs as well as is possible.

In addition to the team scenarios created for you at university, you should also consider the potential of more informal team-working to improve your performance in your studies. Planning is a very broad discipline which embraces a diverse range of areas including finance, design, law, theory, policy-making, critical analysis, decision-making, sustainability, health matters, transport and so forth. It is unlikely that you will excel in all of these areas, but you may find that between a few of your friends and peers you can cover all of the areas. You can then form study teams so you can support each other. This can be extremely beneficial for all concerned, but it is extremely important that you are conscious of plagiarism. Plagiarism is basically where you copy someone's work and present it as your own. This can have very serious consequences at university, including failure and exclusion. Study teams can, however, play an important supporting role so, as long as it is done properly, consider getting together with your peers and friends to maximise your success.

Being at university is about more than developing your academic knowledge, it is also about developing your personal skills; indeed these are actually just as important as the academic knowledge you will gain. It is going to be just as important to be a good team member when you are at work as it is that you know about a particular area of planning law or finance, and the same is the case with your studies. Regardless of your own abilities, if you are working in a team, and being assessed as a team, you need to perform as a team. With this in mind you should ensure that, having undertaken the two activities in this chapter, you identify all of the areas that you could develop to improve your ability to work well within a team. Your time at university is the ideal opportunity to improve yourself and develop your personal and professional skills so that when you enter the workplace you are conscious of your weaknesses and you have minimised them whilst maximising your strengths. You will be given plenty of opportunities to grow personally and intellectually while at university so make the most of it!

A final area for consideration in relation to team-working at university is to think about the role your tutors will play throughout your studies. You and your tutors are a team, the goal being for you to get the degree outcome you want. Each of your tutors will have a different skill area and specialist knowledge which you can draw on to aid you complete your course to the best of your ability. A further consideration in this context is that your relationship with your tutors will have a team dynamic similar in certain respects to the one you will have with some of the more senior practitioners when you enter the workplace. It is important to remember that hierarchies often exist in teams, with some partners having a more senior role than others. Leadership of teams is an important consideration in planning practice, but it will also be of significance to your studies whilst at university.

Leading at university

Where you have a team it is a likely that you will also have a team leader. Sports teams have captains, work teams have leaders, and even friendship groups will be led by one person in many individual circumstances. During your studies you will, as discussed in the section above, be formed into teams. If this is for a small classroom-based exercise it may be that no leader is identified, emerges, or indeed is required because of the direction given to you by your tutor. However, for larger projects a leader will normally be required. A team leader may be appointed, or it may be that it is for the team to identify its own leader through a conscious selection process. In other cases a leader will just emerge by virtue of the circumstance, task requirements and/or the character types present in the team.

Personal attributes like courage, intelligence, initiative, integrity, and will-power are often identified as making for good leadership qualities, but not everyone possesses these character traits. So are leaders born? Or created? It is thought by some that leaders are born, not created. Traits theory suggests that people have innate ability from birth to be a good leader. The majority view however is that leadership can be learned, developed and nurtured.

You will likely find yourself as a team leader at some point during your studies, and this is an excellent opportunity to hone your skills in preparation for entering the planning profession. You will find yourself in both team roles and leadership roles as a planning professional; for example, you will likely find yourself in a number of different teams with differing roles and dynamics, and you will find yourself in differing positions within these teams. For instance, a development management case officer could find themselves with roles in the following scenarios:

- team member of the service area or directorate
- team member of the department
- team leader/member of an area team
- team leader/member of a sub-area team
- application case officer leading a team of specialists and consultants (the hub in the centre of the wheel)
- pre-application case officer leading a team of specialists and consultants
- team member of a consultation group
- team leader of a consultation group
- team member of an advisory group
- team leader of an advisory group.

Of course, it is not only important that you use your university experience to prepare for such circumstances; you should also aspire to perform well during your studies to maximise your potential marks and degree level.

It is generally accepted that there is no one list of traits that make for a good leader. Different people have different characters and use different methods of managing and leading; often reflecting the wider circumstances. For example, is it a formal or informal scenario? Are you working within a set organisational structure and approach? The traits you have will inform the style of leader you are, but so too will the circumstances you find yourself in and the training/support you have.

Effective team-building and leadership

As noted previously, effective teams rarely just happen, they need effective leadership. With regards to an *approach* to leadership, there are numerous schools of thought, but John Adair takes an integrative approach to leadership, team-building and achieving team success; which is ultimately the goal of effective leadership. A holistic view is considered where the three common needs of all teams are defined; specifically, the task, the team and the individual. It is also important to think about the inter-relationship between these factors. The importance of the leader in the context of these needs is clear. John Adair developed a theory based upon this concept, known as the 'action-centred approach'. The model that is used to demonstrate the theory highlights that it is the point where we can achieve overlap between the need to achieve the task, develop the individuals in the team, and build the team where we will achieve success. Effectively there is a 'sweet-spot' where the relationship between these factors is such that they all overlap and therefore a team will be effective (Adair, 2009).

An effective leader is conscious of the action-centred approach and attempts to ensure that all of the elements of the model are considered; the individuals in the team must be supported and developed, the team itself must be supported, and a focus must remain upon achieving the task. During your studies at university you will find yourself working to deadlines and with particular assessment requirements that you need to meet. These are the task and the time-scale within which you must achieve them. You and your peers are the team who must be supported as individuals and as a group to deliver on the task and, ultimately, get the best mark you can from the assessment. All of this will also be relevant when you enter the workplace, of course; planners are always working to deadlines and the success or failure of the project will depend upon the ability of the team and its leader to achieve the task effectively, which means being a successful team that is well led.

The ability of an individual to deliver on the action-centred approach is easier said than done, of course. John Adair's approach to achieving team success does provide further support however by identifying the key functions which a team leader should focus upon and be responsible for to ensure that the task is achieved and the team successful. Adair identifies the following functions:

- Planning – seeking all available information, defining the task, developing a plan.
- Initiating – through briefing groups and allocating tasks.
- Controlling – maintaining standards, influencing tempo, maintaining focus on objectives.
- Supporting – encouraging group/individuals, creating a team spirit, maintaining discipline, reconciling differences.
- Informing – clarifying, providing new information as it becomes available.
- Evaluating activities – feasibility monitoring and testing, evaluating group performance. Adair, J. (2009: 122)

It is not always easy for a leader to carry out all of these tasks though, and this is where delegation of responsibility comes in. Despite this, it is always the responsibility of the leader to ensure that any delegated actions and roles are undertaken successfully. If this is achieved, the team should be in a position to deliver on the task and perform as a group.

Activity

Think about different scenarios where you have been in a leadership position, either formally or informally. Write down a list of all of the strengths and weaknesses you can think of.

In the same way that it is important to be self-aware when working in teams generally, it is also important to be conscious of the strengths and weaknesses that we have as a leader.

Reflect upon the strengths and weaknesses that you have and reflect upon how you might maximise your abilities as a leader. What could you do to improve yourself? How could you be a more effective 'action-centred' leader?

 **tip**

Remember, effective leadership can be learned, developed and nurtured and good teams can be actively developed. Think about people who are seen as good leaders, what can you learn from them? You university library will also have books exploring leadership and team-working. Try to find time to read and reflect on yourself; self-awareness is the first step to personal improvement and it can form a basis upon which you can start to improve your skills and abilities at university, and in turn prepare you as an effective team member and leader for your career in planning.

When you get an appropriate opportunity, try to lead in a manner that you feel makes the most of your advantages.

Effective planning and organisation at university

In the previous chapter you explored time management and how to manage yourself and your work most effectively as you pursue your studies at work. The discussions surrounding effective leadership and team-working in the previous sections of this chapter relate in some ways to how this self-management is translated into a group scenario i.e. you are no longer just managing yourself, but a group of people; there is the same need for conscious planning activity when working as a group. There are a number of very practical tools and methods you and your team can deploy to support the development of a successful team:

1. Understanding the task – your group will have been given a specific piece of work to complete. Does everyone in the group fully understand what is being asked of them? Have you all interpreted the task in the same way? Before you dive in at the deep end and start ploughing into the work, first establish that everyone knows what is being asked of them and write it out in a format that helps you all to agree the full parameters of the task.

2. Task identification – any task you have been set will actually be made up of a number of different elements which can be broken down and considered individually, before reconstructing the component parts and shaping it into a single, coherent and cohesive piece of work. A good way to do this is to write the task down in the middle of a large sheet of paper and then 'pull out' the different elements that you can identify from within. Next, put numbers next to them so they make sense in relation to the order they would come; you need to make sure the structure of the work makes sense.

3. Task allocation – now you know the task in detail, you need to identify who in your group is best suited to which elements. Talk to each other and find out who has knowledge, experience and skills relevant to the tasks set. With this knowledge you can assign people to the tasks identified in the previous step. Do ensure that your allocation of work is fair though, and remember, you can always have sub-groups within a group i.e. two or three people working on one or more of the tasks.

4. Time management – the work you have been set by your tutor will have a timescale attached to it. First, identify this deadline and ensure everyone writes it down. Next you need to work backwards to today's date, ensuring you build in time not only for the actual work to be undertaken, but also for it all to be brought together and put into the final format. If there is a presentation as part of the task, make sure you give yourself time to practise; do not just assume it will be alright on the night! Similarly, if you have printing

or some form of production associated with the task, give yourself plenty of time to do this and make sure you plan into your schedule a trial production phase. As a planning student you will be required to produce many formats of work, including models, maps, plans and drawings. These can all require special printers or production so ensure you factor this into your timescale.

5. Resourcing, skills and information requirements – having planned the tasks, timing and individuals, go back over your strategy and ensure you have enough resources, skills and information to deliver on the promises you are making. Do you really have the time? People? Technical skills (computer software, etc?), Information (books, journals, official publications, primary research, web-based information, etc) ? Money? Equipment? You need to be realistic about what you can deliver.

6. Space and environment management – you now have the tasks, the people identified against the tasks, and the timescale to undertake the work. One area that is often overlooked though is *where* you will do the work. You will all have your own preferred working styles, but you will need to work together as a group sometimes. Think really carefully about where is most appropriate for meetings, practices and group working to be undertaken. Is there study space you can reserve for example? It is easy to get distracted in the wrong sort of environment so it is important that you find a space and environment that suits you all as far as is possible.

7. Communication – once you start to undertake the work it is easy to move off into your own little world, failing to adequately communicate with one another. Ensure that you schedule regular meetings so you can update each other, and think about the best way to share your work as you progress, such as via email. As a planning professional you will often find yourself working in an autonomous manner but, as discussed earlier this chapter, you will still nearly always be in a team of some form. Effectively, communication is therefore going to be important for you as a professional; think about how a planning officer will liaise and work with people who may be on the other side of the city? Country? Or world?

8. Motivation – keeping motivated as an individual and a team can be difficult. If the task is hard, or if the timescale is long, it is all too easy to lose motivation. This is really difficult when you are working alone, but the great thing about working in a team is that you can keep each other going; so keep an eye out for each other and make sure everyone keeps pushing all the way to the end!

9. Maintenance of the aim – as well as being motivated, it is also important to ensure that everyone stays focused upon the aim. By exploring the task initially in detail you will be well placed to do this, but it is all too easy to stray when you start exploring your area of work. As a group you need to ensure that everyone remembers the task and their allocated responsibilities so that everyone produces what is required and the end result is what is needed. Keep monitoring your progress and performance throughout so you change things if necessary.

10. Support – there are two elements here; first, it is important to remember to support each other in the team. Things will not always go as planned and it is important that you are all there for each other, looking out for each other, and providing the necessary support when it is asked for or become apparent as required. The second

aspect here is to remember to work with your tutors throughout your project duration; your tutors *do* want you to be successful in your studies and will be able to provide support as appropriate.

11. Managing materials and outputs – do not under-estimate the final stages when you start to bring everything together. This can take longer than you might expect. Technology can also place its part here, and not in a good way! Merging documents together and building up a single piece of work can be challenging, particularly when you factor in the need to agree upon the final form and nature of the work you are submitting.

12. Testing – test your work before you submit or present it. You should initially do this within your group, sharing your final outputs with each other. This should be an on-going process. Do not leave it to the end in case you are on the wrong track! This links back to the communication point above. It is always beneficial to get an outside view of your work to allow you to reflect upon it more effectively. Try presenting your work to a 'critical friend'; this could be a friend or family member who can give you some constructive criticism. This is also good if you are presenting your work verbally; it can help build your confidence and allow you to identify areas for improvement before the big day itself.

13. Finally, remember to review your performance at the end of the process and learn lessons for next time!

Even with the best planning, leadership and team performance, things will still often go wrong, but the above steps should help ensure that the risk of things not going well is minimised!

Conflict resolution

Planning your group activities, combined with the effective management of the group by the leader using the action-centred method is the best way of ensuring an effective team. However, conflict is always possible and is one of the greatest threats to achieving the task successfully as a team.

The team-working section of this chapter talked about the phases of group development, one of which was 'storming'. Often groups will struggle with conflict in this phase, but actually conflict can occur at any time. The potential for conflict will be minimised with good leadership and support, and your tutor may be able to help with this, but it is also important for everyone in the team to think about their own behaviour and relationships within the group. The first section of this chapter asks you to reflect upon your own characteristics within a team and how you can maximise your potential; equally important is how you each respond to each other, something which is less easy to plan for.

Carl Rogers, a renowned psychotherapist, developed a humanist theory which considers how people can communicate and interact authentically to facilitate an effective team dynamic and avoid conflict. Rogers (1962) presents three core conditions which can be summarised as follows:

1. Unconditional positive regard – this means respecting a person regardless of their views, behaviour and beliefs and instead focusing upon them as an individual with a role to play in delivering the task; ultimately you need to work together;
2. Empathy – this is the consideration of the other person's perspective and considering why they might be as they are; and
3. Congruence – this is about being honest and truthful.

Working within a team and having regard to these three core conditions can help everyone focus upon the task and the necessary steps to achieve the end output without instead resulting in conflict. This links back to the action-centred leadership approach and the importance of focusing upon the task and building the team. The development of the individual can still occur in parallel to this, whilst importantly being conscious of the impact of this upon the other two functions.

Conclusions

In this chapter we have explored team-working and leadership and how you might best work in a group when at university.

Working in teams and performing well as a leader is more difficult for some than others, but everyone has strengths and weaknesses in this regard. What is most important is that you are self-aware and that you take the opportunities presented to you at university to develop your abilities so that you can play your part in a successful team and, when given the opportunity, lead a winning team that achieves the task to the highest possible standard.

Transferring your abilities; throughout this chapter there is reference to how team working and leadership skills will be needed once you enter planning practice and this is a very important point to finish this chapter with. As a planning professional you will work in teams and be in various positions of responsibility and leadership. Your time at university is the time to crack this to maximise your career potential.

Further reading

Adair, Belbin and Handy have all written good books which provide some useful commentary and thought on teams and leadership, including:

- Adair, J. (2003) *Concise Adair on communication and presentation skills.* London: Thorogood.
- Adair, J. (2009) *Effective leadership: How to be a successful leader.* London: Pan Macmillan.

- Adair, J. (2009) *Effective teambuilding: How to make a winning team.* London: Pan Macmillan.
- Belbin, M. (2010) *Team roles at work.* Oxford: Butterworth-Heinemann:
- Belbin, M. (2010) *Management teams: Why they succeed or fail.* Oxford: Butterworth-Heinemann.
- Handy, C (1976) *Understanding organisations.* Oxford: Oxford University Press.

Review points

When reflecting on this chapter you might consider the following:

- working in teams and acting as a leader is challenging and success never 'just happens'
- you have strengths and weaknesses both as a team member and a team; self-awareness of these is the foundation upon which to improve your own performance
- there are practical ways that you can develop yourself and maximise the potential of a team
- this is the time to develop yourself to improve your employability and career prospects.

6

Engagement and Negotiation

Aims

This chapter aims to explain the importance of effective negotiation activity and skills for town planning, as well as to discuss the importance of engagement beyond the planning profession with other disciplines, groups and communities.

Learning outcomes

After reading this chapter you will:

- understand the inclusive nature of planning and the importance of engagement
- recognise the diversity of groups and individuals who are involved in planning
- recognise the importance of effective negotiation to town planning
- appreciate the skills and processes associated with negotiation.

Introduction

It is all too easy to see the activity of planning as a 'closed shop', an exclusive club of professionals and experts who, thanks to their education and experience, can control the manner in which a place changes in an impartial, balanced and effective manner and in the public interest. The reality is very different. Planners, architects, surveys and other built environment professionals are indeed experts, and they are all tasked with managing the evolution of places, but it is an activity to undertake in an inclusive manner, *with*

those to whom the change will have an impact. Only the most arrogant (and ignorant) of planners would say they always know best and should be left to plan on behalf of the nation; planning as a discipline exists to balance interests remember, not to impose the will of a profession or the wishes of private individuals.

With this in mind it is plain to see that planners are involved in engagement and, because views of different people will often contradict, negotiation activities.

Engagement and participation

As noted above, the basis for the system of town planning in the UK, and the reason for the effective 'nationalisation' of land rights, is in order to balance interests. The public health origins of the modern planning system, a reaction to the conditions resulting from the Industrial Revolution, highlights the importance of considering the public interest in what are otherwise broadly private matters. Having regard to the importance of the 'public interest', it is clear that the practice of town and country planning must be one where all persons can be engaged and participate, and where fairness and impartiality drive decision-making, rather than private profit.

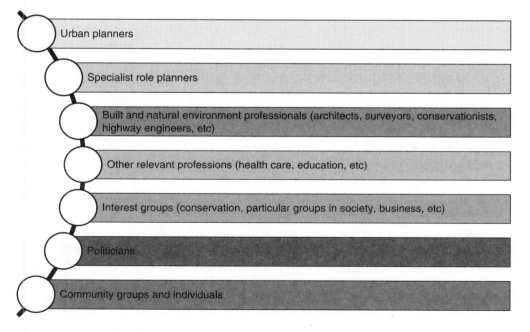

FIGURE 6.1   Examples of participants in town and country planning

Participation in planning comes in many shapes and sizes. It ranges from engagement with other professions through to the participation of the local community in the processes and activities of planning.

You will recall from the first chapter of the book that town planning involves a range of organisations and actors. As identified in Figure 6.1, this translates into a range of participants, supplemented by the wider public and the individual impacted upon in some way by the development proposal.

The way in which these different groups will participate in planning activities will vary significantly, but in planning today this interaction will take place from the very earliest stages of plan and policy formulation; this is one of the core principles behind the 'spatial planning' approach to planning.

Spatial planning is a way of approaching the activity of planning. Planning in the UK was initially focused around managing land use. This activity often took place in a relatively 'siloed' manner, without the integrated approach that has grown up into the spatial planning approach we see today. Spatial planning embraces a cross-policy strategy and solutions approach whereby town planning is one element of the integrated planning and management of all policy areas which impact upon our lives and the evolution of communities. It could be argued that this is far from a new approach to town planning activity which has, to a certain extent, been undertaken in this manner to varying degrees at least since the emergence of the modern system after the Second World War. Nevertheless, the term 'spatial planning' has become common parlance since the early 2000s, reflecting the effective formalisation and mainstreaming of the approach as recognised best practice. Having regard to the ethos of spatial planning it is clear that a participative approach is vital to delivery and place management being effective.

The manner in which participation takes place will vary significantly between the various groups and individuals concerned. This variation has two elements to it; first the opportunity for interaction, and second the nature of the interaction.

Opportunities for participation are often tied to the systems and processes associated with planning. For example, both the local plan and planning application processes present a formal schedule for enabling engagement by the various participants; this will vary between phases of collaborative working between organisations who could be considered 'internal' to the process, to a consultation period where 'external' groups and individuals have the opportunity to participate through providing their comments and input thoughts on the strategies, visions and plans. At different stages in the process, the same group may change from being internal to external in the process. Notwithstanding this, it is important to remember that participation is not tied to the process. It can, and should, be more extensive and participative than this.

You may be thinking at this point that there is a question of power being posed here, with the ability of those 'outside' of the process being given the opportunity to input their views, but not necessarily the power to actually result in change. This is a criticism sometimes raised by members of the public who, despite often being consulted on the future of the area before pen is put to paper, may later feel powerless to subsequently change the nature of the plans presented ultimately by the local planning authority.

Sherry Arnstein (1969) presented a 'ladder' of participation, with citizen control, delegated power and partnership forming the top three rungs and constituting citizen power. In the middle, making up 'tokenism', are placating, consultation and then informing. At the bottom are therapy and manipulation, considered to be non-participation. Fundamentally, the nature of the system is that, in the interests of implementation and delivery, there is a need for a schedule to exist and the processes to be managed. This inevitably leads to planning being undertaken with participation and consultation at its heart but with the local planning authority and local political leaders for the area acting as the 'lead' and ultimate decision-makers. The nature of the system is thus one which aspires to deliver a partnership approach with degrees of delegated/citizen control, but which (generally out of necessity in the context of the nature of the current system and in recognition of the often conflicting views of participants) operates with consultation and government retained power in some cases.

The management of engagement and participation

Having regard to the power relationship noted above, the local planning authority is often at the centre of the various activities that take place since it is they who manage the participation and involvement of the other actors in many cases. This is because, notwithstanding the changes associated with the 'localism' agenda, the local planning authority and political leaders for the area ultimately must make the decisions on many of the questions concerning everything from the vision and policy direction for the area for the next 20 years, to the details of an individual planning proposal.

In relation to the involvement of other governmental and non-governmental organisations (the organisations presented in Chapter 1), this is partly controlled by regulations which specify exactly who must be involved and about what. This is the case for both the preparation of plans and policies and the processing of a planning application. For example, when an area of land is at risk of flooding or pollution, the Environment Agency must be involved. This method of requiring involvement through law acts to ensure minimum standards of competence and effectiveness on the part of the key decision-makers. The involvement of these various actors is encouraged beyond these minimum requirements however, and most local authorities will seek to work with these other groups throughout the various activities taking place.

Beyond the recognised organisations discussed above, the approach to enabling participation by the wider local community is presented by all local planning authorities in their Statement of Community Involvement (SCI). This document, which represents one of the core papers in the folder of planning documentation produced by local planning authorities, presents opportunities for participation and involvement in planning activities. The SCI will:

- identify the range of community groups and organisations which need to be involved and engaged;
- set out a methodology for how the local authority will engage with all of the participants involved in planning;
- demonstrate resource availability and management competence, i.e. that they can deliver on what they say they will do; and
- set out the local authority's policy for community involvement in the plan-making process, and the determination of planning applications.

The local authority therefore sets out very clearly the when, how and who of involvement. Again, much of this is based upon minimum legal requirements but most local authorities will go beyond this to maximise participation wherever possible and viable.

It is desirable, given the role and purpose of planning, for higher rungs of Arnstein's ladder to be used as far as is possible rather than mere consultation, for example. This is an area of debate that you will explore extensively at university and a number of texts and articles specifically address these issues. You should take the time to explore this important area of planning.

Activity

Visit the website of a local authority you are familiar with in England and, through the planning policy pages, find their SCI. Work your way through this document and identify the different methods of consultation used and the circumstances where they are utilised. Now visit a couple of different local authorities on a random basis and find their SCI document; are they very different? Can you find any innovative methods that do not appear to be commonplace?

The nature of engagement and participation

The techniques employed for engagement and consultation purposes are numerous and vary depending upon the circumstances and the 'target audience' involved.

When inviting involvement from other organisations, a letter or email notification is most likely. For wider engagement activities a greater range of options are available.

Notification of the opportunity to comment on a specific planning application or the development of a plan is usually undertaken through letters to neighbours, site notices, adverts in local papers (for larger schemes) and the onward notification that is often undertaken by Parish Councils (notice boards, etc). This process is quite formal and is based upon legal requirements set out nationally. Similar approaches are also used to advise of the opportunity to participate in the formulation of plans and policies. It is very important to stress and recognise the difference between consultation and meaningful participation and involvement in decision-making. Planning sometimes limits itself to consultation activities but this does not have to be, and should not be the case. As noted already in this section, this is an area of planning you should thoroughly explore.

Consultation and opportunities for involvement and participation will place demands upon you as a planner. You will need to have a knowledge and understanding of the legal requirements for involvement, have the ability to phrase and present the pertinent questions/opportunities effectively and, perhaps most importantly of all, be able to interpret and make decisions based upon the information that you subsequently receive back. This last skill goes to the heart of being a planner; the balancing of interests and making a judgement in the public interest is core to the way in which planners manage the built and natural environment. Your written, verbal and visual communication skills will all be tested in these circumstances and as such it is important that, when presented with the opportunities to develop these skills at university, you embrace them fully.

At university you will find that a range of exercises involve thinking about how information is presented, analysed and used to inform a decision. You will also go beyond the more traditional and impersonal processes of interaction though with exercises, activities and, perhaps, assessments which are based around the more interactive forms of participation which are increasingly being utilised by local authorities to facilitate more effective participation in planning.

In parallel with the drive to increase involvement and participation by the wider community in planning activity, there has also been the diversification of the methods employed. Exhibitions have long been used to display information about a new development proposal, and this is still the case today, but increasingly interactive methods of involving people in planning are also used with traditional exhibitions supported by workshops, activity events, discussion groups and debates. Such approaches are not solely used by the local planning authority in relation to new plans or proposals; the private sector also employ these methods to seek opinion, inform and, perhaps, persuade. Indeed, the private sector are often at the forefront of the development of new techniques and technologies to create better and more effective ways of seeking opinion and involvement in new ideas. As a planner you will therefore need to have advanced written, verbal and visual presentation skills; your effectiveness at communicating your thoughts and ideas, or those of your employer, may have a significant impact upon the outcome of any given decision or course of action.

tip

For more information on the different methods of involving the community in planning you should visit www.communityplanning.net . This is an excellent resource with information about methods, techniques and best practice.

Negotiation in town and country planning

With so much emphasis upon participation and involvement you will not be surprised to read that negotiation is a vital skill for planners today.

It is very rare that you will ever find two people with the same view on any planning matter; indeed it can be fatal to mention the fact that you are a planner in any social scenario given the likely heated debate that will inevitably result between anyone who even heard the word 'planning' mentioned. The emotive nature of planning is, of course, very understandable. The nature and evolution of the places we live in, know or otherwise care about are things about which we can be very passionate. As planners we may therefore be responsible for managing change which is controversial and perhaps unwanted by certain groups or individuals.

This scenario sounds like one of conflict, and indeed matters can sometimes get a little 'heated' when key decisions are being discussed or made. But planning is about resolving conflict or, preferably, managing a situation in such a way that conflict is avoided. Negotiation is absolutely central to this process. Mediation between interested parties and negotiation over changes, approaches and ideas is core to how planning manages the built and natural environment.

In Chapter 1 of this book, the nature of the planning system was discussed. As you will recall, planning in the UK is based upon a discretionary system where decisions are made having regard to the local development plan and the policies contained therein, together with any other material considerations. This means that planning is inherently 'grey'. Policy has a degree of flexibility with regards to interpretation and application, and other material considerations can mean that a decision is further open to discussion and negotiation. This is not the case in most of the rest of the world when, once a plan has been put in place, decisions are an administrative process where compliance with the plan is a legal test, not a matter of debate or discussion and where only limited flexibility to stray from the plan exists. In the UK, negotiation therefore exists not only in the plan preparation stage, but also in relation to every element in every individual planning application, proposal, strategy, vision, enquiry or policy.

Negotiation is required where interests are conflicting or in some way differing and, as presented above, the nature of planning is such that it inevitably has conflicting interests and differing views at every scale of activity. For negotiation to occur there must be an existing or upcoming change with an associated 'conflict' and, in the case of planning, such conflict can exist almost anywhere because it is all about managing change (Hargie, et al. 2004). Everyone involved in planning, from planning agents to local residents, will, to varying degrees, be promoting their own interests. The parties involved will perceive their respective positions on the matter in hand as being contradictory or, at the very least, incompatible with each other. Even in a small case, such as a house extension, the applicant, neighbours, the planning consultant and the case officer may be at loggerheads about the acceptability or otherwise of the proposal. Within the planning system, almost every decision that is made will therefore involve a degree of discussion in relation to opposing or differing views on the basis that the intended actions of one party will, potentially, be perceived as adversely impacting upon the interests of another.

Negotiation is an approach to resolving conflict. The act of planning therefore revolves around negotiation and a town planning professional must facilitate effective negotiation to resolve competing views and interests to enable a decision to be made. As a planning professional you will be at the centre of the negotiation taking place and may well be responsible for managing and facilitating it. What makes negotiation challenging is its complex nature; different actors with different positions on a given matter, common interests in some areas, competing interests in other, varying motivations, outlooks, attitudes

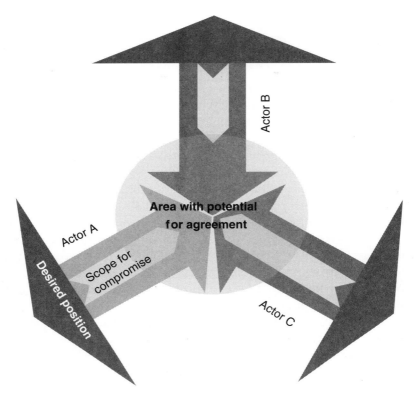

FIGURE 6.2   The nature of negotiation

and so forth. Furthermore, the negotiation context will vary with the structure within which the negotiation activity is taking place; this may be very structured and formal or it may be informal. Understanding the nature of negotiation is therefore important and at a basic level we can see negotiation as in Figure 6.2.

As you will note from Figure 6.2, each actor involved will having varying degrees of flexibility within which they are prepared to compromise on their desired position. Normally there is some area within which agreement on an 'acceptable' way forward may be, even if this is some way from the initial desired position of some of the actors involved.

As you no doubt already suspect though, there are some scenarios where the initial positions taken are so diametrically opposed that there is no overlap for agreement. This is not entirely unusual in planning given the nature of the potential change that can be occurring; some residents will never support a nuclear power station, or a waste processing plant, a prison or a fast-food takeaway in their vicinity regardless of the efforts made to mitigate against any risk, harm or impacts. This can make planning negotiation extremely challenging and difficult and can make the ultimate decision-maker (the planners and the politicians) extremely unpopular because decisions ultimately have to be made and although the public interest is at the core of decision-making, and interests are considered and balanced, some groups and individuals may be disadvantaged in some way. This can be difficult for planners on a personal level but the decisions that are made are important and necessary. If the act of planning is undertaken correctly then the best possible outcome in the given circumstances will be reached.

Activity

Consider the implications of planning proposals for the following new developments and think about the various competing, conflicting or varying interests that might exist between the developers, local residents, businesses and other potential stakeholders. Make notes about how their positions could differ and reflect upon how such differing positions could be approached by a planner seeking a solution – including mitigation:

- a large new residential development on the edge of a small rural village
- a new supermarket in a small and vibrant market town
- a waste incinerator in the open countryside
- the conversion of a shop unit into a betting office in a city centre location
- a new football stadium on a current area of green space
- a park-and-ride site being built on some allotments on the edge of a city
- a new bypass cutting through a sensitive area of countryside
- a fast-food takeaway being planned in a suburban residential area.

Reaching the best possible outcome will often depend upon the negotiation that is undertaken throughout the process of planning. There is no set way to facilitate negotiation or to manage the process but, as with some of the other skills you have identified, there is a foundation that underpins the process that will be undertaken by the parties involved (whether consciously or not) which looks something like Figure 6.3.

Being conscious of, and understanding, this process can help you to manage a negotiation scenario, whether this is formal or not. With this in mind it is also important to approach negotiation in the right manner; being positive, solution orientated, and with an awareness and understanding of the position of the other parties involved. Negotiation is therefore a skilled art and it is an art you will need to develop if you are to succeed at university and in your subsequent career.

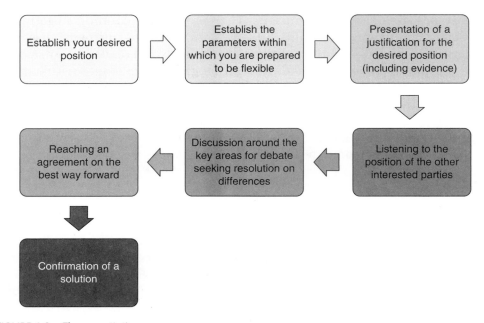

FIGURE 6.3   The negotiation process

Negotiation skills

The only way to really develop negotiation skills is through practical exercises and your university will facilitate this though classroom activities and assessment. Notwithstanding this, there are important ways that you can think about how you might approach negotiation, and some principles that you can apply to your negotiation activities. The next sections of this chapter consider this further.

Being a negotiator

No two people will negotiate in the same manner. Different people, as a result of both nature and nurture, will have different professional and personal traits when it comes to negotiation. Some people will have a co-operative stance, others more competitive. The approaches employed and the characteristics of individuals can have different results in different circumstances but there are 'constants' in negotiation. Research has shown that there are certain traits that are associated with effective negotiation – these include being a trustworthy, courteous and personable person, acting fairly, behaving ethically, and coming across in a sincere manner (Morley, 2006).

Developing and displaying these traits can therefore help you to be a better negotiator and therefore achieve success as a planner. At university you will be presented with opportunities to undertake negotiation activities and you should be mindful of what it means to display the traits identified above. Try to be conscious of what you are saying, how you are saying it, and how it will be heard by the other parties involved. Being courteous, personable, tactful and sincere are interpersonal skills that you can develop with time. If you are conducting yourself as a planning professional, being trustworthy, fair and ethical should go without saying, of course!

Managing negotiation

As a planner you will find yourself at the heart of the negotiation process. If you have a facilitating role it is important that you think about how you can manage the interaction. You need to think carefully about all of the aspects of the pending negotiation. Below are a few of the key questions you might want to ask yourself:

- Is it a formal or informal scenario and what are the implications of this for where the negotiation is taking place and how is it managed? Are there any process requirements?
- What environment is the negotiation being held in? A round table discussion? A formal debate? An informal site meeting? A telephone conversation? Online? What are the implications of this? For example, what will the standard of dress be? A telephone conversation means body language, etc are not involved. An online discussion means only the written word is employed – this, in particular, can lead to misinterpretation in relation to how you are presenting your position, making it difficult to employ the key traits for successful negotiation effectively.
- How do you manage the actual discussion? Timings? Rotation of speakers? Structured and/or controlled questioning? Free discussion and debate?
- How do you make sure everyone is heard and understood fairly?
- How are you ensuring that the negotiation is solution orientated and will lead to a resolution at the end?
- Who are ultimately the decision-makers?
- Practicalities? Does a room need to be booked? Refreshments ordered? Parking or travel arrangements? Technology requirements?

You will become increasing more proficient at managing negotiations as you progress through university and into practice. As with most skills it is not one that you should consider to ever be fully developed; there is always room for improvement and there are always opportunities to learn, develop and prove yourself.

tip

At university and in practice you will find that there are a range of short courses (single days) where you can develop your skills. This might be specific training in the art of negotiation, or it might be to develop your own skills, for example your confidence. Take these opportunities when they are presented to you and you will see the benefits in your negotiation skills.

It is important to remember and be mindful of the fact that emotions may be running high in the negotiations and the art of facilitation is as much about inter-personal skills and emotional awareness as it is about the practicality and knowledge associated with the process and the case in question. Dealing with this side of the negotiation process will come more easily and naturally to some than others but you can certainly develop your skills in this area whilst at university and in practice too.

Employing negotiation skills in practice

Although negotiation occurs everywhere, including in our personal lives, the nature of planning is such that there are certain things to be particularly aware of when negotiating in the planning process. As a start point you might want to think about the following:

1. The success or failure of a negotiation will depend upon the people involved, so make certain you have the right people around the table. Do you have all of the specialists you need? Do you have the right people to have meaningful outcomes?
2. Have you considered all of the important issues? What are the impacts of the proposal and who will be affected by the development? Link this back to the point above and reflect upon who else might need to be involved in the process. Sometimes overlooked but vitally important are the local community for example; how will you engage with them?
3. Think about the most effective approach to negotiations. Confrontation, threats and bullying will undoubtedly be counter-productive.
4. Do not try to 'play the game' when it comes to planning matters; this will also usually be found to be counter-productive in the long-run. Approach the people, activities and processes in a positive, constructive, honest and congruent manner for greatest success and show consideration for your ethical responsibilities as a planning practitioner.
5. Think about all aspects of the proposal from the start, not just the ones you are interested in or focusing upon – what are the benefits? What are the potential negative impacts? How can these be mitigated? Hoping that something will not get considered because you have not highlighted it is a disaster waiting to happen!

6. Use specialists where necessary and appropriate. Nobody knows it all and getting the right people around the table is key.
7. Think about the logistics and practicalities. Plan well for meetings and take notes and minutes. Agree what the outcomes and action points are from negotiations to ensure that they are productive.
(Collins and More, 2009)

Conclusions

A publication by the Academy for Sustainable Communities called *Mind the skills gap: The skills we need for sustainable communities* (2007) identified the skills that were considered to be required but in short supply across the spectrum of built and natural environment professions. For planners, negotiation skills were highlighted as a weakness. And yet, as we have seen, negotiation is an important part of the activity of planning and where it is ineffective, outcomes can be compromised. The ability to create a vision, policy, strategy, masterplan or detailed design proposal is important, but if it cannot be implemented it is impotent; worthless. Negotiation is one of the key tools to support implementation; overcoming the barriers that present themselves and finding solutions so that change can be managed successfully.

Throughout your studies you will learn about the role and value of negotiation and be able to practise the skills so that you enter practice with a competence in this field. Once in practice it will be important for you to develop your skills so that as the work you become involved in becomes more complex and challenging, you have the ability to respond, deliver, and manage change effectively and appropriately.

Further reading

As with other skills discussed in this book you will find that there are both planning books and generic skills books that will be helpful to you. You might want to consider the following to support your learning and skill development:

- Hargie, O. (ed.) (2006) *The handbook of communication skills*. Second ed. London: Routledge.
- Hargie, O (2011) *Skilled interpersonal communication: Research, theory and practice*. Fifth ed. Hove: Routledge.
- Hargie, O. Dickson, D and Toursih, D. (2004) *Communication skills for effective management*. Basingstoke: Palgrave Macmillan.
- Healey, P. (2010) *Making better places: The planning project in the twenty-first century*. Basingstoke: Palgrave Macmillan.

- Morphet, J. (2010) *Effective practice in spatial planning.* London: Routledge.
- Parker, G. and Doak, J. (2012) *Key concepts in planning (key concepts in human geography).* London: Sage.
- Rydin Y. (1999) 'Public participation in planning', in Cullingworth, B. *British planning – 50 years of urban and regional policy.* London: Athlone Press, pp. 184–97.

Review points

When reflecting on this chapter you might consider the following:

- planning is a participatory activity undertaken in the public interests – engagement with stakeholders, including the local community, is therefore central to good planning
- planning, by its nature, often involves competing and conflicting views. Planners must engage with, and manage, this situation to ensure effective participation and good decision-making
- negotiation is complex and multi-faceted. It is key to resolving and managing conflict and implementing change in the built and natural environment and planners are at the heart of this process.

7

Spatial Analysis

Aims

Understanding places and spaces is at the heart of town planning. Our ability to understand the nature of a place, and appreciate the implications of future change, are vital to appreciating the impacts and repercussions of policies, strategies, plans and new development. This chapter will introduce you to the core spatial analysis skills, techniques and knowledge you will need for your studies.

Learning outcomes

After reading this chapter you will:

- recognise the importance of understanding places
- appreciate approaches to spatial analysis
- recognise how you can undertake spatial analysis
- understand how you can develop your skills and their application in planning practice.

Introduction

No two places on earth are the same. The geology, flora, fauna and environmental conditions all vary significantly between locations. Humankind has also shaped our environment, from the earliest influences of hunter-gathers, through the processes of industrialisation, to today's population – people create, destroy, change and shape the world in which we live.

Town and country planners are at the forefront of how places change and evolve. Regardless of the legislative processes employed by any given nation, the art and science of planning informs, guides and manages the evolutions that take place.

To enable planners to be involved in this process they must have spatial analysis skills; the ability to understand places and the implications of change in order that they can deliver healthy sustainable communities.

The nature of spatial analysis

Planning is essentially applied geography. It is the practical and pro-active part of the geography family. Traditionally planning was aligned towards the human geography side of the family, but over the decades the increased knowledge and understanding of the environment and sustainability has brought planning more centrally into the field of geography.

For planners to truly understand places and undertake effective spatial analysis they must therefore appreciate the multi-dimensional nature of our environment. Spatial analysis is therefore not just about understanding the site, it is about understanding place.

Understanding places

It is all too easy for planners, architects or other built environment specialists to focus upon the site that is the subject of their interest, but when we think about places it is important that we truly appreciate the context in its broadest sense.

Places are like onions; they have layers. The development you are interested in might be confined to a site, but even in a small town that site sits within an immediate area, a neighbourhood, a town, a county, a region, a country and a continent. Each of these layers will have a uniqueness that will be an influence on the nature of place. The nature of the physical environment (including transport infrastructure), natural environment, society and beliefs, history and the economy will all vary and influence each layer differently. Each of these factors will inform the site of interest to some degree or another and will require consideration.

The first step to undertaking spatial analysis is therefore not to get on site; it is to research the area. These means trying to understand the influence of all of the factors identified in Figure 7.1.

As a planner you need to try and digest this context, analyse it and be able to be informed by it in the manner in which the space is subsequently managed.

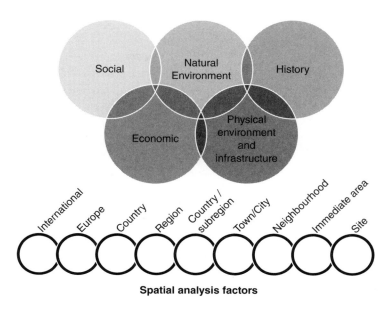

Spatial analysis factors

FIGURE 7.1   Influence examples

It is very important to recognise that no two places are the same and no solution can be applied universally. All of the influences will create a uniqueness that should inform the solution.

It may be the case that planning is the practical and pro-active application of the geography discipline, but planners must be more than geographers; they must also be historians, scientists, economists, anthropologists, sociologists and designers all rolled into one.

You may well have developed many of these analytical skills, particularly if you have studied a related subject area at school or college, but at university you will not only need to demonstrate a sound ability, but also demonstrate it in a manner relevant to planning. From your first year at university you will be taught about the history and nature of places. You will also be supported to develop your analytical skills such that when you come to undertake a plan or proposal for a site or area, you start with the influences and work your way down to the site, rather than 'cutting out' the site, planning it, and dropping it back into its context. This latter approach doesn't work!

For new places to be successful they must understand their context. They need to understand and recognise the influences that inform the place so that when a place changes, it does so in a way that is successful. As a practitioner it is your responsibility to ensure that places change and are managed in an appropriate way; you cannot do this if you do not truly know and understand the place.

Activity

Think of two places or areas you know; one that you think is successful, one that you think is unsuccessful. Thinking about the influences discussed in this chapter, reflect upon why the place is how it is. Why does the successful place work? Why is the unsuccessful place not working? What role does the economy (retail/commercial/industrial, etc), the buildings, the spaces between the buildings, transport, population make-up, history and natural environment have in each case? Could past change have been approached differently leading to an alternate approach? With this in mind, think about the implications for how these places could change in the future – this is what planners do!

Analysing places: assessing impact

Once we understand a place, we need to analyse it. We can start to think about how we can manage change in that place and start to think about impacts.

Town planning is all about balancing and managing impacts. Delivering sustainable development means enabling economic growth and the delivery of new communities whilst preserving, conserving and protecting the natural environment and built heritage. Achieving this balance is a very difficult thing to do and requires some tough decisions to be made, but making the right decision can only occur if we have analysed the place of interest and considered the impact of a proposed development.

All development has an impact in both the immediate area and the wider area. These considerations are relevant whether you are involved in a small development proposal or considering site allocations in a local plan in which you are identifying strategic development sites for the evolution of an area for the next 20 years. A proposal might generate traffic, it could bring unwanted competition into an area, there might be an unacceptable environmental impact, the implications upon residential and/or visual amenity and landscape could be problematic, it could be an inappropriate use for the location due to the nature of the proposal or the nature of the area *for* the proposal. Likewise the proposal itself could be considered flawed by virtue of the design solution proposed or the financial viability of the scheme. There are multiple factors to be considered and the impacts must be assessed and balanced. It is the responsibility of the planner to come to a conclusion as to whether the proposal is acceptable/appropriate and viable or not.

At university you will learn how to analyse place, assess impact and make judgements. You will also make proposals yourself where you will be required to justify your approach and solution having regard to your understanding of the place and your analysis of it and your proposal. These will be vital learning opportunities which will be at the core of your future career as a planner.

Analysing places: assessing viability

As mentioned above, management of places and spaces needs to consider viability. The finances of managing change are complex but it is important that planners have an understanding of financial viability and business. Whether considering a development proposal or creating a strategy in a local plan, planners have to be aware not only of the *build* costs, but *all* costs associated with new development proposals. This means considering any planning obligations (charges) that would be levied by a scheme, the implications of, for example, affordable housing to the viability of a scheme, land values and local variations in viability based upon the economic profile of a given area. There is no fixed measure of viability against which a planner can operate universally; even within a small urban area costs can vary significantly and thus so too can viability.

Understanding development finance and viability is necessary since the management of places must be grounded in reality; aspirations must be realistic and planners must consider what can actually be delivered. Failure to do this can lead to delivery failure and undesirable outcomes. Notwithstanding this, it is important to remember that the lack of viability for a scheme should not necessarily override other factors; viability is *one* factor to be weighed up when making decisions about planning matters. It must be balanced against all the other relevant factors, including all of the environmental and social impacts. Planners must consider the long term and the public interest, not base decisions upon private interests. This runs to the very heart of the principles of town planning.

Your university course will provide you with a foundation in development finance and viability. This training will ensure that you enter the planning profession with the basic skills you need in this area. Once in work you will find that there are opportunities to improve these skills, including further training and education if appropriate, but you should also find support from property experts within your organisation or through partnerships.

Spatial analysis: the site

Although you will be given support as both a student and planning professional to understand and analyse place, you will also be expected to have the ability to undertake some of this analysis yourself.

A key skill for all planners is site analysis. Whether searching out a new site for allocation in a local plan, searching for a development site, or determining a planning application, it is important that as a planner you can assess the suitability of a site and locality for development.

A good place to start with a site is with the basics. For example, how big is the site? In planning we tend to work in metric areas (although sometimes you will still come across acres). The hectare is the key measure for site size. One hectare is 100 metres by 100 metres, or 10,000 metres square. Once we know the area of a site we can think about the practical question of whether what is proposed for the site will fit acceptably, not forgetting the need to allow for landscaping, amenities, access and parking arrangements and so forth. Planning policy will guide the scale of suitable development too; for residential development, for example, the number of residential units expected to be delivered per hectare will be identified.

But let us not get ahead of ourselves here. The physical size of the site is only one factor. The topography of a site will also be key. What are the ground conditions (soils, rock type, etc), for example? Is it suitable for development or will extensive engineering be required? What is the drainage like on the site? What about the flora and fauna found on the site and what are the implications of this for what is being proposed? The physical attributes can impact upon the viability of a site for a proposal; for example it may be environmentally sensitive or it may be prone to flooding.

It is also the case that the site might not be a greenfield site. If the site currently has, or once had, other development on the site, what is the implication of this? Is there contamination on the site? Is there planning policy which seeks to retain an existing use or fix a proposed use?

Access also needs to be carefully considered. You will typically receive guidance from a specialist in relation to the access arrangements but thought will need to be given to private motorised transport (cars and motorbikes), servicing (deliveries, maintenance, etc), pedestrian movement by persons of all abilities, cyclists and public transport accessibility. The suitability of the site from a safety perspective is important, but of equal importance is the sustainability of the location and access arrangements. Will people be able to access the site in a safe manner and utilise sustainable modes of transport? The impact of the proposal in relation to the wider area also needs thought; will the proposal add or create congestion, for example? Local planning authorities will create guidance to inform decisions about these matters; there will be guidance on the number of parking spaces per unit or square meter of space created, requirements for cycle parking and pedestrian/cyclist access arrangements, servicing needs, access to public transport and so forth. Not that *an* impact equates to an *unacceptable* impact. It may be that the way in which the development is brought forward can make the impact acceptable, or changes to the infrastructure in the wider area, typically funded or carried out by the developer, could bring about changes such that the impact is within acceptable limits.

Neighbouring uses and the implications for an area are also an important consideration. The impact of the proposed development on the local area needs thought, for example the environment implications of the new development, the impact upon local residents, the impact on the visual amenities of the area, or the impact on local retail centres. Similarly the appropriateness of the area for the new development must be taken into account; it would not be acceptable or appropriate to locate new housing in the middle of an industrial area in many instances!

Activity

You can begin to understand site analysis techniques and impact analysis just by visiting somewhere locally and thinking about the implications of change.

Find an area of land near where you live that is either undeveloped or in need of regeneration. Visit the site and make notes on the physical attributes of the site. Write down a description of the site thinking about site size, location, access, topography, boundaries, surrounding uses and buildings, flora and fauna, microclimate and use. Write down what considerations these attributes will have for any proposals to change the site.

Planning places

If the idea of analysing a place and assessing impact feels overwhelmingly difficult then fear not, planning is not a discipline that operates without guidance and structure. As you will recall from Chapter 1, planning policy exists at the national and local level to guide new development. Local plans guide development spatially, and planners do not operate alone; they are part of a team, working with a wide range of built environment professionals and the local population who will provide specialist advice and guidance. For example, if a client is seeking to develop a piece of land, a planning consultant will, once they have researched the area and begun to understand the nature of the place, be able to review the thematically relevant national planning policy, review the local plan and policies to assess the stance of the local planning authority, liaise with highway engineers, architects, landscape architects, surveyors and planning specialists, talk to the local community and liaise with any necessary organisations such as the Environment Agency or the Highways Agency depending upon the nature of the site. All of this support will help the planning consultant to analyse the place and assess the impacts and viability of the options. Similarly, a local authority planner when assessing a planning application will be able to draw on the knowledge and views of local residents and the expertise of a range of specialists to enable him or her to make an informed decision upon the acceptability of the proposal.

Activity

Using the same site that you identified for the previous activity, look at the local council's website. Find the planning policy/forward planning section and identify the 'local plan' for the area. This will come in different forms and using different names depending upon where you live and when the document was produced, but look at the documents that are available. For a site you are familiar with, try to work out if there are any restrictions in place that will limit what you can do (the 'proposals map' will help you here). Now look at the main policy document (which could be called the 'local plan' or the 'core strategy') and try to work out what types of development might be supported in the area you have identified and any restrictions that might exist. With all of this in mind try to write out what you think the site could be used for and what the key considerations will be for any new proposal from the perspective of the planning policy context.

The steps you have taken in this and the previous activity are effectively the beginning of the real process for planners analysing the potential for a site and considering the acceptability of new development options.

Spatial analysis and mapping

Elsewhere in this book you explore the *role* of maps and other forms of visual communication, but in the context of spatial analysis it is important to first understand *what* maps are and *how* they communicate information. This chapter has already explored how we analyse places, but mapping is a key part of how we then communicate the nature of places to others.

At a basic level, maps communicate information visually; they are a graphical representation of a place as it was, as it is, or as it could be.

As an information source, maps are vital to planners. It is arguably the best medium for communicating information about the nature of places. Maps can tell us about elevation, gradients, geology, vegetation, patterns of built development, transport networks and places/points of interest or significance.

There are a wide variety of map types. Common types include physical maps (which show a graphical representation of the physical reality), road maps, political maps, economic maps, resource maps and climate maps. Each communicates different information. In reality a map can be created to communicate almost any type of information desired, making them an exceptionally valuable communications medium.

Maps are all drawn to scale, accurately representing the real world in a scaled form. The ratio of this scale reflects the difference between the actual scale and the drawn scale. So 1:1 is full scale i.e. 1cm on a map = 1cm in reality, whereas 1:10,000 would mean that 1cm on a map is 10,000 centimetres (100 metres) in the 'real world'. Scales are talked of as being large or small scale. The smaller the difference between the map and the reality, the larger the scale of the map is considered to be. So a 1:10,000 map is a larger scale than a 1:50,000 map.

Maps are typically based around a grid arrangement to aim orientation, location finding and directions.

In the UK there is the 'British National Grid' which gives every 100km square a unique reference. Grid squares are made up of 'northing' lines (vertical) and 'easting' lines (horizontal) and each is given a unique two letter reference. Each grid line is also given a number, and each grid square is divided into tenths. Using this system it is possible to create a unique two letter and six figure grid reference for any given point in the UK.

Ordnance Survey (OS) is the 'official' producer of maps in the UK. As an organisation, Ordnance Survey can trace a history back to the late eighteenth century when, for reasons of ensuring the effective defence of the Realm from attack, it was decided that accurate mapping should be created. The Board of Ordnance (Ministry of Defence today) undertook to carry out this work and commenced a survey; the Ordnance Survey. Today, OS is an agency of the UK government and continues to provide accurate mapping for the nation (Ordnance Survey, 2013).

Activity

In the UK, Ordnance Survey mapping is the best way to learn about maps and grids. Go to your local library and find a Landranger Ordnance Survey map for your area. Complete the following tasks:

1. Find the British National Grid square letters (look in the corners of the map).
2. Find a precise point you know and look down to see which 'easting' square the point is (eastings are always quoted first).
3. Do the same to find the 'northing' square number.
4. Now try to break down the square into tenths and accurately identify the point in the grid where the point of interest you have identified is located.

(Continued)

(Continued)

5. Now write this down in the following order:

   a. Grid square
   b. Easting square
   c. Easting 'tenth' within the square
   d. Northing square
   e. Northing 'tenth' within the square

The letters and numbers will obviously be unique to your point, but you should have something with a format like this: *SO 704 386*

Being able to identify a precise location is very important when you are trying to communicate a location. This is a skill you can easily practise so you should try to develop your mapping ability as early as you can in your studies; it is a basic skill that will serve you well throughout your studies and into planning practice where, for example, you will be required to identify sites using the correct reference.

There are some basics factors that you should also be aware of when it comes to professional maps. For example: maps should be drawn with north at the top of the page (be aware of the difference between true north, magnetic north and grid north); a scale should be provided for the map; the date that the map was drawn and revised should be clearly indicated; and a suitable key should be included to identify how features in the map are communicated visually.

Gradients are another important factor when considering the nature of a place. Contour lines help us to appreciate the gradient of an area. Contour lines are drawn every 10 metres of height change and will be identified by a height number in metres. This is the height above sea level in metres. So, a contour with a '50' inserted onto it means that everything along this line is 50 metres above sea level. The closer the contour lines are to one another, the steeper the gradient. The levels on a site are clearly important and as such our ability to understand and communicate levels is a key skill.

The manner in which maps convey information will vary depending upon the mapping product you are using, but Ordnance Survey effectively provide the national standard for map symbols. General features, water features, roads, railways, rights of way and tourist information points will all be identified using standard symbols that are used across all types of OS maps and many other providers of mapping use the OS symbols as the basis for their own visualisations.

Activity

Look at an OS Landranger map again and find the key. Now try to find the following on the map:

- trunk road
- parking
- a place of worship
- a public house
- a wood
- a public right of way.

You will have noticed that some of these features have subdivisions, for example places of worship are differentiated by the type of addition, and the public rights of way differentiate between types, such as footpaths and bridleways. This highlights the level of detail that is provided in these maps and the extent of the information that can be gleaned from them.

Specialist software and equipment

As discussed elsewhere in this book, Information technology (IT) plays a key role in visual communication, but IT also plays a part in how planners manage information, and specialist IT packages enable planners to manage, seek and communicate information.

E-planning is the term given to the introduction of electronic systems to support planning practices. This process gained traction in the UK following the election of the Labour government in 1997 and in 2002; the government launched its e-government strategy which included e-planning. Part of the e-planning project was to enable greater access to information by putting documentation online for open-access purposes. Another aspect was the introduction of electronic processes associated with submitting, commenting upon, and determining planning proposals, and a further element was to enhance information communications technology (ICT) capabilities for planning practitioners. This has meant that national and local government planners are now able to undertake more activities electronically, including the generation of reports and other written outputs with integrated mapping and plans. Such capabilities are typically supported by specialist software packages in the public sector that also enable documentation and information management and the integration of Geographical Information Systems (explained in Chapter 10). Outside of government, organisations will typically use 'off-the-shelf' packages, such as those available from Microsoft and

Adobe, to manage information and communicate information. This is discussed further in Chapters 9 and 10.

Photography is an important skill for a planner to develop. Photographs are an important way of showing a current site, helping to express a point or aid orientation. The development of digital photography has enabled planners to integrate photographs into other mediums, such as MS Powerpoint or a written report, and potentially use a photograph as the background for a computer image of a new proposal. Developing basic photography skills, and the ability to transfer images onto a computer and then use them with other software packages, will be an important set of skills whilst at university and in practice. As a student and as a practitioner you will be asked to produce written work and presentations which will necessarily include photography so it will be worthwhile to practise these skills. You don't need a particular type of camera; just a basic compact digital camera will give you what you need to get started.

tip

If you are not very confident at photography or the use of images, look into short courses at your local college or university. Short courses, ranging from one day to a series of evenings, can be a great way of developing these skills. This is also something to think about doing if you already enjoy photography but would like to take your skills further.

Safety equipment is also something you will need to become familiar with. As a planner you will find yourself on a building site, in a derelict building, or in the middle of a very muddy field! In each case you will need to ensure that you are dressed appropriately. Commonly you will find yourself wearing hard hats, florescent jackets and protective footwear, such as steel toe-capped boots. Usually you will not be expected to purchase these yourself though; your university and your employer should provide you with everything that you need; indeed they are required to by health and safety legislation in most cases.

As a student you will also undertake accompanied and unaccompanied site visits. If you are going with your university they will give you the information you need and make certain that safety has been considered. If you are going on an unaccompanied trip however, think really carefully about where you are going. Are the public allowed access? Are there any dangers on site? Is it a safe area for you to be in alone? Always tell someone where you are going and how long you will be, take a phone and, if you can, try to have a friend or family member come along with you. You university will tell you more about best practice for site visits and you will find when you get into work that your employer has processes and procedures that you need to follow to make sure you are dressed appropriately and that your wider safety has been considered.

Other equipment you will find yourself using includes the humble tape measure, laser measurers, measuring wheels and scale rules.

Tape measures are important when measuring the potential size of a new proposal and you will find that they have value when considering small alterations particularly. Tape measures have clear limitations though and even large fabric tapes have their shortcomings when measuring sites or potential large development footprints. In such circumstances you will find either a measuring wheel or a laser measurer very useful.

A measuring wheel is, as the name suggests, basically a wheel on the end of a stick. As the wheel rotates it measures distance, displayed on the wheel bracket or handle. A measuring wheel is great for measuring lengths and distances along the ground. Where they fall down a little of course, is measuring vertically! In this case a laser measurer is the solution.

A laser measurer works by firing a laser beam out from a hand-held device; when the beam hits something it returns the distance to the readout on the device. The issue with a laser device is the need for something to be at the other end to break the beam; this can limit their use for measuring both heights and distances, but this limitation can often be overcome with a little imagination!

A scale rule is important when working with plans and drawings. A scale rule is a like a traditional ruler but has conversion scales to work with so, for example, it will show you 1:50, 1:100, 1:200, 1:500 scales to help you interpret and draw to a recognised scale. There is more discussion about drawing to scale in the next chapter of this book.

Finally, you may find yourself using other equipment such as Global Positioning Systems (GPS), used for orientation and position-finding, or a theodolite – a piece of surveying equipment used for measuring angles. Where you need to use these, either at university or in work, you will be given the necessary training so that you are able to use the equipment as required.

Conclusions

In this chapter we have considered some of the core professional skills that will be at the heart of your career. Town and country planning plays a very important role in managing change in our built and natural environment and to be competent at this we must understand the places we are working in, be able to analyse the implications of change and their viability, and be in a position to understand the practical implications of change for the site and immediate area.

The skills discussed in this chapter range from the very technical to the relatively general but all will form part of your studies and most will become central to your activities as a planning professional. You may have experience of some of these skills from your previous studies but it will still be important to engage fully with these elements of your programme because you will certainly find that, even if you have ability in the activity in question, the application of the knowledge will be different.

Through the development of the skills discussed in this chapter you will have the ability to manage places and spaces effectively, balancing impact, making the right choices and delivering sustainable development.

Further reading

You will find a variety of books from different disciplines will be useful to further develop your knowledge and skills in the area of spatial analysis:

- CABE (2000) *By design: Urban design in the planning system towards better practice.* London: Commission for Architecture and the Built Environment.
- LaGro, J. (2008) *Site analysis: A contextual approach to sustainable land planning and site design.* Second ed. London: Wiley. This gives a good overview of site analysis. It is written for the American market though and you should be aware of this when reading it.
- Marshall, S. (2004) *Streets and patterns: the structure of urban geometry.* London: Routledge.
- Moor, N. (2011) *The look and shape of England.* London: The Book Guild.
- Tewdwr-Jones, M. (2012) *Spatial planning and governance.* Basingstoke: Palgrave Macmillan.
- Taylor, N. (1991) *Development site evaluation.* London: MacMillan. This is a very good text for developing analysis skills for sites, but it is a little dated in places. The principles explained in the context of site analysis remain valid however.

For a real estate perspective and to read more about the issue of viability, see:

- Harvey, J. and Jowsey, E. (2004) *Urban land economics.* Sixth ed. Basingstoke: Palgrave Macmillan.
- Ratcliffe, J., Stubbs, M. and Keeping, M. (2009) *Urban planning and real estate development.* Third ed. London: Routledge.
- Squires, G. (2012) *Urban and environmental economics.* London: Routledge.

Review points

When reflecting on this chapter you might consider the following:

- before we can understand the implication of change and actually start to 'plan', we must first understand a place
- understanding a place means that we have to learn about a place; its history and the nature of the place today – what makes it what it is?
- as planners we need to analyse impacts and consider viability. We also need to be able to look practically at the nature of the site and its physical attributes and be able to consider the implications of these
- mapping is a key tool in developing and communicating understanding of a place
- a range of specialist equipment is used by planners to help them undertake spatial analysis and to do so safely.

8

Understanding Plans and Drawings (by James Burch)

Aims

- At the end of this chapter you will be able to:
- understand the different purposes for which planners use drawings
- understand the conventions of scale drawing and how expressing a place at varying scales allows a planner to analyse and interpret different aspects of that place
- understand different conventions of plan, section and elevation that a planner uses to understand a planning proposal
- practise drawing yourself, enabling you to look at and understand places more accurately and with greater empathy.

Introduction

Be it when developing a proposition oneself or in contributing to another's planning proposal, the art of planning is a creative process, and making, understanding and discussing drawings is central to this creative activity. This chapter seeks to show how you can use drawings to help you plan and it will hopefully encourage you to practise drawing yourself.

Drawings verses pictures

Before we begin to discuss the different ways in which drawings contribute to the art of planning, we should try and understand what drawings are and what the purpose of drawing for planning is. To aid this understanding it is helpful to first make a distinction between a *drawing* and a *picture*. The purpose of any drawing or picture is to communicate visually. It is a common view that drawings and pictures are one and the same but this is not the case and it is important that as planners we appreciate the difference. In planning and design we need to think about drawings as a more particular visual form that has a different communicative purpose to that of a picture. As planners our interest in drawings is not simply pictorial. In the art of planning, a drawing should be understood as a working tool that makes a small contribution to a greater goal. For these purposes, drawings are valued for their practical use, they should do a job for us and not be considered special or valuable things in their own right.

So put simply, drawings, for a planner, are not pictures. A *picture* is the final outcome of a creative process and something to behold of itself as a work of art. The picture is the final statement in its maker's creative process and when we look at a finished picture we seek to appreciate and interpret the complex set of ideas and meanings its maker seeks to communicate. We will all have a subjective reaction to this depiction that might be pleasing or disturbing (something beautiful might not necessarily be pretty!). Contrary to this, drawing for planning aims to be clear and objective, it is not an end result and it does not have to be beautiful. In the art of planning, drawing is part of a creative process – one communication within a much longer conversation that aims for some shared objective agreement. It leads us on to further work, in plan-making for example or the evaluation of a building proposal. Its job is to help the people using the drawing (be they the drafter or the reader of it) to define, understand and develop an idea. This distinction between a picture as a work of art with aesthetic value and a drawing as a working tool is of course more subtle and complex than is portrayed here, but it is an important distinction for us to make. If we simplify the difference further we might say that we think *about* a picture we look at; but we think *with* a drawing that we make and discuss it, using it to help us form a future plan. So, when thinking as a planner, try not to judge drawings as pretty pictures and please do not get hung up on attempting to make your drawings beautiful. Remember instead that drawing is a useful skill you should cultivate in order to communicate and discuss your plans. You should not be scared of drawing. It does not matter whether or not your drawings are beautiful, it does matter how they describe your ideas. And finally, everyone can learn to draw, it is a skill not a talent.

Drawing conventions

In order to understand any problem we need to approach it from different angles and use these different viewpoints to inform our understanding of how we might begin to solve it. Different types of drawing – *drawing conventions*, as they are called – give us these viewpoints. As there are different tools for specific jobs so there are different drawing conventions that we use to aid our investigation of the different aspects of planning. In working to a convention we set basic rules with which to organise what we are looking at. Choosing and using these rules carefully helps us define more clearly the aspect of a problem we seek to analyse; and, because planners' drawings are tools for communication, applying these rules consistently is important so that everyone can understand the drawing. Conventions are the language of drawings and it is helpful in a conversation if we are all speaking the same language!

We can say that any drawing convention has three key aspects:

- projection
- scale
- editing.

We will think about each of these aspects in more detail and then, for the next part of this chapter, we will look at how a range of drawing tools use these conventions to analyse and communicate a planning problem.

1. *Projection* – plans, sections, elevations and perspective views are all forms of projection. Each of these conventions has its own precise manner of projecting the three-dimensional world into a two-dimensional description on a page. Another way of thinking about this might be as a frame of reference or more literally as a view through a frame. Imagine you are carrying a picture frame holding a sheet of glass, say, a metre square. If you stand in the middle of a street looking at a group of buildings opposite and you hold the framed-glass in front of you, you could draw the buildings you see onto the glass. When you have finished your drawing you would have something approaching an elevational projection of those buildings (see Figure 8.1). It follows that if you flew up in the air with your framed-glass and looked through it down to the ground you could draw something approaching a plan projection of what you see below. The 'something approaching' is important to remember. Different projections follow precise conventions for the measured relationship between drawn elements. An elevational projection defines height and width measurements in proportion (to a similar scale) but does not describe depth, whereas a plan projection defines width and depth of building in proportion (and to a similar scale) but does not describe height (see Figure 8.2). These two conventions of plan and elevation flatten the three-dimensional world into two dimensions by omitting a third dimension. Perspectival conventions seek to describe the relationship between three dimensions and thus they give proportional relationships between height, width and breadth – but possibly not always at a similar scale.

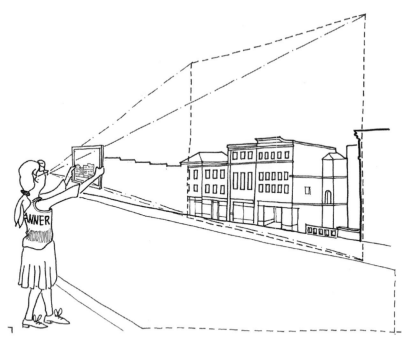

FIGURE 8.1   Street projection as an elevation

FIGURE 8.2   Street projection as a plan

2. *Scale* – this is the proportional relationship between life-size and drawn-size that a drawing defines. Going from life-size and getting progressively smaller, typical scales you might be familiar with are 1:1, 1:50, 1:100, 1:200, 1:1,250 and 1:5,000. A drawing ratio of 1:1 means that what is drawn is measured at the same size as it will appear in real-life. A (literally) life-size 1:1 drawing might be useful in the discussion of the fine architectural detailing of a new building in a designated conversation area. Here, in order to evaluate how it will relate to other existing details in the conservation area, the exact size and sculptural qualities of the new detail can best be communicated at 1:1. If we were to draw a strategic master plan of a new neighbourhood at 1:1 this would be time-consuming and ultimately unhelpful to the kind of planning analysis needed for that problem. A much smaller scale will be appropriate, perhaps 1:5,000. If, as in this case, life-size is drawn at a 5,000th of its actual size, detail is removed from the drawing and this simplification reveals broader relationships between areas and locations in and around this neighbourhood that it might be important to consider in a new planning initiative. As we can see from these examples a completely different order of information is revealed at 1:1 than at 1:5,000. These different orders of information are pertinent to different problems and choosing a scale of drawing is therefore an important aspect of defining the type of thing you wish to analyse – whether these things be the finest detail (1:1), detailed decisions (1:50, 1:100 and 1:200), matters of location and connection (1:500 and 1:1,250) or broad strategy (1:5,000). It follows that making this decision about the scale you are drawing at is an important aspect of editing.

3. *Editing* – a 200 millimetre long wood cylinder encasing a thin filament of brittle graphite (your humble pencil in other words) will never capture everything about the world around you. And nor should it. All drawings edit out information and that process of leaving things out is central to the activity of drawing. Indeed we might see the editing process that drawing demands as one of its most useful aspects, because in order to make a decision about a problem, one must decide what to include to aid the analysis and what to exclude. As we have seen from the above, a choice of drawing scale immediately excludes some and includes other information, therefore choosing the scale of work forces a decision on what aspect of a problem we are focusing on. The choice of plan, section and elevation demands similar choices of editing. In the task below and the drawn example to follow we should keep this in mind and consider carefully how the choices of projection and scale help us self-consciously edit the aspect of a problem we seek to explore.

This editing process might sometimes lead us to choose drawing conventions that reject scale and projection but that focus in other ways on communicating an idea. These are diagrammatic drawings or ideograms. You will see examples of this form of drawing throughout this book, where *diagrams* are used to show how different concepts relate to each other. A diagram can be understood as a very precisely edited drawing that seeks to reduce aspects of a problem to their essentials.

Activity

Forget for a moment the drawing conventions we have discussed above. Take a sheet of plain paper and a pencil (or ball-point pen if this feels more comfortable) and draw your route from your to home to somewhere that you are familiar with, maybe your local cinema for example. Think of and then draw what you remember in your minds-eye of this journey. Make a series of drawings to explain the details of what you did on the way, your route and any remarkable moments you experienced en route. Draw these as naturally and straightforwardly as you can. Remember what we said towards the beginning of this chapter; your drawings do not have to be beautiful, but they do have to communicate your ideas as best as they can.

Once your drawings are finished take a short (tea?) break. Take this moment to review the discussion above, about projection, scale and editing, and think how you have used these conventions in developing your drawn description of your route. Take a fresh sheet of paper and look through your drawings noting each convention you have used and for what part of the journey you used it. When did you draw in plan, section, elevation or 3-D sketch and when did you draw at larger or smaller scales? For example, to show a bus journey did you draw the bus and how did you draw it; how might you describe a climb up a hill or some steps; if there are left and right turns along road routes how did you describe these? Ask yourself why that particular convention felt most appropriate for that aspect of the journey and why that might be.

Hopefully the activity above has given you a greater sense of the way different drawing conventions and scales help you communicate your ideas more clearly.

Scales

We are now going to look in more detail at how changes in scale and drawing convention can be used to look at different aspects of a planning proposal. We are going to look at a hypothetical proposal on a real site in Park Street, Bristol, so that you can see the role different scales play in the activity of planning. This is a central street that links Bristol's civic quarter of the Cathedral, Central Library and Council House at the bottom of a hill, to the University and Museum at the top of the hill. The street is steep creating pronounced level changes, one of which is a vacant lot – no. 4 – that sits at the bridged intersection of Frog Lane running approximately 5 metres below Park Street above and perpendicular to the line of it. It turns a corner and the proposal is to design a dry public house for teenagers on this site. We are now going to look at a series of drawings that describe this proposal.

Note: Because of the size of the book these drawings are not presented here at their correct scale. Each drawing has been reduced by the same ratio to fit the format of the book. However, you should still be able to make a comparison between scale drawings and the types of information different scales and drawing projections bring to the fore.

1:5,000 Strategy plan

FIGURE 8.3   1:5,000 strategy plan, central Bristol

No. 4 Park Street sits centrally (as a tiny black dot) on this plan drawing. The small scale of the drawing locates the site within the city centre and this allows us to relate the proposed site of the building to neighbouring areas of Bristol. At this scale we can look at the drawing and start to ask questions about, for example: transport – how easy will it be for teenagers to access this building; user groups – which neighbourhoods can access the building most readily; and perhaps the location of other similar youth centres.

Beginning at a 1:5,000 scale we can draw simplified abstractions that help us understand these key issues.

1:1,250 Location plan

FIGURE 8.4   1:1,250 location plan, Park Street, Bristol

This drawing shows the building in its more immediate surroundings and is the usual scale of location plan submitted with a Planning Application. From this drawing we can see what planners term the *urban grain* of an area, which means the pattern and density of building in an area. When locating no. 4 Park Street at 1:1,250 we can see a dense linear pattern of streets and also a particular characteristic of Park Street where the eastern side of the street comprises a long linear terrace with only two relatively narrow breaks in this line. Contrary to this, the opposite side of Park Street is broken by a series of roads making perpendicular connections into Park Street. This characteristic of Park Street will be useful to us in considering the design of a new corner building at no. 4.

tip

Unless stated otherwise, plans are always presented with north running directly up the drawing or page. Plan drawings in this chapter all follow this convention.

121

1:500 Roof plan

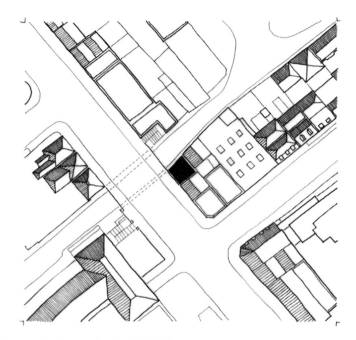

FIGURE 8.5   1:500 roof plan, Park Street, Bristol

This scale allows us to look at key simplified characteristics of buildings within a small local area. At this scale we can see the pattern of pitched roofs directly surrounding the site of no. 4.

1:200 Street elevation

At this scale, key patterns of detail can be focused and compared. This is important when considering the context that a location defines for a site. Commonly, as for this example, a 1:200 street elevation shows how the rhythm of window openings and façade modeling create the characteristics of the street. Looking at this 1:200 Park Street elevation we can see a long flat elevation with parapets (horizontal tops that conceal the roofline from the street). Park Street rises steeply and each building steps up the hill creating a regular rhythm of window openings and a jagged top profile to the elevation.

FIGURE 8.6   1:200 street elevation, Park Street, Bristol

There are very few projections on the buildings on this side of Park Street, the wall is flat with light modeling provided by simple windows with restrained classically proportioned windowsills and pediments.

Urban diagram – not drawn to scale (NTS)

The next two types of drawing in this series act as a pair created with a slightly different intention to the scale drawings we have looked at above. The preceding drawings present information about Park Street at a scale and within a particular convention so that we can understand characteristics of Park Street and measure these with respect to that street and its surroundings. The diagram here and the sketches that follow use three-dimensional drawing to make statements about the characteristics of Park Street and do this in order to make an argument about how we might think about the future plan for no. 4 Park Street.

In our observations on the 1:1,250 plan above we noted the difference between the eastern side of the street, which is a long almost unbroken line of building, and the western side where the street elevation is broken by a series of perpendicular street connections. This diagram reinforces this observation and makes the point that the urban form of the street can be argued to be a plain backdrop of flat buildings that contrast with a collection of interesting corner buildings on the western side, each with its own architectural character. Which leads us to think: should no. 4 be considered another interesting corner?

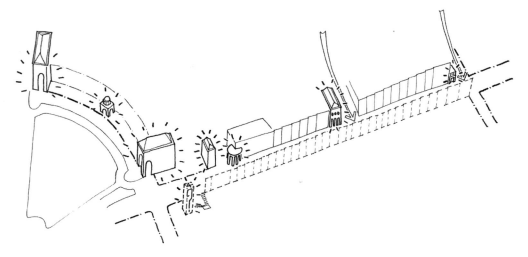

FIGURE 8.7   Urban analysis diagram of Park Street, Bristol

Sketch studies of corners – NTS

FIGURE 8.8   Sketch study of Charlotte Street's intersection with Park Street, Bristol

FIGURE 8.9   Sketch study of Great George Street's intersection with Park Street, Bristol

These two drawings are perspective site sketches that seek to record some of the characteristics that the existing 'interesting corners' present to us. The first corner is very casual, scruffy perhaps, where the corner building presents a single storey in stucco-work with a timber-framed first floor above. The second corner is grand, taller than its adjacent buildings and decorated in a Venetian Gothic style. In each case a contrast with the street terrace is made, but very differently.

Activity

The 1:200 street elevation shown above identifies a gap where the no. 4 site sits and, as we have said above, identifies some of the parameters we can consider in proposing a new building on this street. Then the diagram and sketches make a drawn argument to us that different-looking corners are an appropriate architectural approach on Park Street. With this information in mind, how would you like no. 4 to appear on to Park Street? Thinking about a building's elevations as its appearance can be useful. Ask yourself how you like to appear in public. What you wear and how you behave portrays your role in society

(Continued)

125

(Continued)

and your attitude to other people. So, how would you like to see a dry public house for teenagers to appear on a corner in Park Street – a street where we've identified that corners are visually interesting?

Copy the 1:200 elevation drawing shown on the previous page (you could enlarge it on a photocopier perhaps) and draw in your own proposal for no. 4. Draw three different versions, each time thinking about a different appearance of no. 4 to the surrounding street – perhaps a noisy building, a polite building or an unusual building. We could make a good argument for all these different options on this street.

1:100 Elevations

FIGURE 8.10   1:100 design elevation of no. 4 Park Street, Bristol (design by Yannis Hajigeorgis)

1:100 is the usual scale for planning application drawings for a building. At this scale one can see clearly the overall design proposals for a building and relate them to the immediate context. In the drawing, the design for the Park Street elevation of no. 4 is shown in the immediate context of adjacent buildings. The design is by Yannis Hajigeorgis – a student of Architecture and Planning at The University of the West of England who undertook the design of this teenage public house as a first-year design project.

1:50 Section

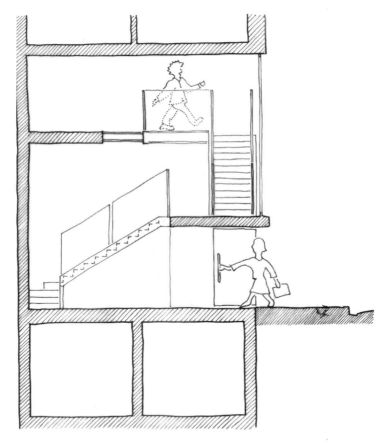

FIGURE 8.11   1:50 design cross-section through no. 4 Park Street, Bristol (design by Thomas Harper)

This final drawing offers us finer detail of the profile and form of a planned building. The design was prepared by another Architecture and Planning student, Thomas Harper. This drawing gives us information about the modeling of the building façade, that is, how the line of the windows, walls and sills step in and out. In this case we can see that Thomas' building is quite flat, in order to follow the façade modeling elsewhere on Park Street.

In most circumstances it is unusual for a planner to use drawings at larger scales except when key matters of detail are under consideration (as in the 1:1 conservation detail discussed on page 118).

The different scales employed in planning are therefore used for different purposes, with each scale of drawing helping to inform, communicate and support the process of planning. Every planning application will include plans and drawings to some degree and these will vary from a simple layout plan for a change of the use of a building, to a comprehensive set of plans and drawings for a major development proposal. The range of plans submitted will equate to the nature of the development and the associated need for information of all forms to be communicated.

Activity

Access the planning application pages for a local planning authority in England which you are familiar with. Find the area that allows you to search for planning applications and find any planning application for some form of physical (i.e. building) development. You should find that all the plans are available online. Look at each scale of plan and any drawings submitted and reflect upon the role they play in enabling you to understand what is being planned and what the implications of the proposal are. You should be able to see clearly the purpose of each plan and, in combination with the other application documents, be able to understand the nature of the development proposed and the potential implications of it.

Drawing at university

As noted elsewhere in this book, different universities will place different emphasis upon different areas of planning. At a university, like the University of the West of England for example, you will find planning students working alongside architecture students in modules that require drawing skills, the development of which has been supported through other modules and tasks. Elsewhere there may be less emphasis upon design skills but may have more property and real estate content. As with all things, it is important that you pick a course that is suited to your preferences but you will find that design skills and drawing will be a part of your studies and you will be supported to develop your skills in sketching and more technical drawing.

Technical drawing, producing the plans that are found in this chapter and that you saw through completing the third activity in this chapter, are increasingly produced using computer-aided design software. There is more on this in Chapter 10 of this book.

Conclusion

This chapter has given you an introductory understanding of plans and drawing for planners. We discussed the purpose of planning drawings as part of a communicative process, not as an end result, and we introduced the key aspects of scale, projection and edit that inform our choice of convention when drawing. No. 4 Park Street, in Bristol, provided an example of the way drawings might be used to communicate ideas of what is planned for a location. Obviously this is only a brief introduction and you will need to look elsewhere to broaden your understanding of drawing.

Further reading

The following books might help you start:

- Cullen, G. (1961) *Concise townscape*. London: Architectural Press. This is a classic study of how diagrammatic and observational drawing can be used to develop design strategies in urban environments.
- Farrelly, L. (2011) *Drawing for urban design*. London: Laurence King. This book on urban design shows a great range of drawing approaches and techniques that are used to study cities and develop planning ideas.

Cullen (1961) and Farrelly (2011) offer useful methods for studying cities through drawing, but you will need some confidence to apply their ideas and examples. In order to achieve this you need some drawing skills – and the only way to learn this is by practising drawing. A good way to start is to take drawing lessons. Alternatively there are also many 'how-to-do-it' drawing books. Treat these books with a degree of caution. Many of these teach you to copy other good-looking drawings rather than teaching to draw what you see; and, as we have established, drawing pretty pictures is not the purpose we identify for drawing. Our drawings are working tools that help us look at and understand problems. Two classic books that will help you with this latter purpose are:

- Edwards, B. (2012) *Drawing on the right side of the brain: The definitive*. Fourth ed. New York: Tarcher. Edwards argues that drawing is a way of thinking that you can learn and, first published in 1979, successive editions of this book have developed an excellent drawing course you can follow to achieve this.
- Ruskin, J. (1991) *The elements of drawing: Illustrated edition*. Edited by Bernard Dunstan. London: Herbert Press. John Ruskin was one of the most important art critics of the nineteenth century and this book, written in 1857, presents his course on drawing as a series of letters. Bernard Dunstan's edition gives the book extensive illustrations and a more contemporary commentary.

Review points

When reflecting on this chapter you might consider the following:

- there is an important difference between pictures and drawings – as planners we use drawings as part of the process and art of planning
- drawings and plans come in varying scales, each of which plays a role in supporting knowledge, understanding, analysis, and decision-making
- each scale is used for different purposes and together they provide the information we need from the macro to the micro
- as planners we must have the skills to interpret plans and drawings to ensure our decision-making is effective and well founded.

9

Giving Presentations

Aims

This chapter aims to improve your verbal communication skills and your ability to deliver effective presentations during your academic study. The chapter also aims to help you to understand how enhancing these skills will improve your practice performance and success within the planning profession.

Learning outcomes

After reading this chapter you will:

- be able to identify effective verbal communication traits
- understand how to deliver effective presentations
- begin to develop the skills so you can deliver high quality presentations
- appreciate the transferable nature of the verbal skills you will develop at university.

Introduction

Verbal communication is all about how you interact with other people. This could be an interaction on a one-to-one basis, but it can also be through meetings, briefings or presentations which each have very different dynamics. Your performance and effectiveness in these scenarios will impact upon your performance as a student, but will also be a core factor in your professional development and success.

How you interact with other people will also affect your personal and professional relationships at an individual level in a fundamental way, significantly impacting upon your future in the very broadest sense.

The focus of this chapter in this respect will be how to deliver good presentations, but basic interactions with others will also be considered briefly.

The importance of good verbal communication

From a purely academic perspective, how you verbally interact with other people will have a significant impact on your ability to achieve success at university in placements, tutorials, workshops, seminars and presentations. It will also affect your performance at interview when you come to apply for jobs after completing your course.

Town and country planning is a discipline that depends upon effective interactions between people within the profession, and between practitioners and those who interact with the planning system, including politicians, businesses, community groups, interest bodies, third sector organisations and the general public. The settings will vary too; you might find yourself in an informal 'round-table' discussion, or a formal committee scenario. In all cases, effectiveness in these different circumstances will be important to you as a professional working within the planning field. For the system to function, and for the art and science of planning to be effective, good verbal communication skills are vital. The effectiveness of the way in which you communicate information verbally could be an influencing factor in the outcome of a planning decision, in the position taken by a given group, or in the selection made by a potential client. As noted by Hargie et al.:

> The ability to capture the attention of an audience and deliver one's message in such a way that it is received with interest and changes beliefs, opinions and actions, is one that has been valued down the ages. (2004: 151)

The basics of verbal communication

Your choice of words and the actual way in which you deliver your message are equally important to ensuring that our communication is effective. John Adair (2003: 33) suggests that there are six basic principles of effective speaking:

1. be clear
2. be prepared

3. be simple
4. be vivid
5. be natural
6. be concise.

You may find some of these easier than others. For example, telling someone to 'be natural' is like telling someone in a stressed situation to 'relax'. It is often easier said than done. You will obviously be communicating with others while at university from day one, but you will also find that there will be more formal evolutions, such as seminars and presentations, from an early stage too. Overcoming your fears and being able to 'be natural' is therefore something you will be able to work on throughout your studies with a view to graduating as an effective communicator. Your university will support your development so this is not something to be worried about. Whilst at university you will be given opportunities to develop your verbal communication skills and this is very much a transferable set of skills you will carry into the workplace.

Adair's six principles are a good foundation upon which to start thinking about how you interact with other people. Although geared towards more formal speaking scenarios, they are actually not only relevant to such situations – considering these principles can also be used to improve how you approach other situations, such as tutorials, seminars and workshops.

 **tip**

Make a note of Adair's principles and try to have them in mind as you approach each opportunity to demonstrate your verbal communication skills in an academic setting. Reflect upon your own communication effectiveness in the conversations that you hold; perhaps you can already see areas in your own skills to improve?

Presentation skills

Whether the situation is a formal presentation or an informal workshop, your commentary is a presentation of some form or another. You will tailor the specifics to the circumstance, adapting the formality of the delivery and so forth, but the same skills and concepts associated with delivering your piece will underpin everything you do.

Non-verbal communication

Where do you start when it comes to presentation skills? The answer does not relate to what you say; it's about your body language. We communicate through our bodies with factors such as our posture, eye contact and mannerisms telling the audience a great deal about how nervous we are, how interested, and how scared! So the best place to start is with our bodies. Burns and Sinfield (2012: 320) provide some advice about how to create a positive body language which can be summarised as follows:

- Face towards the audience.
- Keep facing the audience even if your presentation is supported by a visual aid such as MS PowerPoint. Turning away from the audience breaks your connection with them.
- Stand or sit straight, but try to relax and be natural so you do not appear stiff and uncomfortable.
- Do not hold anything in front of your face, again this will break your connection with the audience.
- Look engaged and smile, this can help build a positive bond with the people you are talking to.
- Do not tap your foot, click a pen, or make repetitive and distracting gestures since they can be very irritating!
- Do draw people calmly into your presentation with brief welcoming gestures and an open stance.
- Do not cross or hold your arms defensively in front of your body. Present an open posture.
- Do stand in a relaxed manner, but don't slouch!
- Do not stand there with clenched fists or look as if you want to be somewhere else…even if you wish you were!
- Do dress appropriately for the situation. This might be very formal, or could be a little more relaxed. Always dress to look professional though.
- In a group presentation, do not act as if you dislike or disagree with everybody else on the team…even if you do!
- Do act calm, confident and in control. Think about how a duck looks while swimming on a pond; even though the legs and feet are going almost manically fast, they still look serene from above the waterline. Try to ensure that externally all is well, even if internally you are finding the situation challenging.

Activity

Stand in front of a mirror somewhere private so you do not have to worry about being seen or heard. Take your time to look at yourself; what is your posture like? What do you feel you are communicating just by the way you are standing? Try moving your limbs, head, and your body into different positions and think about how it changes the message you are communicating. Try to find a posture that is relaxed but upright, open, communicative and professional. Practise talking to yourself and think about the gestures you are making and the energy and emotion you are communicating. Yes, you probably feel embarrassed and a bit silly doing this, but we often look without seeing. Starting with these basics will give you the foundations to build further skills.

As with Adair's principles, some of the aspects of developing effective body language and non-verbal communication skills are easier read than done, but practising helps and you will find that as you do more presentations, your body language improves. Once you are in planning practice your body language will be important; your audience will 'read' you based as much upon your body language as what you actually say.

Support and tools for giving presentations

When it comes to actually delivering the presentation there are also some handy things that you can think about to help you deliver effectively and successfully. You will develop your own tools, like using cue-cards with notes on, to support yourself. Stella Cottrell (2008: 108) suggests a range of things that will help improve how you 'manage' your presentation, your delivery and the impact it has. Although some of these are more relevant to formal presentation scenarios, many will also be valuable in less formal situations:

- Use a clock to time yourself. This will help you keep to time and adjust your content as you progress through your talk without being cut off or rushing. Do think about where you locate the clock though. A presenter who keeps turning to look at the time does not give a good impression!
- Wait until everyone is settled and quiet before you start speaking. If the room is still noisy when the time has come to start, do not just dive straight into your presentation in the hope that they will quieten down. Speak loudly but in a friendly manner and advise the group that you are going to start.
- Tell the audience whether you would prefer questions at the end or during the talk. Having questions at the end will stop interruptions during the talk which can cause problems with flow and timing, but if a more interactive and discursive environment is desired you can invite questions as you talk.
- If possible, speak from cue-cards, from a poster or from memory, rather than reading. The talk will flow better and will be easier to listen to. However, if you are unable to give the talk in any other way, write it out in full and read it. If you do this, think about where you will put your notes, how well you can see them, the lighting and so forth.

- Remind yourself to speak more slowly and loudly than you would usually, and tailor this to the room size and whether you have a microphone. If you can, test any equipment before the start of the session so you do not come across too loudly or quietly at the start.
- Do not apologise for anything you feel could be better. Act as though you are quietly confident that your talk is excellent, and you will be half way to convincing your listeners. This links back to the 'duck' analogy mentioned in the previous section of this chapter.
- Look up. Make eye contact with at least two people in your audience but move your eyes around the room. Try to connect with your audience without anyone feeling like you are staring at them!
- At the beginning, summarise what you are going to say, and in which order. The following section of this chapter talks about structure in more detail, but having a logical approach and 'signposting' your talk is important for the audience and their ability to engage with your content.
- Go through your cards and/or MS PowerPoint slides. Make each point clearly and avoid flicking back and forth.
- Pause and take a breath after each point. This gives your audience time to absorb the point. It also makes you look professional, calm, natural and confident.
- At the end, briefly sum up what you have said.
- Prepare a good line to end with. If you're not sure how to end, simply smile and say thank you. Try to avoid saying things like 'well…erm…that's it'!

tip

Practise, practise, practise! Nobody is beyond improvement when it comes to presentation skills. Practise on your own, in front of family or friends, or ideally video yourself. Videoing yourself can work very well; watching yourself back can be quite a painful experience but it is one of the best ways of seeing potential areas for improvement. The more you practise the better you will get; try different tools and techniques and you will work out what works for you; the result will be a better presentation.

If you have already read Chapter 10, try combining your verbal presentation skills with a visual aid, such as MS PowerPoint, and practise this too. If not, try this later.

Presentation approaches

Presentations follow the same structure principles as your written communication will. This is discussed in much more detail in the subsequent chapters, but in brief your work will be based around the following simple structure:

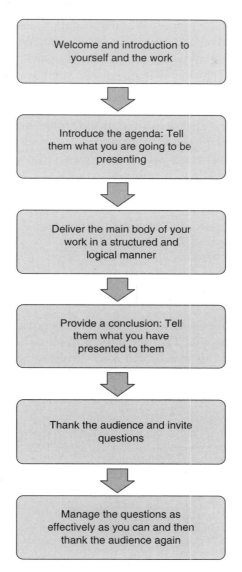

FIGURE 9.1   Presentation structure

Using this basic structure will ensure that your presentation has a logical approach, improving the effectiveness and impact of your work.

Questions

In Chapter 8 of this book there is more discussion about structure, but the key point here is that the main difference between written and verbal communication is the interaction that takes place. When you submit something in writing you will get written or verbal feedback at some later point. With a presentation, there will be questions and interactions at the time of giving the presentation so you need to prepare for this. The key is making sure you have the detailed knowledge and understanding to support what you have presented. If you have prepared fully this will not be a problem, but some people have better memories than others so think about how well you can recall the things you have learnt, and also think about how you are impacted by pressure. It can be seen as good practice to take more extensive supporting notes with you so that you can refer to them if possible. This can help you give a fuller answer.

As a final point about questions, if you do not know the answer, be honest and say you are not certain. Offer to come back to them with the answer at a later stage and take their contact details after the event has finished. This looks much better than waffling or guessing!

Presentations in practice

In planning practice there will be a number of scenarios that will require you to present in front of people. The discussion in this chapter should help with your skill development but it is worth also thinking about the unique nature of the presentation scenarios you will experience as a planning professional.

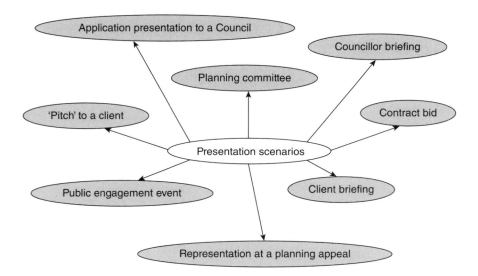

FIGURE 9.2   Presentation scenarios

The scenarios you will find placing demands upon your presentation skills will vary significantly (see Figure 9.2).

Looking at the range of scenarios that exist can be daunting but, thinking back to Adair's six principles on effective communication, it can be seen that these essentially all have their foundations in preparation and the importance of this transcends the different scenarios you will be presented with. Adair advises that:

> Preparation is helped by asking the Who? What? How? When? Where? Why? of the speaking occasion to focus on the audience, the place, the time, the reasons giving rise to the occasion, the information that needs to be covered and how best to put it across. (2003: 34)

Thinking about these questions when preparing for a presentation is a good method of tailoring your work to the circumstance. It sounds obvious but it is easier to focus on what you *want* to present, rather than thinking about what you *need* to present. These will not always completely match up. Your audience will vary significantly in knowledge and understanding in each of the scenarios presented in Figure 9.2 so even the language that you use, including the technical terminology and abbreviations, will need some thought. Similarly the physical environment, the technology available, the time allocated and so forth will all be significant factors. Having regard to this diversity, reflecting on Adair's questions (in parallel with the application of the fundamental skills for delivering good presentations discussed above) will prepare you well for delivering presentations and communicating effectively in practice.

Activity

Pitching your presentation can be difficult but a good way of seeing how this is done can be seen by watching some television. Find some programmes that cover the same subject, like science, and see how they are delivered and presented differently. For example, children's television, early evening 'popular science' programmes and more technical/academic programming of the type often supported by the Open University can all be covering the same subject area, but the manner in which the information is communicated varies greatly. This is also the case with planning, and the use of children's television in this activity may not be as inappropriate as you might be thinking; community consultation is an area of significant importance within town planning and engaging with children and young people is important as part of this, so we need to think about the appropriateness of our communications approach.

Preparing for practice

Your university planning programme will prepare you well for planning practice. All of the tutorials, presentations, workshops, informal discussions and even social interactions you participate in at university will support the development of your non-verbal and verbal communication skills and enhance your effectiveness in planning practice. In addition, and as with other forms of assignment such as essays and reports, you will find that presentations, seminars and workshops will often be organised to simulate real-world scenarios. All of this will ensure that you are not on the 'back foot' when you enter work, and for that matter when you are applying for jobs in the first place. It is common now for job interviews to include presentations, discussions and activities, so improving your skills at university is very important; it will not only help you in work, it will also help you actually get a job.

There are other things that you can do to help prepare yourself for practice. Local, Parish and Community Council meetings and consultations are all held on a regular basis; going along to these can help you appreciate how things are done in practice.

Activity

Local planning authorities will host planning committee meetings most months. These are public discussions so you are free to attend them. Find out when the next planning committee is being held and go along to listen. This will give you a good insight of the day-to-day scenarios where planning professionals need to present to, and interact with, a committee.

The complex nature of communication

As a final point, it is important to remember that verbal communication is rarely one-way. Even when someone is delivering a formal presentation there will usually be an opportunity for questions and interaction between the presenter and the audience. It is therefore important that you do not forget the importance of listening skills. Effective listening skills are just as important as the verbal communication skills that have been the focus of this chapter. You will be a better team member, leader, student and professional if you are a good listener. It will not only help you personally learn, understand and develop, but it will also help improve the output (Adair, 2003).

Conclusions

In this chapter we have explored verbal, and non-verbal, communications. The chapter has focused on more formal presentation scenarios but, as is noted throughout this chapter, the fundamental principles of effective speaking and presentation skills underpin all forms of verbal communication.

Effective verbal communication skills are not only vital to success at university; they are also going to be fundamental to your success as a planning professional. At university you will be supported to perform in a range of verbally assessed and informal verbal communication scenarios. In turn, these will prepare you for the variety of circumstances in your professional career in town planning where verbal communication skills will be vital to your effectiveness.

Further reading

John Adair is a well-regarded author on the subject of communication, leadership, team working and management. The text referred to in this chapter is written with both students and professionals in mind, but it provides a good insight into effective communication skills:

- Adair, J. (2003) *Concise Adair on communication and presentation skills*. London: Thorogood.

Also referenced in this chapter, Stella Cottrell has written a range of excellent study skills books for students. The book used in this chapter is another good general text and includes some useful content on verbal communication skills:

- Cottrell, S. (2008) *The study skills handbook*. Third ed. Basingstoke: Palgrave Macmillan.

A huge range of study skills book are available to support students at university. Take time to look through the different options that are available because you will find that they are written, structured and presented in different ways and some will suit your own learning and reading style better than others.

You will also find that all of the major publishing houses, including Sage, have a range of more detailed texts to support you in particular areas, including verbal communication skills, but another good general text is:

- Burns, T. and Sinfield, S. (2012) *Essential study skills: the complete guide to success at university*. Third ed. London: Sage.

Review points

When reflecting on this chapter you might consider the following

- verbal communication skills are important to success at university
- the skills developed at university will be transferable as you progress into planning practice
- verbal communication skills range from informal communication to formal presentations
- in planning practice verbal communication skills are vital to your success and effectiveness and that of the project and your organisation
- practising presentations skills will help develop your competence, effectiveness and impact.

10

Presenting Your Work

Aims

To improve your ability to produce successful visual communication outputs during your academic study and to understand how this will support your practice-based activities within the planning profession.

Learning outcomes

After reading this chapter you will:

- understand how to communicate your ideas visually in an effective manner
- recognise how to present your ideas visually
- understand how to develop your visual communication skills
- appreciate the transferable nature of the visual communication skills you will develop at university.

Introduction

Visual communication tools are about how you communicate your thoughts and ideas to an audience; this could range from Microsoft PowerPoint to the use of professional tools such as AutoCAD. As you will note from the aims of this chapter, there are two elements to visual communication skills; the first is how you can communicate your ideas visually, the second is how you then actually present your ideas visually. These sound very similar but as this chapter will demonstrate, they are quite different.

Town planning is a visually dependent discipline; whether presenting a strategic vision or a detailed building design, we need to communicate our plan visually. Similarly, we need to communicate that visual representation of our ideas to an audience; this is the presentation part of the visual communication.

Communicating your ideas visually

This section is all about how you translate something from being an idea in your mind to something other people can see and understand. Much of what we want to communicate we can talk or write about; but sometimes what we are trying to express needs a different medium of communication to improve the clarity, understanding and effectiveness of the communication. There are a range of ways that you can translate your ideas from these thoughts in your head to something that has been externalised in a visual manner. These are discussed through the following sections of this chapter.

Traditional drawing and sketching

Chapter 8 of this book has explored the use of plans and drawings in general. It is important to remember that the 'manual' creation of drawings and sketches can, despite the growth of electronic systems and software, be the most effective way of expressing yourself and communicating your ideas. Manually created drawings and sketches can be a very visually stimulating experience since they can communicate emotions in a way that electronic impassive outputs sometimes cannot.

Manual drawing and sketching is not the possession of the architectural profession. As a town planner the importance of plans and drawing is clear and, as discussed in Chapter 8, they are central to the communication of visions, ideas and strategies at the strategic and site specific level.

Each university will approach this area of the discipline differently so although all will embrace drawing and sketching, each programme and planning school will teach and support drawing and sketching skills differently. Some universities, like the University of the West of England, position their planning programmes in the same department as the architecture courses and this relationship is reflected in the teaching content on some of their programmes (though property development orientated planning courses are also available). In other cases, planning may be in a stand-alone school, such as at Cardiff University, or it could reside in a real estate and planning orientated department, as you will find at the University of Reading. You should look carefully at what you want from your course and factor this into your university and programme choice.

In all cases, drawing and sketching will be present in your course, but the extent to which they are included in the syllabus, the prominence they are given, the scale at which 'design skills' are taught, and the manner in which these skills are utilised in assessment and project work will vary. All planning programmes from accredited schools will give you an insight into this craft and the tools you need to enter the profession with confidence, but every course has a slightly different focus. This is something you should reflect upon when you select your course to ensure your personal preferences are reflected in your studies. You should also be aware that it may be possible to transfer between courses (and sometimes even universities) in certain circumstances and you might want to explore this if you feel your course is not offering you what you want.

Digital mapping

The use of mapping has always been important to planning. From the masterplan or vision overlaid onto a map to a locational map for orientation purposes, mapping is a key tool to how we communicate our ideas.

Historically planners would have relied upon paper maps, often annotated by hand, and copied/printed for wider distribution. Today, mapping is digital. This allows for endless opportunities to vary the map contents to allow you to communicate your message. You may only want to show a site location, but digital mapping allows you to alter the information contained within a map. These 'layers' can be added and removed so that you can create the map you want, with only the information you need included.

A range of different mapping packages are available and your university will, usually through the library services, provide free access to software provided by, for example, DigiMap, which uses Ordnance Survey mapping. There are also free mapping systems such as MagicMap (which is supported by the Department for Environment, Food and Rural Affairs), which can be used to produce very effective outputs. You can use packages like these to create maps that can be used in your project work at university.

Other software can be used for the creation of certain mapping and imagery products. For example, Google Maps and MS Bing, which both have relatively simple street-based mapping and associated satellite imagery, can enable you to create useful visual outputs.

In planning practice you will find that your organisation has access to mapping software to meet your professional needs, though the systems will vary between organisations.

Geographical Information Systems (GIS)

Geographical Information Systems (GIS) is related to digital mapping. It is a system that enables you to combine mapping and data. A great range of GIS software packages exist. The line between a digital mapping package and a GIS system is somewhat blurred, but essentially GIS systems allow for both data analysis and the communication of data through mapping. Software such as the aforementioned MagicMap can be termed a GIS package due to the use of data within the layers and options. Your university will provide you with access to some of the packages but others are freely available on the internet. You may find that your course, to some degree, utilises GIS in teaching and assessment.

Whilst at university you will find that your programme may have modules that teach and assess your mapping (and GIS) skills but you will also be able to access other tutorials and courses that can teach you the skills required to produce effective digital mapping across a range of software packages. The ever increasing importance of technical skills for planning professionals is such that you should seek out such opportunities and embrace them. This will enhance your CV, your employability, and your effectiveness as a practitioner.

Mind-mapping

Mind-mapping, also known as spider diagrams or mind-webs, are a diagrammatic method of expressing your ideas visually. A mind-map may be for your own personal use or for presentation purposes. They are normally used to express concepts, breaking them down in a logical and understandable manner. They can be used for problem-solving, helping you to overcome an identified challenge, or for communicating a concept or vision you have already worked up.

The best way to explain a mind-map is to see one. Figure 10.1 is a very simple, incomplete example to show the beginnings of what would become a very large and complex mind-map!

As you will see from Figure 10.1, from the central idea or premise you then work out, breaking the core down and expanding outwards. Elements will be inter-connected across the entire mind-map, which makes some extremely complex!

There is no set way that you have to work when creating a mind-map. Some people will work from the centre writing along each line, rather than linking boxes, to create a map that looks a little like tree branches spreading out from the centre. Others will use a boxed version as demonstrated in

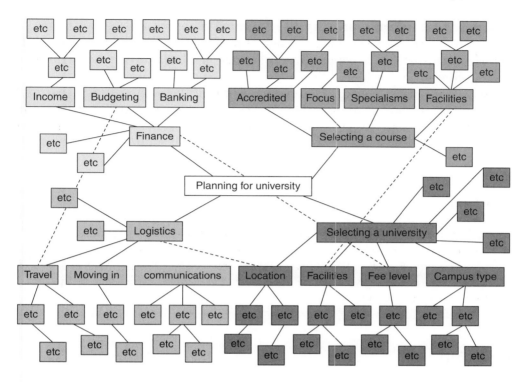

FIGURE 10.1 Mind-map example

Figure 10.1; and in some cases a combination of the two works well, with linked boxes and text on each linking line. Similarly, a mind-map may be a rough diagram drawn out in your notebook, or it could be a beautiful creation that you produce using software such as MS PowerPoint or a more specialist drawing package. This will be dependent upon the use of the output, i.e. personal or presentation to an audience (see section below). Regardless of this question, the approach and principles of this simple but expressive tool are the same.

tip

A number of mind-mapping tools are available online which you may find useful. Put 'mind-map' into a search engine and see what is offered. Some are free but others are chargeable.

You may find that the primary use for mind-mapping during your time at university is to help you make notes. However, there may be assessments where you are asked to communicate an idea or plan that you have through a mind-map.

You can therefore develop your own style to suit your own study needs, but do be aware if there is an assessment, that a mind-map can be presented in different ways and make sure your submission reflects the assignment requirements.

Activity

Practising mind-mapping is a good way of developing the skill. Thinking back to Figure 10.1, try making your own mind-map using a style of your choice either for your upcoming application for university or for your personal development for your later years of study if you are already studying your course. Break each part down as far as you can and find as many links as possible.

Modeling

Making physical models is a good way of communicating your vision for a site, area or whole city. Often associated with architecture or construction-based courses, models are also used in planning to help visualise a project. Models can take various forms and can be made of anything – you may find yourself making a complex wooden model or it could be something constructed out of recycled materials. As a planning student the range of model outputs you produce could vary significantly, from a 'speed planning' event where you use random materials to create a vision in a time-limited activity, through to a model of a development proposal that is days or weeks in the making.

Once you enter practice you will find models are used extensively to communicate a development proposal more expressively and these can be particularly useful for consultation events or presentations. This is discussed in a little more detail later in this chapter.

Computer Aided Design (CAD)

Computer Aided Design is the use of software to create a computer-generated image of your idea. These computer systems can support the visualisation of an idea and, increasingly, can actually inform the development of a design solution. At one end of the spectrum, CAD systems are 'simple' drafting tools where the computer is passive in the process. They enable the creation of an idea in plan form and are the computerised realisation of the traditional manual drafting of design proposals. At the other end of the spectrum are 'intelligent' systems of CAD. These are packages that can offer design solutions (to varying degrees) for consideration, informed by data based upon regulations, client requirements and so forth. These systems have evolved greatly since the 1960s when the very earliest software was first developed (Kalay, 2004).

CAD systems therefore vary significantly having regard to the varying roles they can play in the design process. A range of software packages are available, some of which are available for free. Widely used packages, such as AutoCAD, can be relatively expensive but you will typically find that you can access these at university or work if you need them for the work that you are doing. Other systems, such as Google SketchUp, can be downloaded for free. The complexity of these systems varies but your university will support you to develop the skills that you need to use CAD if this is appropriate for your programme. In some cases you will be offered CAD as a specialism or an additional module/course. If you are offered such an opportunity it is worth trying to take it up because a working knowledge of CAD is another good skillset to have. CAD does not have to be scary, systems such as Google SketchUp are very simple and easy to use and, whether CAD forms part of your course or not, becoming familiar with such software is useful. You might find it adds to your ability to communicate your ideas visually.

Activity

Get yourself online and find Google SketchUp or another similar piece of **simple** free CAD software. Practise using the system and learn how to create simple buildings. Try to draw a simple house first, then try more complex buildings and places. Designing things using CAD can be fun, so keep playing around with the software and improve your skills so that you can use it to support your university work. You can build on this if you want, by learning how to use more complex software packages.

Photographs

Finally, don't forget the power of the photographic image. Whether showing a current situation, or electronically integrating an overlaid image of some form of change, a photograph can be a powerful and effective way of communicating your message.

Presenting your work visually

The first section of this chapter is concerned with how you can realise your ideas through visualisation tools. The following sections explore how you can now present these ideas visually. The difference is that this section is looking at methods of presenting your ideas to an audience, either with or without a verbal presentation, rather than how you realise your idea in a visual manner.

Showing your outputs: Digital

Using projectors and monitors to present your work has been commonplace for many years now in both education and in the workplace. The overhead projector is not commonly used today but a modern visualiser is a useful way of showing drawings or sketches produced on paper. More common in planning though is the use of computer-based software systems. These may be packages that allow scanned-in work to be shown through a computer projector, or the work may have been created electronically in the first instance.

The dominant piece of software for electronic presentations is MS PowerPoint, but there are a range of other packages that are available including Adobe Photoshop, Prezi and Keynote (for Apple computers) for more complex outputs. Some of these systems, such as MS PowerPoint, are very easy to use and with the latest versions you can create quite advanced presentations; indeed it is possible to do basic design work using the software if necessary. Other systems are a little more difficult to use or can be less familiar, such as Adobe Photoshop, but the results produced with such packages can be visually quite stunning. At university you will be expected to have, or to quickly develop, skills in MS PowerPoint. Other packages may be introduced through your studies but you will be able to access support of some form to help you develop the necessary skills with these applications.

You may well have become familiar with these packages before you reached university, but you will find that the work you will be expected to produce will be more complex and demanding. Producing a presentation using a system such a MS PowerPoint is actually very easy; producing a *good* presentation is far more challenging!

The principles behind the creation of good presentations transcend the software you are using. Some packages will give you more tools than others, but the basics behind the design of a good output is the same. Some of the basic points to be aware of include:

- Think really carefully about the colour scheme of your presentation. Keep it simple and consistent.
- Avoid using unnecessary animation, sounds and effects; these can be really annoying for the audience!
- Use contrasting colours so the text and information is clear and easy to read.
- Think about the size of any text. It needs to be large enough to be read at the back of the room you are presenting in. Knowing the presentation environment is important for this too.
- Consider how many words are appropriate for each slide. Remember, the text should be supporting what you are saying so do not put everything you are going to say on the slides, just the key facts and points you are making. You might not even need words.
- Keep borders around the slides unless you are presenting photographs, graphics or diagrams. When presenting text think about how you would present on a piece of paper.
- Think really carefully about the balance between text and imagery. The ability to show photographs and images is a great strength of electronic visual aids and they can really add to a presentation. If you use them, think about the size – there is nothing wrong with having a slide that is filled by a single high impact photograph or image. Notwithstanding this, providing important facts, figures, dates and so forth in the text can be really helpful for the audience. As a student you will appreciate this when you are trying to take notes in lectures!

Using electronic visual aids to present your work can be really helpful. It can improve the impact of your work, aid memory/note-taking, and can enable you to communicate things that are difficult to explain in words. There are 'health warnings' with the use of such software though:

- Anything electronic can go wrong! Ensure you are not entirely dependent upon your electronic presentation because this could lead to a very problematic and embarrassing situation if something fails to work. You should always be prepared to present without a visual aid if necessary.
- Ensure your presentation actually works with what you are saying, not against it. A presentation can distract from what is being said, undermining the impact of the content you are delivering.
- Failure to consider and deliver good practice can lead to a presentation that is entirely undermined by the visual aid used; it almost will not matter what you are saying!

Activity

Practise producing presentations of different lengths and formats using MS PowerPoint. Vary the length from 5 minutes up to 15 minutes and practice inserting images, diagrams, and photographs into your work. Make the content about anything you want, the important thing is to get the technique right. Show a friend, family member or teacher/professional your work – get feedback on its design and see how you can improve it. Once you have read Chapter 8 of this book, try practising delivering a presentation using PowerPoint in support.

When you enter planning practice you will be expected to have IT literacy in, at the very least, the Microsoft family of software, including PowerPoint. Of course, if you are proficient in other packages this will further aid your employability and you should seek out opportunities where possible to develop such skills. Importantly though, in addition to a basic competence, you will also be expected to understand the principles of creating good presentations so a focus on this will serve you well.

 **tip**

Observe how your teachers and lecturers present work to you; some will be better than others but good practice will be obvious to you because of the way you feel and respond to the delivery. You will also find watching things like BBC, Channel 4, Channel 5, ITV or SKY news helpful; presenters will regularly (and often unnecessarily) use graphics and visual presentations to support an item and you will be able to see how they communicate the information to you. Take note of things like the colouring (which will be brand specific), fonts, level of details and so forth. Try to watch the different channels and reflect on the different styles and approaches. This will reflect upon the audience being targeted by the producers – something you should be mindful of yourself.

Electronic visual presentations are not limited to MS PowerPoint style outputs though. You should think about other mediums that can allow you to present your ideas, such as video. Additionally, design software such as CAD can create virtual worlds that you can 'fly through'; such presentations may be complex to create but they can be visually stunning and support the communication of your vision significantly.

Showing your work: Physical outputs

This is the presentation of work that you have produced as a display or installation of some form. This may be a presentation board or panel with your drawings, sketches and diagrams on, a portfolio, or an area in which you can display models, installations, panels and audio-visual work.

On the face of it, the idea of presenting your work on a board or panel might seem simple, but the reality is that there is real skill in creating a presentation display that has the impact you want.

At university you will find that there are circumstances when you will be asked to create something very visual for an assessment. You could be asked to hand in a portfolio folder with sketches, drawings, plans and so forth inside, or it may be a 'crit' (critique) where you are asked to pin up and display your work for consideration by your tutors and/or peers. Such a 'crit' may be accompanied by the need to deliver a verbal presentation, but this will not always be the case. Portfolios are also briefly mentioned in the next chapter of this book because there is overlap in their role as both a visual and written communications medium. At university you will be helped to create an effective portfolio submission because you might not be familiar with how to do this in the manner that will be expected on your programme.

If you are presenting your work via a physical visual display, you need to think really carefully about order, positioning, fixings, colouring and sizes. As with verbal presentations, which are discussed in the next chapter, you need to think about whom your audience is and what their needs are. Is your assessment a simulated scenario? If so, do you need to tailor your content and presentation style to a particular audience? Things like font size and positioning are very important having regard to how large the audience for the work will be, how far away they could be standing and so forth.

While you are studying at university you will find that there are assessment scenarios where a physical display is required; but you could also find that your work is also included, in some form, at the end of year show where your planning school is presenting the work of students to family, friends and professionals. In either case it is important that you understand what is being asked of you; what are the criteria against which your work must adhere to? Learning these skills will prepare you for planning practice where there will be multiple scenarios involving physical presentation displays.

As a practitioner you will need to present ideas to other professionals, clients, politicians or members of the public. Whether you enter private practice or the public sector there will be consultation events and circumstances where you are presenting work through a physical display. The skills you learn at university will help you develop the skills to deliver a professional, effective and high impact presentation.

tip

Keep your eye out for exhibitions, shows and consultation events in your area, whether they are planning related or otherwise. Take yourself along and reflect upon how the material is presented. Think about the details, the colours, sizes, fonts, and positioning. There is an art to effective displays and appreciating the techniques used in professional presentations and exhibitions will help you develop your own skills.

Conclusions

Visual presentation skills will be familiar to you from school and college but at university you will find that the demands placed upon you to produce high quality, professional and complex outputs will be significantly higher. This is important because your course is preparing you for planning practice where effective visual communication skills are so important.

Take the time to work on your abilities and you will see positive results in the quality of your outputs and the marks that you receive. In turn, these transferable skills will be relevant throughout your professional career.

Further reading

A large number of study skills book are available to support students at university and professionals in practice. Explore the different options that are available because you will find that they are written, structured and presented in different ways and some will suit your own learning and reading style better than others.

A good general text is:

- Burns and Sinfield (2012) *Essential study skills: The complete guide to success at university.* Third ed. London: Sage.

You will also find that all of the major publishing houses, including Sage, have a range of more detailed texts to support you in particular areas, including visual presentation skills. Some aids, such as GIS, CAD, and presentation software packages have a wide range of guides available to aid your development. Some good examples of such texts include:

- Vander Veer, E. (2007) *PowerPoint 2007: The missing manual.* London: Pogue/O'Reilly.

This is very much a 'how to' guide that will help you learn how to use this software package. MS Office software guides are generally numerous and range in complexity. Your local bookshop will have some different options for you to look at, including 'Dummies' (and similar) guides and official Microsoft products. Information is also freely available online to help you develop your skills.

- Heywood, I. et al. (2006) *An introduction to geographical information systems*. Third ed. Harlow: Pearson Education Limited.

An academic book, this text provides an excellent introduction into all things GIS, from the basic concept and fundamentals to more detailed and technical information; this is a good place to get started.

- Kalay. Y. (2004) *Architecture's new media*. Cambridge, MA: The MIT Press.

This is a very thorough, well-written and presented academic text which provides a detailed history and comprehensive insight into CAD. The range of CAD software packages available means that you will be best looking at books for particular packages once you know which ones are used and/or favoured by your university, but this book explains all of the principles meticulously.

Review points

When reflecting on this chapter you might consider the following:

- town planning is inherently visual and a variety of visual presentation mediums are utilised to support the art and science of planning
- ideas can be communicated using a range of methods, from traditional pencil and paper drawing through to complex software tools such as CAD
- CAD is becoming increasingly 'intelligent', although the communication of ideas is all about translating what is in your own head into a medium that is understandable to a given audience
- in addition to translating the ideas and communicating them visually, there are also methods of presenting work, such as MS PowerPoint presentations
- visual presentations can be high impact and persuasive, but they can also compromise an idea and must be used with care.

11

Reports and Essay Writing

Aims

To improve your ability to create effective written outputs during your academic study, and to understand how this work will support the requirement to produce a variety of written material in planning practice.

Learning outcomes

After reading this chapter you will:

- understand the nature of different written outputs
- appreciate how to structure and approach written work appropriate to your studies
- recognise your own abilities and identify areas for further development
- understand the application of the skills and knowledge in professional practice.

Introduction

It is vital through both your academic and professional career that you are able to communicate thoughts, ideas, opinions and facts as appropriate to your role and the circumstances in question. The way in which you communicate will vary depending on the circumstances; it may be through a visual presentation of some form, as explored in the previous chapter, or it may be through some form of written work.

Through your planning degree you will be expected to produce written work for a wide range of scenarios. This is important as you will inevitably be required to produce high quality written outputs on a regular basis once you are in practice. Your academic studies will therefore be structured so that not only will written assessments test your academic ability, but they will also prepare you for the sort of work you will be undertaking as a planning professional.

An overview of the types of written output

As a student you will have three main types of written output; reports, essays and dissertations. These outputs will be set as assignments for a number of your modules to test your knowledge and understanding and to give you an insight into the form and content of written outputs you will ultimately be producing once you have entered practice. The principles discussed in this chapter are relevant to dissertation writing, but Chapter 12 specifically looks at this very particular form of output. Portfolios are also briefly mentioned since again the principles are relevant, but they are not the focus; when creating a portfolio you should read this chapter alongside Chapter 10 in recognition of both the visual and written nature of a portfolio.

Essays

Essays are discursive tools that are used to enable the writer to present an argument in a structured and formal but flowing manner. They are written using the 'third person' and supported by extensive referencing. In planning practice you will rarely be required to produce an essay, but they are a very important method of assessment at university since they allow you to present an opinion piece supported by evidence, thereby demonstrating your knowledge and understanding of the subject and your ability to present an argument (Burns and Sinfield, 2012).

Reports

A report is similarly formal, but is more overtly structured in style and flow, with headings and sub-headings creating a very ordered and linear piece of work. As a student you will be required to produce reports but the practical nature of this form of assignment means it will serve a slightly different function in some regards, allowing you to present findings following an investigation of some kind, for example. Reports are the form of assignment that will translate most directly into your practice work. Planners will use reports extensively and for a variety of purposes and the ability to write reports effectively is a vital skill (Burns and Sinfield, 2012).

Dissertations

The final form of 'traditional' assignment you will come across is the dissertation. These are extended reports that are focused around a single piece of research. As a student you will typically undertake a single module that is based around a dissertation output. In relation to your subsequent practice work, your dissertation will be extremely important as this module will develop your research skills and enable you to deliver an extended report to a deadline and to a professional standard (Burns and Sinfield, 2012). It will also enable you to pursue an area of individual interest which you may wish to develop in your early career. Further guidance on writing a dissertation is provided in Chapter 12.

Portfolios

The portfolio could be considered as a non-traditional form of assessment in the sense that many academic subject areas will not employ this assignment format. A portfolio is essentially a large folder in which sheets of paper, typically A3 or above, are compiled to form a project or proposal submission. Portfolios are used when more design/visual work is involved in the assessment, making the more traditional forms of essays and reports less suitable and appropriate. As a planning student you will be involved in projects that involve design work and the use of imagery – this will typically be submitted for assessment in a portfolio. The portfolio is therefore both a means of presenting your visual outputs and your written outputs.

Think back to the work you have produced previously at work, school or college. You will have written essays and reports before, and you will probably have created a portfolio of work for a project, even if it was given a different name. What you produce at university is not going to be radically different, but it will be more challenging because of the standard of work expected and the advances you will be expected to make in your written communication ability.

Activity

Look back at the work you have produced previously at work, school or college. Undertake a critical review of your work and think about your strengths and areas for improvement based upon the feedback you received. Before even thinking about the planning subject area, knowing the general areas in your writing skills that require development will allow you to focus your efforts on improving the outputs you produce. The contents of this chapter, together with support that you will find elsewhere, will help you address the areas for improvement that you have identified.

Written communication: The process

Regardless of the type of assignment output you are producing, the stages you will go through to produce a successful piece of work will essentially remain the same. Burns and Sinfield (2012: 271–30) present ten stages for the creation of successful assignments:

1. Preparation.
    The old adage that proper preparation prevents poor performance is true. Whether writing an assignment for university or preparing a planning statement for a planning submission it is essential that you work through and plan what you are going to deliver. A key part of this, and a very useful tool to employ as a student, is the action plan. An action plan will effectively outline the steps you will need to undertake to deliver on the question or output requirement, including the necessary research, any reading and how you can access it, and the timetable/schedule against which you need to work. As a planning practitioner and student you will also need to think about dependency relations; who else will be involved in the work? Who are you dependent upon for content or information? This is something you will need to think carefully about. Managing collaborative working can be very challenging. You may find Chapter 5, 'Leadership and team-working' helpful with this.
2. Following the action plan.
    It sounds obvious but if you have gone to the effort of making a plan then make sure you follow it! A key element of this will be developing and building the research and evidence base. As a student this will likely mean an extensive review of both academic and practice-based material that will be in both hard copy and electronic formats. As a practitioner you will also need to undertake research, but this will likely be practice-oriented content rather than use of academic sources. Do not forget too that your work may involve primary research, that is to say undertaking research yourself directly rather than using material produced by someone else. As both a student studying town planning and a planning practitioner, you may find yourself undertaking site surveys, interviews, questionnaires or facilitating working groups or workshops to generate the evidence you need to produce your work.

3. Review the notes you have made.
    When you have undertaken the research, do not just assume that this means you have everything you need. Go back over the notes you have made and reflect upon whether you have all you need to answer the question. Also consider whether you have both sides of the argument covered if this is appropriate for the scenario you are working with. Spend some time thinking about everything you have learnt before moving on to the next stage; let your mind work with all of the information you are offering it.

4. Plan the structure.
    Once you have processed the information and you are happy that you have all you need, think about the structure you need to work with. This is discussed in more detail in the next section of this chapter.

5. Write the first draft.
    Writing the first draft of any piece of work can be the most challenging. The daunting prospect of filling a blank sheet of paper can feel quite overwhelming. But remember, you are not starting with nothing, you already have a structure and the evidence you need to complete this work; it is just a matter of filling in the gaps. If you undertook the previous four stages fully you can relax and let the words come. Do not try to make the first draft perfect, just go with the flow and write whatever comes into your mind. Do not think about the word limit at this point, you can go back and review and edit what you have written later. The first task is to get what is in your head and in your notes down into the draft; you can tidy it up afterwards.

6. Leave it.
    Walk away from the work and leave it. This will allow you to come back to the work with a refreshed and calmed mind.

7. Review, revise and edit.
    In reality this might prove to be the trickiest part of the process. You will find yourself presented with something that requires revision and editing. The most important thing here is to give yourself plenty of time to work with what you have produced. Save different versions, play around with the content, and slowly piece together what you hope is your final draft. Then do it again until you are happy with what you have.

8. Proof-read.
    After leaving your work to one side again, do not forget to check over your work with fresh eyes. Look for repetition, typographical errors, structural issues and so forth. Give yourself time to do this properly in an environment that is conducive to being thorough; you may well normally work with the radio on or music playing but it is important that you remain focused during this process. Small errors can make work look unprofessional or rushed; such an impression will impact on your mark as a student and will adversely affect the strength of your argument.

9. Hand in...
    ...in time for the deadline! If you hand in work late as a student there will be a penalty of some sort, either to your mark or your ability to pass the module/course. As a practitioner the penalty could be a lost contract or a loss of influence of a planning decision. Potentially your job could be jeopardised as well!

10. Review feedback.

At the end of the process take the time to go back over the mark, feedback or decision outcome and reflect upon what you could do differently next time to improve. Even the most experienced planner will continue to learn with every project they are involved in.

tip

Keep guidance like the ten steps above to hand when you are actually doing your assignments so you can refer to it as you progress through your work. It is all too easy to just get caught up in what you are doing without really thinking about how you are doing it.

As both a student and a professional you may find that some steps can, and indeed should, be undertaken with the support of peers and colleagues. As a student you must of course be aware of the issue of plagiarism, but proof-reading for example is something which will benefit from a second look. As a planning professional, your work will likely be more collaborative, but even when you are undertaking work on your own you will find it helpful to have your work reviewed or edited by a colleague. It is sometime difficult to see the errors or potential for improvement in work we have written ourselves and having support from an appropriate associate can help improve the quality and impact.

Sky Marsen (2007) suggests in her book *Professional Writing* that it is essential that you have a clear idea of the audience you will be addressing through the report, what the actual purpose of the report is, and what format the report is required to be in. Marsen's book is geared towards writing for business, industry and IT but these points are key considerations for both students and planning professionals and will actually apply to almost any piece of written work you are involved in. The following seven questions are suggested as being particularly pertinent:

- **What do your intended readers already know?** In the context of being a planning professional this is particularly important – a planning report will be read by both planning professionals and lay persons.
- **Why will they read this document?** It is not only practitioners who need to think of this; as a student you may find that your assignment is designed for a certain audience. Indeed, your assignment may actually be a 'live' project for part of your university, in which case you will be writing a practice output (for which you will be assessed) for a very particular audience.
- **What do they need to know? What do they *not* need to know?**
- **What is actually needed from this output?** It is all too easy for a piece of work to evolve into something that suits your own knowledge or interests, but the work is for a purpose;

what are you actually being asked to produce? And what, therefore, is the appropriate content?

- **How much detail do they need? How much of the big picture do they need?** There will always be a balance to be struck, depending upon the word limit and audience, between providing contextual discussion and detailed commentary/analysis. Knowing what is wanted from the assessor/audience is important to how you strike this balance.
- **What purpose is the document serving?** For example, does the document inform? Analyse? Clarify? Persuade? Will it be used as the basis for a decision? Questions such as these will impact upon the manner in which you present and 'angle' your work and therefore they need some thought at the planning stage.
- **What is the standard way of presenting the information your audience requires?** i.e. what are they expecting to read? Is there reason to vary this format? As discussed previously in this section, the format will vary depending upon the assignment type. The use of plain English in the presentation of information will also be important in some circumstances, such as when writing information for the public or councillors.
(Marsen, 2007:3)

Effective written communication is a skill that develops with time, practise, and experience. The written products required as a student and as a planning officer will vary depending upon your specific role or the module learning outcomes, and the purpose of the report. Similarly, different organisations and institutions will have their own format and style for reports.

Following the stages set out by Burns and Sinfield (2012), and considering the questions posed by Marsen (2007), will allow you to produce effective academic work, but they will also apply to the work you will produce as a practitioner. The principles will remain, only the nature of the output will vary.

Structuring your work

When considering how to structure your work it is important to remember the difference between the structural approach you take, and how you structure your work in the presentational sense.

As a student you will be directed by your tutor in relation to the structure that is required. In some cases, such as your dissertation or a report-based assessment designed to simulate a practice-based scenario, you will find a rigid structure within which you will need to frame your work – there is a little more discussion about this in the next section. In other cases you will be given more flexibility. Not that you will necessarily have a formal structure to actually present; if you are writing an essay then this will be free flowing, unencumbered by titles and heading. An essay still needs a structure though, with a beginning, middle and an end.

Ineffective structural approaches can be fatal to the impact of a piece of work because the argument can be lost in the confusing approach employed. It is important that work is logical and understandable to a reader and much of this comes down to how the author presents the content; the order and framing.

All work will, at a fundamental level, utilise the same structural approach. At a basic level all work has the following:

- An introduction – this will explain the purpose of the work, the context and the approach. In some cases, before the introduction, you may also provide an 'abstract'. This is effectively a summary of the contents of your work. This approach is usually taken in formal submissions such as professional reports or dissertations at university. You would not provide an abstract in an essay for example.
- The main body – the contents of the work. This will include all of the discussion, commentary, analysis, critique, results and argument as appropriate to the task. This section may be broken down into sub-sections, particularly in a formal report or dissertation. Whether formal sub-division takes place or not, it is as important that this main body is logically approached as it is for the work as an entirety. Think about the order of the contents and the way to present it. Is there a logical flow? Does it build up in the right manner?
- Conclusions – where the contents of the main body is drawn upon to present the key outputs of the work. After the conclusion you may present 'recommendations'. These will be looking to the future. These are typically used in reports where an investigation has taken place and the remit involves looking forward, rather than just reflection.
- Referencing and bibliography – identifying the evidence base that informed your work.
- Appendix – normally reserved for formal reports, dissertations and the like, this is where copies of supporting material can be provided.

As noted previously, this structure may be overt (a report) or covert (an essay), but in all cases a logical and coherent approach which follows these basic principles of structure should be followed. By working with this basic structure you can then flesh-out the work into any format you wish and in accordance with the guidance provided to you by your tutor or in the assessment details.

As a student you may find guides to writing helpful. Your university library will have a range of these and most bookshops will sell guides. Specialist guides for students like Peter Redman's *Good essay writing: A social sciences guide* (2001) can really help you to improve the structure, approach, effectiveness and impact of your written work.

As a planning practitioner you may find yourself working within a very rigid structure. A planning committee report, for example, will have a very clear and fixed structure for you to work with. A typical written report by a local planning authority for a planning committee might have a structure something like this:

- Application information, including applicant, agent, site address and political ward.
- The nature of the application, i.e. what development is proposed.
- A description of the site and locality identifying key attributes of relevance to the development proposed.
- Any relevant site history, enforcement history or background of note.
- Consultations carried out and the responses received.
- The planning policy context.
- The case. This will begin with a consideration of the acceptability of the proposal in principle, i.e. when tested against the planning policy context identified. The case is then normally broken down into thematic areas such as residential amenity, visual amenity, conservation, highways and so forth.
- The recommendation of the planner based upon the discussion presented.
- Any suggested conditions or the proposed reasons for refusal (if a planning obligation is involved this will be presented too).

In contrast to this, and unlike a rigid local authority report structure, a planning statement produced by a consultant will be tailored to the needs of the client, case and circumstance. That said, there will be accepted structures and presentational approaches that you will be expected to follow.

Written communication methods

There are basically two ways you can create a written output. Manually (you write it yourself by hand) or digitally (you write it on a computer). By now you should be familiar with the most commonly used software packages, such as Microsoft Word, and will likely have used them extensively at school and/or college. You will find, however, that at university and subsequently in planning practice, you are expected to produce written outputs to a higher standard than you are used to. For this reason it is important that you do not under-estimate the need to be competent with packages such as MS Word and Excel (communicating figures can be important as a planner) so that you can communicate information effectively. You might find that there are certain skills, such as referencing, inserting pictures, tables or graphics, or formatting your work to a set criteria, which need a little attention before you are truly competent. Numerous guides (online, embedded in the software, and books) are available to help you to develop the necessary skills in the software that you will use.

It is typical for employers to spend additional time desk-top publishing their outputs in order to deliver the most creative and polished of outputs. Applications within the Adobe suite are perhaps the most common and it is likely that computers within your department will have such programmes already installed. Student pricing does exist to purchase your own copy but you may want to explore cheaper alternatives as well.

Look in the library or online for guides about key software like MS Word and Excel. Look through these guides and reflect on how able you are to use the packages to their full extent. If there are areas you could develop, take the time to do this.

Written communication at university

At university you will be assessed in a variety of different ways. You will find that there will be a requirement to do presentations, 'crits' and scenario-based activities as discussed in the previous chapter, but essays and reports will likely be a dominant form of assessment type for some modules; though the nature and format of these will vary greatly of course.

Town planning is an interesting area to study at university because it is both an academic subject and a profession. Consequently, there are vocational elements within your course, but also theoretical content and the nature of your written assessments will reflect this. Typically you will find that there is a requirement to produce essays in connection with assessments that are looking for subject-based debate and discussion, generally with a theoretical underpinning. These could be considered to be 'traditional' forms of assessment of the type usually associated with academic study.

Other modules, however, will require the submission of a report or portfolio; these will often be assessments with more practice-orientated content. You may find yourself asked to produce a report or portfolio in a scenario-based assessment, effectively role-playing the part of a planning consultant, local government professional or third sector organisation. These assessments will vary greatly in format, form and output requirements in an attempt to simulate the variety of outputs that you could be involved in producing as a planning practitioner. For example, you may be asked to produce a planning proposal submission with plans and planning statements, or a consultant's report in response to an intended plan.

In some cases there will be an accepted way of producing and presenting your work to meet the requirements of your university. The dissertation is the best example of this. You will normally be required to produce a dissertation in the third or fourth year of your studies. Although in many respects the dissertation is a great opportunity to pursue research into an area you are particularly interested in, your university will likely have an accepted approach for you to work with in relation to both the process of undertaking the research, and how you present your work.

Activity

Many university courses, particularly postgraduate programmes, will require you to submit a short essay or statement to demonstrate your suitability for acceptance on the course. In your own time, try to write a short essay of about 1,000 words that would fulfil this requirement using the 10 stages listed in this chapter and having regard to Marsen's questions. Using this process, and thinking about these questions, is good preparation for how you can approach all of your written work in the future.

Regardless of the work you are producing, the ten stages outlined by Burns and Sinfield (2012) will hold true in all of your written work and you can always use this as a framework. That said, in each circumstance you will need to think very carefully about the questions posed by Marsen (2007). You will be given guidance by your tutor concerning the presentational approach you should take, structure and so forth, but part of the assessment and academic rigour for the assignment will be your ability to consider the audience and output requirements associated with the assignment in question. When considering the steps of Burns and Sinfield (2012) therefore, the importance of the planning stages is clear.

As with many of the other aspects of developing your written communication skills, these stages and questions will serve you well in practice when similar stands will be required of you, albeit in slightly different arrangements and formats.

Plagiarism and referencing

In all cases, whilst at university you will need to develop your writing skills to ensure that you produce academically rigorous submissions; this means being conscious of things like plagiarism, and understanding how to reference correctly.

Plagiarism is effectively when you present someone else's work as your own. At university plagiarism is taken very seriously and failure to adhere to the requirement to reference fully and completely will lead to some form of action on the part of your institution; this can be a really serious matter.

Having regard to the importance of plagiarism, but also recognising the need to demonstrate the academic rigour of your work, learning how to reference is very important. Different universities will have different approaches to referencing, but you will probably find that the institution requires you to comply with the provisions of the Harvard, Chicago or MLA systems. In some cases, specialist approaches may be used, such as the Oxford Standard for Citation of Legal Authorities (OSCOLA). In all cases you will find that your university provides support through the library, tutorials and/or workshops. It is important that you learn how to reference properly from the earliest stages of your university career or you will find that your performances, and marks, suffer.

Written communication in the workplace

Once you enter the workplace in a role within the built environment professions you will find many of the skills and techniques you developed whilst at university will be directly transferable. Most courses will also have provided you with real world experience, or simulated scenarios, which will mean you are competent at producing the forms and standards of practice output that will be required of you.

The work you produce in practice will, to a certain extent, vary depending upon the area of practice you enter. In the public sector you could find yourself writing planning policy or creating case officer reports for delegated or committee decision-making purposes. In the private or third sectors you could be producing planning reports/statements relating to policy or development proposals, or preparing development briefs for clients. Whichever sector you enter though, you will find that there are accepted formats, structures and approaches that you will need to work with. These may be nationally accepted approaches, such as the preparation of a statement of case or proof of evidence for a planning appeal, or an internal arrangement to ensure consistency, clarity, branding, conformance with legislation and so forth.

In addition to your assessments preparing you with the skills to write effectively, you will also find that your university studies will have prepared you for another factor which defines practice working – collaboration. Writing planning practice reports will, even when led by a single person, typically require input and involvement from specialists inside and outside of your organisation. The nature of planning means that support from specialists will be essential to the production of comprehensive outputs. The team work and leadership skills developed at university and discussed in Chapter 10 of this book will help prepare you for this work environment.

Activity

Look at the website of a local planning authority that you are familiar with, perhaps the one for where you live, and one for a planning consultancy. Explore the planning pages and look at the work that is produced; on the local authority pages this will include 'Policy'

(Continued)

(Continued)

sections with policy documents, and the pages for planning applications submitted – this is particularly useful because if you look at a few random applications you will be able to access the officer's report and all of the material submitted by the applicant and/or their consultants. These documents might include a design and access statement, a report on consultation and public engagement and an environmental statement. Make yourself some notes that consider how the work is presented, what the structural approaches are, and what the language is like. Take note of the differences between the local authority outputs and those of the planning consultancy; think also about why they might be different. Write down where you found the information too. Going back to these sources can be helpful when you are producing an assessment that is simulating practice outputs, or indeed if you are working on a 'live' project. Downloading good examples is also worthwhile to develop your own library of best practice.

Regardless of the circumstances you find yourself working in, however, if you embrace the assessments and opportunities offered to you during your studies at university you will find that you are prepared for most eventualities, and that the fundamental principles introduced to you in this section transcend the various scenarios and will underpin all of your output, enabling you to have confidence in your ability to produce competent and high quality written outputs.

Improving your writing skills

Writing essays and reports at university can be very challenging. Writing in an appropriate manner, with effective structuring, formatting, grammar and punctuation, is a skill that takes time to develop. Referencing too can be difficult to get right and may be something you have had limited experience of previously. Your university will expect you to deliver these standards from the very first submission, but equally they will assess you based upon the level you are expected to be at so first year students are not expected to produce written work to the same standard as final year students. More importantly, universities will all offer some form of support to help you develop your writing skills. Support may be provided through the library, via tutors, or using a structured taught programme of graduate development sessions. These may be optional but you should take every opportunity available to develop your skills and maximise your potential; this will not only improve your performance at university, but will also provide you with the fundamental skills you will need when you enter practice.

tip

Universities will keep at least some of the dissertations produced each year in their library, either in hard-copy format or as an e-copy. Look at a few that have been produced by past students on your programme and think about how they are written, structured, referenced and so forth. This will give you a good insight into the work that will be expected of you. Make sure you look at a few so you can appreciate the differences and find good examples to learn from.

Conclusions

In this chapter we have very briefly explored written communication at university and the application of your study outputs in practice. The nature of the work you produce at university may be different in some respects to what you have done before, but the high and carefully managed standards and requirements expected of you are important because, as demonstrated in this chapter, what you do at university will prepare you for the demands placed upon you in practice. This chapter has identified the nature and range of written work expected of you, but it has also identified the underlying principles and approaches that will give you the ability and confidence to produce the necessary work in university and in practice.

Further reading

A variety of study skills books are available to support students at university. Take time to look through the different options that are available because you will find that they are written, structured and presented in different ways and some will suit your own learning and reading style better than others.

A good general text is:

- Burns, T. and Sinfield, S. (2012) *Essential study skills: The complete guide to success at university.* Third ed. London: Sage.

You will also find that all of the major publishing houses, including Sage, have a range of more detailed texts to support you in particular areas, including writing skills. For example:

- Redman, P. (2001) *Good essay writing: A social sciences guide.* London: Open University in association with Sage, London

In addition, do not forget to explore what your university has to offer. In addition to taught and tutor support, most universities provide online support, such as the University of the West of England's 'myskills' and the University of Ulster's online Information Skills module.

Review points

When reflecting on this chapter you might consider the following

- a diverse range of written output types are used for assessment purposes at university
- each form of written communication has a different character to it
- but each form of written communication is also underpinned by the same fundamental principles and requirements
- the work that you produce at university will demonstrate your ability for assessment purposes, but they will also prepare you for planning practice and, in some cases, simulate or deliver 'real-life' practice outputs.

12

Writing a Dissertation

Aims

This chapter aims to introduce the role for research in the context of preparing a dissertation or major project. It will help you to think about a possible topic and how these interests can be framed around an integrated set of aims and objectives. The importance of including a clearly defined question will also be introduced, as will the general approaches and styles for undertaking research.

Learning outcomes

After reading this chapter you will be able to:

- formulate some key aims and objectives for your study
- recognise the importance of having a clearly defined research question
- demonstrate a basic understanding of the different approaches and styles that exist for undertaking research
- consider the type of data collection techniques that might be relevant to your study
- develop an appropriate structure for your dissertation
- appreciate what is meant when we talk about taking an ethical approach to research.

Introduction

The previous chapter referred to some of the skills that you will need for effective writing and offered some examples of the type of work you will need to produce. Of these, the dissertation was identified as being particularly significant, not only in terms of the number of words that you will be expected to write (in the order of 10,000 for an undergraduate programme, more for a postgraduate course) but also in terms of the level of credit that such a module is typically assigned. Some students are often apprehensive when faced with a dissertation but these concerns are misplaced; producing a good dissertation may well become a highlight of their university career. A successful dissertation demands a variety of skills and it is for this reason that employers often ask about the type of study you undertook and the grade you were awarded.

Some students see a dissertation as an extended essay or report. They may be right to some extent, but a dissertation also requires you to *research*; to obtain new information or to gain a better understanding of the subject you have chosen to study and draw meaningful conclusions from your work. This is an important life skill, particularly in town planning practice where you are likely to be asked to undertake some kind of investigation yourself, or appraise the research outputs of others.

Some aspects relating to research will be familiar to you. Indeed, in Chapter 2 we referred to the need to 'research' relevant literature before starting a piece of work, and to critically assess how this work had been composed. However, other aspects, such as the need to administer a questionnaire or undertake a survey, may be quite new to you. While a range of texts relating to research exist, with a selection being highlighted as we proceed, the chapter should prove a useful guide as and when you start your dissertation or major project.

Understanding the task

It might seem obvious but the first thing you should seek to do is to understand the task in hand. Again this message has been discussed in previous chapters but it is particularly important in the case of a dissertation given its significance and the timescale that you are likely to be given to complete it; you may have up to a year so it always possible that certain details will be forgotten. Early answers to the following questions might therefore be useful:

- What are the timescales involved? When should I expect to start to work and what are the important milestones along the way?
- How is the dissertation to be assessed? Are all of the marks to be allocated to the final submission or are there interim points of assessment too, such as creating some kind of research proposal or demonstrating progress through an interview or seminar?
- How long should the dissertation be? Does the word count include tables, appendices and such like?
- What can the dissertation cover?

- Is there a particular approach I need to take? Am I expected to create new (primary) data or can I use and analyse existing (secondary) data?
- What help will I receive along the way? If I am allocated a supervisor what help can they provide me? How many times am I expected to meet them?

Practice in relation to the last of these questions will vary but it is likely that you will receive some guidance along the way. This assistance might include a series of seminars concerned with different elements of the dissertation process and/or an individual tutor. Having an individual tutor is particularly useful and they can act as a critical friend along the way, offering advice and alerting you to things which (in their view) might be going wrong! Tutors might be allocated randomly or on the basis of their teaching and research interests. Each supervisor is likely to take a different approach to their students and you may find that some tutors are more hands-on than others. You should seek to make a good impression on your tutor and attend when and where necessary. You should take the lead in initiating this contact by identifying dates on which you would like to meet, presenting an agenda for each session, and writing up some basic notes after you have met to ensure that future actions are sufficiently clear for both you and your tutor. Many students often choose their dissertation tutor as a future referee which is a good idea as they will be well-placed to speak of your qualities after working alongside you during the course of the project.

Thinking about your topic

This can come quite naturally for some students, but for others it can be difficult. You may be spared this task if your department issues a list of topics or questions but the trend is still largely for this thought process to be led by you. Where choice does exist you are likely to be given significant flexibility with the only requirement being that your study fits within the confines of planning (and any other subject that you might be studying alongside). In coming to a decision you might be influenced by the following:

- A module, lecture or seminar that you found interesting.
- A piece of coursework that you did well in and/or an assignment that you felt could have been taken to a greater level of detail.
- A personal interest that also relates to planning (e.g. the role of planning in delivering and protecting sports pitches).
- Recent work experience or a period of employment that has highlighted areas of worthy study.
- A recent change in policy or legislation or some other contemporary change relating to planning.
- Some other kind of topic or event that has been in the news (such as the promised legacy associated with the recent Olympics).

Unless you have a clear topic in mind from the very beginning, it is useful to 'brain-storm' potential ideas. The goal of this initial stage should be to identify some broad themes which could include such things as:

- retail development
- climate change
- conservation
- regeneration
- the use of public space.

The next stage is to think of some topics or issues relating to these themes. For instance, those associated with retailing could include:

- out of town retailing
- retail-led regeneration
- revitalising the high street
- town centre management
- temporary or pop-up retailing
- shuttering retail stores
- indoor markets
- enhancing village services.

Clearly these topics can be broken down even further by identifying particular issues that could be examined. So a project examining the efforts to revitalise a high street could look at the role for pedestrianisation, traffic management and street art, or at strategies for supporting independent retailers.

To be able to do this you will need to do some research by referring to the type of resources that we outlined in Chapter 2. Not only will this help to galvanise your basic understanding of the topic but it will help you to identify current research agendas and areas where some kind of investigation might be worthwhile. Your intention should be to add value to this existing work or to try and fill perceived gaps that seem to exist. For example, your study could assess the relevance that some kind of conceptual framework has in explaining a phenomena or process local to you (such as the process for preparing a plan in your town or city).

Activity

Have a think about the type of areas you would be interested in reading or finding out about by putting a key word or phrase in the middle of an A4 sheet of paper (or larger if you have something available). Other words, in the form of sub-topics, can then be placed in circular fashion around the phrase to reflect the full extent of the subject area. Try to develop a bulleted list of headings underneath two or three of the sub-topics you have chosen (or more if you would like). These headings might reflect your current knowledge of the subject or the strands of research that are being undertaken by others. Once your list is complete take one of the headings and think about the study you might want (or be able) to do. Use separate sheets of paper to do the same for some of your other headings.

Although some topics are more popular than others you should try and think of something that will endure your interest over the course of the project. Selecting an under-studied topic might help to get your work, and your perceived ability, noticed but do not pick anything too obscure as finding information could become problematic. Think about the resources you have available; examining urban growth in a district of Buenos Aires could lead to an excellent study but would you have the financial resources to travel there or have the time to undertake fieldwork and conduct interviews? Your approach to undertaking the research will need to respond accordingly.

Focusing on topical issues is, as we note above, a popular choice but remember that your colleagues might be having the same ideas as you! This could lead to you chasing the same resources or the same people. While the developer of a major shopping centre may be interested in helping the first student who contacts them, it is unlikely that this enthusiasm would be maintained as further students came forward. Issues that become live as you begin to formulate your ideas may be particularly attractive but you may experience a dearth of relevant literature to begin with. Instead, resources may come forward sporadically during the course of the project as other researchers begin to bring material forward; keeping up with this can sometimes be a challenge.

 **tip**

You may be tempted, given the timescales involved, to delay starting on your dissertation. This may be because you want to focus on another piece of assessment, or possibly because you cannot relish making a start. The sooner you start the better you will feel; your confidence will increase dramatically once you get some words onto a page. To do well you will need to devote a significant amount of time each week; programme specific activities on certain days to ensure that you remain on track.

Setting out your intentions

You can begin to develop your specific intentions once you are comfortable with the topic you have selected.

Aim of research

An important first step is to outline the general aim of the research. Work up some ideas by using a further sheet of A4 paper. At the top of the page write:

The aim of this study is to...

Complete the rest of the sentence by playing around with some of the words you came up with through your initial brainstorm. If we imagine a student, James, working on this basis, we might find ourselves with the following:

The aim of this study is to examine the type of skills and competencies that local community groups need to create a neighbourhood plan.

Such an aim is clearly quite topical at the time of writing this book, with James' interest mirroring some of the debate and discussion that has taken place around the Government's push towards community action and neighbourhood planning.

Research question

The next step is to convert your aim into a research question that will sit at the heart of your study. This might be quite easy but it can also be problematic and quite frustrating. However, it is worth giving it a go and coming up with something since you can always tweak it later. It is fair to say that the question you eventually settle on can make or break a dissertation so it is important to get it right.

A research question that builds upon James' aim for a dissertation could be:

What type of skills and competencies does a community group need to create a neighbourhood plan?

While this question has opted for 'what', other possibilities exist, such as:

- How...?
- Why...?
- When...?
- Which...?
- To what extent...?

Once you have your draft question in place, apply some critical reflection. How might it be improved? Are there elements that seem ambiguous? Similarly, think about what your answer might look like. In the case of James' dissertation, the reader might be expecting to see a list of skills and competencies which have been judged (following the collection of data) to be perhaps 'essential' or 'desirable'. To support your principal question it is important to develop some sub-questions which can provide some useful elaboration and place your research into its wider context. An initial set for James' dissertation could include:

- Why are neighbourhoods being asked to produce a plan? Is such a step a significant one? Have communities been asked to get involved with plan-making before? How is the latest initiative any different? What type of barriers have groups faced in the past?
- What do we mean by a neighbourhood plan? What does such a plan seek to achieve? How does it compare, in product and procedural terms, to other types of plans and how do they fit with legislation? How are neighbourhood plans supposed to be produced according to relevant policy and guidance? What support exists and what role are other key stakeholders (such as local planning authorities) expected to take?
- How do local residents produce a neighbourhood plan? How are community groups defined in the legislation? How can a neighbourhood plan reflect the wider opinion of society?
- What do we mean by a skill and a competency?
- What skills and competencies are typically required when creating a plan? Has the mapping of these been undertaken in the past and, if so, by whom and for what purpose?
- What skills and competencies might a community group expect to have? How might these vary and how might these attributes be assessed? What skills and competencies do community groups think they need to produce a plan? Has any such group spoken out already about what is needed, perhaps through some kind of article or another piece of research?
- What do other stakeholders think? Do planning officers have a view about the most important skills and competencies?

Other questions could be added to this list but it is clear, whatever the final number, that some kind of information will need to be found. This represents the next important stage, the 'how-to' stage. In thinking about this you will need to think about the resources you have available. While James' question could be the subject of a major government-funded research project, the reality is clearly quite different in that James will be undertaking this in a fairly short amount of time with a range of other competing demands in the background. The question that James proposes above could be interpreted as a project for gauging views *from anyone* (irrespective of their location) about the skills and competencies required for neighbourhood planning. However, such an approach would clearly be a massive undertaking. A better idea would be to tighten the parameters of the research by clarifying what you will, and what you will not, be investigating in the opening pages (or indeed, paragraphs) of your dissertation. The research question can also be tweaked, so James' original question could be re-worked to:

What type of skills and competencies does a community group need to create a neighbourhood plan? A perspective from those preparing neighbourhood plans across the city of Bristol.

Such an amendment would provide additional clarity; it identifies how views will be sought from those groups directly involved (rather than more general residents), and from a particular location, the city of Bristol for example. Further clarity might be needed to explain certain points. For example, while the generic term 'community group' is used in the question, it would be worth explaining how the legislation is more detailed in that plan-making powers are bestowed to Parish Councils and especially formed 'neighbourhood planning forums' (DCLG, 2011). Similarly, some explanation might also be needed around the word 'preparing'; at what stage of the plan-making process will groups be contacted? Lastly, while the emphasis is clearly given to the views emanating from the communities involved, some initial indication might be useful to explain how the views of other stakeholders will be obtained as well to provide a further perspective (such as from planning officers).

Building upon your sub-questions you should also develop a list of objectives which should be expressed as a statement, e.g. to investigate the stages by which a neighbourhood plan is produced.

Setting a hypothesis

You might also decide to state a hypothesis – in essence, this is a view about what you think the situation might be. A (controversial) example for James' dissertation could be:

Community groups do not possess the necessary skills and competencies for creating a neighbourhood plan.

Sometimes a hypothesis can focus on the nature of a relationship, e.g. *the distance that one lives from a railway station has a significant influence on their decision to use a train.* It also common, in these situations, to have a control or a so-called null-hypothesis, e.g. *the distance that one lives from a railway station has no bearing on whether they use a train.* While hypotheses are useful for some studies, particularly those involving numerical data and statistical analysis, it is usually the case that a list of objectives and questions will suffice. However, this is something to discuss with your supervisor.

Project title

Finally, you might want to give your project a more succinct title. This need not be presented in the form of a question but may be something that grabs attention. For instance, an example for James' dissertation could be:

Equipped to engage? The role for community groups in neighbourhood planning.

Research design

Once you are clear about what you want to achieve it is important to start thinking about how your research can be progressed. In doing this you will need to consider your basic approach to collecting information or data (a plural noun, the singular of which is datum) and the practical steps or methods that your study will use to do so.

Quantitative and qualitative approaches to research

In terms of approach, Bell (2010) refers to a general distinction between quantitative and qualitative research which offers different views about the nature and scope of knowledge and the type of methods that are most appropriate. While some studies are entirely quantitative or qualitative in their stance, others are less distinct; indeed, some use both approaches.

Quantitative research is heavily aligned to positivism as a research philosophy, the traditional approach of the natural sciences where the researcher seeks to observe, quantify and measure in a way that is objective and free from personal values and beliefs. Quantitative approaches allow for statistical analysis and typically seek to emphasise the relationship between one set of facts and another; they are particularly useful for testing hypothesises. Similarly, they also shy away from exploring phenomena that cannot be directly sensed or recorded, such as fears or hopes. Data is typically sourced through a fixed and clearly defined approach; a plan for collecting the data is set out in an early stage and is pursued with little deviation, even if problems are encountered. A good example of this could be a series of traffic counts where data is obtained at certain points of the day. The raw data could be analysed and statistically tested and compared to situations elsewhere quite easily.

In contrast, qualitative approaches care less about creating and testing specific hypotheses or coming to statistical conclusions. Instead, their common intention is to try and explain the meaning of social phenomena by understanding the worlds in which they are located. As Robson (2007) explains, 'qualitative research is an umbrella term covering several different research traditions' which have a broad alignment to interpretivism, a position that challenges the scientific approach promoted by positivism. Bell (2010) refers to qualitative data as being 'non-numerical and unstructured'; words are a common source of data. Researchers are viewed more humanly, with the recognition that their observations are likely to be shaped by their personal background and the thoughts, beliefs and values they subscribe to. The methods for collecting qualitative data are usually quite flexible and are often revised as and when information is compiled. An interview is a good example where questions might be re-ordered or re-worded as the session progresses.

Research styles

In addition to distinguishing between quantitative and qualitative types of data, the literature also refers to a number of research styles that can be applied to the design of a project. Each style is associated with a particular suite of techniques or methods for collecting information but, as with the use of qualitative and quantitative data, a study can change between styles as different objectives are pursued. The styles to be considered below are those that involve:

- a case study
- a survey
- action research
- an ethnographic study.

Case studies are a popular choice for a dissertation or major project. The actual case can be anything and could be a place, an organisation, or some kind of policy or initiative. As Yin (2008) explains, including a case study can be useful for challenging a thought or theory, for highlighting something of particular interest (such as a specific approach), or for presenting new ideas and insights. Investigating a case can be undertaken in a number of ways and might involve textual analysis, interviews, or some kind of survey. It is important to explain why a particular case has been selected and what other options were considered. Similarly, a view also has to be given as to whether the conclusions arising from the study can be applied to other cases elsewhere.

Building a study around some kind of **survey** is also quite common and can yield both qualitative and quantitative forms of data. As Aldridge and Levine (2001: 5) explain, *'each survey is unique'* and can be designed and administered in a variety of ways. For example, a survey could examine building types along a street or record the number of people using a local park. Another type of survey might seek to collect local views about a local event. A questionnaire is a popular option which can be undertaken face to face, online, over the phone or via the post.

Action research goes beyond studying a phenomenon but seeks to change it in some way; it is a style that seeks to tackle real-life problems by developing appropriate solutions. To be successful, such an approach requires the direct involvement of the people the research focuses on; all parties need to be signed-up and committed to the goals of the project. It is a good style for those working in practice and who want to initiate change in their internal environment. The style allows for a variety of methods to be used, with the majority involving the collection of qualitative data.

An ethnographic study is based upon the careful observation of participants over a period of time. A range of methods can be used, each with the intention to understand the life and customs of people living in a particular culture. Examples might include participant observation, interviews or the completion of some kind of diary.

Referring to these styles, and the others that exist, might be useful to you in shaping how your research is to be pursued. Each style comes with its own literature which provides a useful account of some of the tried and tested techniques, and some general advice for ensuring that common pitfalls can be avoided. As we have already said, some of your research objectives may be better suited to some styles than others but it is worth mapping the options you have. For instance, the styles mentioned above could generate some interesting ideas for James' dissertation on neighbourhood planning – he could:

- develop case studies on community groups preparing a plan. Cases could be chosen on the basis of location (e.g. from different parts of Bristol), the plan-making stage at which they are at, or the number of members each group has;
- devise some kind of survey which could be circulated to those groups preparing a neighbourhood plan. A further survey could be prepared to collect the views of the other parties with an interest in neighbourhood planning; or
- seek to become a member of a community group himself and develop his research from 'within'.

Research techniques

In addition to setting out the basic approach to your research you will also need to think about your methods for collecting data. Some of these have already been mentioned above but three of the most significant include undertaking some kind of:

- documentary analysis
- questionnaire
- interview.

Documentary analysis forms an important part to any dissertation and contributes to a number of key sections. The principal goal is to find as much as you possibly can about your subject, thereby giving you detailed knowledge of the central themes and the research agendas connected with it. Much of this material will need to be set out in a literature review – a major undertaking within your written submission. The review will need to draw from the skills that we spoke about in Chapter 2 in that a variety of resources will need to be brought together and critically analysed. Particular attention needs to be given to identifying relevant theories and concepts, while significant (and possibly quite contested) terms will need to be defined. To work well the review will need to be carefully structured, with texts being included as and when specific themes are covered; the review should not appear as an annotated reference list where each source is considered alphabetically in turn.

Returning to James' work, his literature review on neighbourhood planning might be structured as follows:

- An insight into the basic goals of planning in England and the role that development management and plan-making have in delivering these goals.
- A more detailed summary of the types of plan currently produced, with reference being made to the introduction of neighbourhood-based plans.
- A review of the stages for creating a local or neighbourhood plan and the skills and competencies that the literature identifies as being necessary for their production.
- A summary of the role that community groups have had in plan-making in the past and the barriers that they might have faced in trying to become involved.
- A brief account of some of the research that has, or is currently underway, in relation to the concerns of the research.

In addition to the literature that you will need to draw from to develop and justify your research design, it is probable that you will need to review and analyse a range of documents in order for you to respond to some of your more detailed research questions. This type of analysis may be necessary to develop a case study or to provide a useful accompaniment to an interview. For example, in terms of our dissertation on neighbourhood planning, James might decide to look at the terms of reference for any community group being studied, or any minutes arising from some kind of design workshop.

tip

During the course of your dissertation you will need to look at a variety of texts. As you do this it is important to make an accurate record of the resource; this could be done by means of an online tool (such as RefWorks) or by typing the reference out using the standard required by your institution. It is also important to try and categorise your texts. To do this, create a new file in your word processing package with a number of blank pages. On each page include a word or phrase relating to the intended structure of your literature review. As you find a resource, provide details of its title on the relevant keyword page. This will enable you to have a list of documents that you can refer to (and tick off) as sections of the review are written around each of the keywords.

It may be the case that some of the literature you find is unable to provide the information or level of detail that you need. For instance, while James might have found some basic minutes of a meeting on the internet, they may say very little about what James is trying to study, i.e. the skills and competencies that are needed to create a plan. This may encourage James to use other investigative techniques, such as approaching people to be interviewed or devising a simple questionnaire.

Undertaking some interviews is a good thing to do as speaking with the right people can really add some interesting perspectives to your research. Meeting people in this way is also a great way to network which may be helpful in an employability sense. Interviews take time to plan; for them to be successful you need to:

- have a clear idea of who you want to talk to and for what purpose
- arrange a date, time and place that is convenient to both you and the interviewee
- provide full details of the project and explain to the interviewee why he or she has been contacted
- give an indication as to the number of questions there will be and how long the discussion is expected to last
- carefully think of the questions that you will need to ask and consider how they should be phrased (e.g. should they be open or closed questions)
- ensure that you do some basic research on the interviewee and/or their organisation
- be on time and present yourself professionally
- keep reminding yourself of what you want to achieve as the interview begins by referring to your notes and/or your draft list of questions
- ensure that the interviewee understands what is being asked of them by explaining key terms or aspects that appear confusing
- check on the day of the interview how long your interviewee can talk to you for

- seek to take some good notes during the course of the interview or audibly record the conservation (in which case, permission should be sought)
- reflect and write up your notes of the session as soon as possible thereafter in order to ensure that the discussion remains fresh in your head.

Similarly, to implement a successful questionnaire you should seek to:

- design a questionnaire that is succinct, appropriately focused and attractive in its presentation
- start with simple questions first
- consider the best way for distributing the questionnaire. Could it be delivered through the post or be made available online? Could it be administered over the phone?
- undertake a pilot to ensure that your instructions for completing the questionnaire are clear and your questions are unambiguous
- think about the questions you want to ask and the type of answers you want in reply. Are you expecting some of kind or numerical entry or are you giving the respondent the opportunity to give their answer in some kind of category (e.g. age groups). Plotting responses on some kind of scale (e.g. from poor to excellent) might be useful for some questions
- consider how your returned questionnaires should be analysed (e.g. whether some kind of statistical analysis can be applied)
- have a back-up in case your response rate is poor. That may be likely but could depend on the length, subject and form of the questionnaire. However, if you only get ten questionnaires returned it will be difficult to make any reasoned conclusions on what you have observed.

Ethical considerations

When considering what to study it is important to think about your research in ethical terms as well. In essence, your project should seek to do good without doing harm; any study should seek to protect the rights, dignity and health and safety of both you and your participants. While you may be clear in your mind as to what represents ethical and unethical practice, certain events or issues may arise inadvertently (perhaps as the pressure to complete the project builds). You will need to identify and reflect upon possible issues as and when you devise your research but take care to ensure that your initial conclusions remain sound as details of the study are developed. Although you should refer to the relevant literature, some important precautions would include the following:

- Take care to ensure that your participants understand the project and that they give you written consent to confirm their involvement.
- Agree up-front how a participant's involvement is to be recorded. It may be necessary to keep certain details anonymous.

- Store personal or sensitive information in a way that satisfies the requirements of the Data Protection Act. Careful thought should be given as to whether this data is actually required but, where it is, ensure that it is deleted after a prescribed period of time.
- Take particular care if your project seeks to involve children or vulnerable people. If this is envisaged then you should expect to provide full details to your university's ethical standards committee.
- Protect yourself by ensuring that you interview people or conduct a survey in an appropriately public place. Always let people know what you are planning to do and when you are expecting to return. Remember to take a mobile phone with you and appropriate identification in case somebody challenges you about your intentions. Extra care should be taken if you are contemplating some kind of street survey or if you intend to visit (possibly isolated) sites. Where any risk is anticipated it is important to side with caution.
- Ensure that information is faithfully reproduced and appropriately referenced in your work. Do not be tempted to alter any of your data, even if it would strengthen some of your conclusions!

Writing up

While much of this chapter has focused upon the *process* for undertaking a good dissertation, there is also an obvious *product* in the form of the study that will need to be submitted and assessed. There is no need to say too much on this since some excellent guidance was included in the last chapter. However, it is perhaps important to restate the need for your work to be appropriately structured, proof-read and visually presented. With regards to the first of these, your dissertation could be structured like this:

- A title page, with details of your name and university course. You might want to include an image to add visual interest.
- An acknowledgements page.
- An abstract, which provides a summary of the research, including the key conclusions being made.
- A contents page, with sections clearly labelled. You will also need a list of tables and figures.
- An introduction, which offers background and context to the study and outlines the basic aims and objectives of the research and the questions to be addressed.
- A literature review, which examines resources relevant to the principal interests of the study. It should refer to key theories and concepts and refer to past research and the methodological approaches that these studies abided by.
- A methodology, which justifies the study's basic approach and the philosophical and ideological stance that it takes. Specific techniques for acquiring data are explained.
- The results and findings of the research with appropriate discussion and analysis to relate the findings of the study to relevant literature.
- A conclusion, which draws the study to a close. It might also be appropriate to list possible recommendations.
- A reference list and relevant appendices.

Conclusion

We hope that this chapter has whetted your appetite for producing a dissertation or large-scale project. While such an output often generates a series of fears and concerns, handing in your final submission can be a real moment of pride. You will need to work hard to achieve the type of grade you are looking for but try and enjoy the experience as best you can. Although this chapter has spoken about research in the context of preparing a dissertation, it is a skill that underpins planning practice. Whatever your job, it is likely that you will need to undertake some research yourself. This is likely to vary in size, from researching the history of a site to possibly contributing to a detailed (and high value) survey of housing supply. You will also need to evaluate the research of others, asking critical questions such as how the data was collected and how it was subsequently analysed.

Further reading

As you develop your ideas for your dissertation or major project, you will undertake some further reading on some of the themes outlined in this chapter. The following texts provide some useful introductions and will direct you to other relevant sources:

- Bell, J. (2010) *Doing your research project: A guide for first-time researchers in education, health and the social sciences.* Fifth ed. Maidenhead: Open University Press.
- Denscombe, M. (2010) *The good research guide: For small-scale research projects.* Fourth ed. Maidenhead: Open University Press.
- Robson, C. (2007) *How to do a research project: A guide for undergraduate students.* Oxford: Blackwell Publishing.
- Robson, C. (2011) *Real world research.* Third ed. Bognor Regis: John Wiley and Sons.
- Walliman, N. (2004) *Your undergraduate dissertation: The essential guide for success.* London: Sage.

The following texts provide more focused guidance in relation to certain themes:

- Davies, M. (2007) *Doing a successful research project: Using qualitative or quantitative methods.* Basingstoke: Palgrave Macmillan Ltd.
- Dochartaigh, N. (2012) *Internet research skills.* Third ed. London: Sage.
- Oliver, P. (2010) *The student's guide to research ethics.* Second ed. Maidenhead: Open University Press.
- Ridley, D. (2012) *The literature review: A step by step guide for students.* London: Sage.
- Yin, R. (2008) *Case study research: Design and methods.* Fourth ed. Thousand Oaks, CA: Sage Publications Inc.

Review points

When reflecting on this chapter you might consider the following:

- a dissertation provides an excellent opportunity to explore something that is of interest to you
- it is a project that you will need to control and effectively manage
- a successful dissertation requires the application of a variety of skills and competencies
- a good dissertation can provide a solid foundation for undertaking and interpreting research in the future.

Part three

Planning Practice

13

A Career in Town and Country Planning

Aims

To explore the options that are available to you after your studies and to outline the type of sector or organisation you can find work with. It will outline the mechanisms by which candidates are selected and appraised in relation to the skills and attributes they possess.

Learning outcomes

After reading this chapter you will:

- appreciate the options that exist once you complete your course
- understand the different types of work that exist in the planning sector
- develop an understanding of the skills and attributes that are likely to be sought by employers and the steps that you can take to demonstrate how you have applied them through work, study or your personal interests
- identify the mechanisms by which candidates are selected, with particular emphasis being given to the role of CVs, application forms and interviews.

Introduction

The time at which you decided to apply for a university place may be relatively recent; for others it may be more distant. However, you may recall some of the angst you encountered at the time. You may have queried whether university was right for you, whether you wanted to follow friends and move away from home, or whether you should apply to one university and not the other. These were key decisions which have hopefully served you well to date. Since then you may have enjoyed a fairly predictable trajectory with the structure of your life being determined by the structure of your academic year.

This predictability begins to dissipate as you enter your final year of study and your attention begins to turn to life beyond university. You may think this change is daunting. However, you may also look at it as being an exciting opportunity, creating a new turn in your life. Finally you can begin to apply the skills, theories and techniques that you have been acquiring and earn the level of pay that reflects the hard work and commitment you have given to date in your studies. Many students have a clear idea of what they want to do and take early steps to achieve their plans. Others do not, and simply wait for the end of term to think as things quieten down.

Options after study

Once you finish your degree there are three general options available to you:

1. To look for new or different employment opportunities. This job may be in the area of your degree, town and country planning, or another area altogether. The job may be an actual 'graduate' position or be one that you treat as a short-term fix; it pays the bills and keeps you busy but does not reflect your career ambitions.
2. To gain further qualifications or to engage in research, at either your own university or a different institution.
3. To have time out and travel. You might do this alone, with a partner or with friends, for a period that could vary from a few months to a year or more. Your tour may be purely for leisure purposes or you may decide to interject your travels with either some paid or unpaid work.

tip

Your university's career service will offer a variety of services which you will be able to access. In addition to advertising current and future opportunities, and convening employer fairs, most will also review your CV (curriculum vitae) and any application form you are thinking of submitting.

Undertaking further study

A number of students choose to continue their studies each year by taking a further taught course or by registering for a research-based qualification (such as a doctorate by research). Further postgraduate study can be useful in developing your skills in a particular area of practice and can help you stand out from the crowd. Engaging in further research may enable you to develop an area of personal interest, perhaps by building upon a previous project that you may have completed earlier in your degree.

tip

Ask staff from within your department about the opportunities for pursuing further research. They may be aware of future studentships or viable funding streams. A good place to look for research and university-based positions is www.jobs.ac.uk.

Becoming a researcher may be useful if you are intending to pursue a career in academia, while certain organisations (in both the public and private sectors) are also keen to recruit students with specific research-based training. Rather than undertaking further study, you might also be interested in becoming a paid research assistant or some other kind of opportunity in a university. This may be ideal for the time immediately after your studies. You may also be interested in engaging with other forms of study or training to help boost your knowledge and confidence. These might involve professional short courses, conferences or distant learning programmes. These could help to develop certain technical skills, such as GIS or project management or your use of a certain graphics package.

Finding a job

This is perhaps the most common of the three options. While some students consider this to be the easiest route to take, success is heavily dependent on market conditions and the extent to which employers are looking to appoint new staff. This contextual difficulty is often accentuated by personal factors such as uncertainty over the type of work you want to do, the type of employer you want to work for, and the areas of the country (or world) you want to work in. Some students are somewhat complacent in their attempts to get a job by thinking that their degree is the sole requirement in getting their ideal job. This confidence, in the most part, is generally misplaced. Having a relevant degree can help you secure an interview but it will certainly not guarantee you a job.

tip

If you are interested in working abroad then the website of the Royal Town Planning Institute offers some useful advice. Another useful resource is the International Society of City and Regional Planners (ISOCARP) which is a global association of experienced professional planners, founded in 1965. Particularly useful is the association's International Manual of Planning Practice which provides concise comparative syntheses of planning systems and practices in 101 countries worldwide.

Thinking about your ideal job

You may be lucky and find that a job comes your way with very little effort on your part. Such a scenario might happen if, for example, a previous temporary employer contacts you about a full-time and permanent position becoming available. For the majority of people the reality is often quite different and will require you to direct significant energy in both looking and applying for work. It is tempting, particularly at the start of the process, to apply for any job that appears broadly 'acceptable'. However, a better approach is to think about what you *want* to do and consider the steps that might be necessary to get there. It may be useful to think about:

- the type of sector you want to work in. Are you looking for a post that offers wide-ranging experiences or do you want to build upon a particular interest or specialism? Example sectors might include conservation, economic development, environmental consultancy, regeneration, retailing, transport, urban design, or waste and utilities
- the employer you may want to work for. Do you want to work for your local planning authority or maybe another one that you have heard good things about? Were you particularly impressed by a guest speaker talking about their company or are you looking to return to the place where you were able to gain some work experience?
- the area of the country or world you want to work in. Do you want to remain close to home or where you have been studying? Or are you free to move anywhere?

You may have answers to some of these questions but an element of research might be needed for others. For example, looking through the professional press may help to identify sectors that appear to be growing and the companies that appear to be taking advantage of this growth. You might also be able to pick up such things as whether a company is looking to expand. Some magazines and websites also include career profiles which are useful to reveal the journey that others have taken to get their ideal job.

Looking for vacancies

Opportunities can be advertised by a variety of means, including:

- your university's career service, which may post jobs on its website or have a file of available opportunities in its office
- graduate recruitment fairs, which are often organised by a university during their main teaching terms. These may be open to all job seekers or just the students of the hosting university
- the professional press which, in case of planning, would comprise the fortnightly 'Planning' magazine
- job centre websites, such as the graduate prospects website (www.prospects.ac.uk), Local Government Jobs (www.lgjobs.com) or Haymarket's 'planning jobs' website (http://jobs.planningresource.co.uk)
- company websites, with positions either being advertised year round or at certain periods (to coincide with the commencement of some kind of graduate recruitment programme). Some companies may not post specific opportunities but may invite you to send your CV to them should a position arise in the future
- national and local websites, although the job pages are increasingly being replaced by online resources such as those mentioned above
- social networking sites, such as LinkedIn and Facebook. A growing number of students are being contacted on the basis of their profiles and the networks they have established. While this source of recruitment may increase in the future, it is obviously important to ensure that opportunities appear legitimate before passing any personal details to those trying to make contact
- recruitment specialists, who may be able to offer a variety of posts (of varying length) once you register with them
- staff from your university, such as those in your careers' service or your lecturers.

It is important to note that jobs are not always formally advertised. If an employer can find a good candidate without spending large amounts of money on advertising then they will. If they choose to take this informal route then employers might ask existing staff to encourage their friends or acquaintances to join. They may also contact the planning schools to see if staff can suggest anyone who might be appropriate. Students may then be contacted direct or the opportunity might just be advertised on a course webpage or distributed by email.

Since this informal approach to recruitment continues to play an important role in planning practice today it is important that you network as effectively as possible. The chances of hearing about a job will increase the more people you meet.

Keep a record of everyone you meet. These contacts could include outside guests delivering a lecture or planners that you might meet or hear speak at a conference or seminar. You can either keep their details in a 'work' address book or include them in your electronic or online organiser. You can also buy dedicated books or boxes within which business cards can be neatly stored. To help with your networking, you might also want to print your own business cards which you can get online or at a local print shop at relatively little cost.

While you should try and develop your own list of contacts, an easy way to network is to join existing groups and associations. There are many such groups on the internet or on the same social networking sites mentioned earlier. The Royal Town Planning Institute (RTPI) also hosts a range of online communities which you can join as a student member. Contributing to the debate on these sites will help to get you noticed and may just open up job opportunities.

You may be tempted to do your job-hunting alone. However, the more help you get the better. Friends and family can be invaluable in spotting possible jobs if you give them some basic briefing. It is also tempting to be competitive with your friends but in reality that may be unproductive; you may not want to work for the same type of employer in the same part of the country! There may be times when you do want to apply for the same job. In these cases it is best to be honest and acknowledge that the final decision to recruit will be taken by others. You are likely to remain friends whatever the outcome.

Demonstrating skills and attributes

When looking to appoint new members of staff an employer will want assurances that you can deliver against the requirements of the job being advertised. They will need to be convinced that you *can* deal with the work that is there to be completed, or that you *can* add value to some aspect of their business or organisation. Recruiting new members of staff represents a sizeable investment; they will not proceed if they sense that there could be risks associated with your appointment.

It is for this reason that employers take a variety of steps to understand the skills and attributes you have to offer. These two words are frequently used in recruitment and, by referring to the Cambridge online dictionary, can be defined as follows:

- A **skill** is a particular ability to do an activity or job well. Examples would include your ability to work with others, to effectively manage your time, and to solve problems.
- An **attribute** is a quality or characteristic that someone or something has. Examples would include such things as your confidence, your level of enthusiasm and your willingness to learn.

Before you start looking for work it is often useful to undertake a personal audit in order to see how you score against the key skills and attributes that employers are looking for. It is also important for you to begin identifying examples where these qualities have been demonstrated. These can be taken from your education, your hobbies and interests, your personal circumstances, or from any work experience you have accumulated. This is what the activity in Table 13.1 seeks to do.

Many jobs are advertised with a formal job specification that details the tasks associated with the position and the responsibilities that the successful candidate will be given. An accompanying personal specification is also provided to outline the skills and attitudes that will need to be shown by the individual. Such a checklist can tell you about the knowledge you are expected to have, or the types of qualification or experience that the postholder will need to demonstrate as having. Boxes 13.1 and 13.2 provide specifications relating to a role in planning policy at a local authority. The activity below builds on this information and gets you to think about what might be needed in planning consultancy.

Activity

Consider the job advert below for a graduate planner in consultancy. After reading through the short job summary, begin to think about the other types of skills and attributes that might be necessary to make your application successful. You may want to undertake some broader research, perhaps by looking at actual jobs being advertised or by referring to the websites of relevant planning consultancies. Set out your thoughts in your note pad. As with the policy offer job that is set out in Boxes 13.1 and 13.2, can you think of the type of skills and attributes that might be classed as being 'essential' or 'desirable'? What type of work might you be undertaking? Who might your clients be and what type of work might they require you to do?

TABLE 13.1 Audit of key skills and attributes

Have a go at completing the template below which encourages you to think about your personal skills and attributes. You may want to complete this informally in your notebook but there may be merit in working it up into a more formal document that you include as an additional element to your portfolio (see below).

I have skills in...

	As demonstrated through...		
	My education	*My work experience*	*My hobbies and interests*
Written communication			
Verbal communication, including delivering presentations			
Team work			
Self-directed learning			
Problem solving			
Leadership			
Project management			
Research and investigation			
Numeracy and data management			
Critical thinking and reflection			
Using IT			
Networking			
Commercial awareness			
I am...	**As demonstrated through:**		
Motivated			
Confident			
Loyal			
Creative			
Hard-working			
Adaptable			
Positively minded			

Box 13.1 Job specification for a local authority role in planning policy

The text below, which was adapted from an actual advert, shows how key responsibilities are outlined. These details relate to the personal specification set out in Box 13.2.

Post Title: Planning Policy Officer
Directorate: Planning and Transport
Team: Planning Policy
Responsible to: Planning Policy Manager

Purpose of job: The job will require you:

- to assist in the production of the Council's Local Plan and other planning policy documents
- to assist in the review and interpretation of policies
- to assist in the maintenance of the Local Plan evidence base.

Key responsibilities. You will need:

1. To assist in the development of planning policies and the Council's Local Plan documents
2. To assist in the preparation of reports to the Council's Executive and Local Plan Working Group on progress in implementing the Council's planning strategies
3. To assist in monitoring the effectiveness and compliance with planning policies, including the provision of statistics, performance information and comparative indicators and their analysis
4. To carry out research into planning and other relevant issues, including the implications of legislation and initiatives by Government and by other local authorities or organisations
5. To assist in the interpretation of planning policies, including making observations on planning applications
6. To assist the preparation of planning strategies and Supplementary Planning Documents
7. To prepare material for public consultation, assist in undertaking consultation with outside bodies, organisations and the public and to analyse responses in relation to planning policy work
8. To represent the Council, as directed, at planning and other relevant groups, including those involving local authority associations, government departments, government agencies and non-statutory organisations
9. To assist with the maintenance of the Local Plan database and other associated resources
10. To prepare diagrams and illustrative material for the Local Plan
11. To assist in ensuring all procedures are followed and targets met
12. To answer queries from all sources and to deal with correspondence to a satisfactory conclusion under supervision
13. To carry out such other duties as may, from time to time, reasonably be required.

Miscellaneous. You will also need to:

1. Follow the Council's staffing policies at all times which relate to such things as dress code; flexi-time; email and use of the internet
2. To attend training and team meetings when directed
3. To undertake all relevant administrative and clerical tasks associated with the post
4. To remain committed to delivering effective customer service at all times.

Box 13.2   Personal specification for a local authority role in planning policy

As an accompaniment to the job specification included in Box 13.1, the local planning authority also produced a specification for the type of person that the team was looking to appoint. A distinction is made between 'essential' and 'desirable' qualities. The shading and asterisk below denotes where a quality *should* be present.

	Essential qualities	Desirable qualities
Degree in planning or closely related subject	*	
Eligible, or working towards membership of the Royal Town Planning Institute	*	
Relevant work experience		*
Knowledge of local government and the processes for formulating and implementing policies, proposals and plans		*
The ability to write reports and letters	*	
Communication and presentation skills	*	
Competent in using numbers		*
The ability to negotiate with partners both internal and external to the authority		*
Knowledge of Microsoft Word and Excel, or other word processing and spreadsheet packages, and Microsoft Outlook	*	
Ability to lead others	*	
To be a team player	*	
Use of own initiative	*	
To persuade others	*	
Reliable	*	
Ability to prioritise work	*	
Ability to accept change/to be flexible	*	

Planning Consultant (Bristol)

We are looking to appoint a recently qualified planner with experience in development management to join our small but successful team in Bristol.

The successful candidate will assist with a busy workload and advise on development proposals, preparing planning applications and promoting sites for development through the local plan system. You will need to be enthusiastic and hard-working, have excellent written and communication skills and be able to demonstrate competency in team-work and project management. We are looking for people who can combine creative thinking with commercial realism.

We are a large and growing national consultancy which is multidisciplinary and benefits from a wide client base. The successful candidate will be rewarded with a very competitive salary package. Benefits include a company car or discounted rail travel, pension, private medical and dental care, and an attractive share scheme.

To apply for this position please send your CV, with covering letter, to our recruitment manager.

The benefits of work experience

In completing the exercise above you might have struggled to think about some good examples of your working life. This may be the case if your employment to date is somewhat limited, but all jobs should be able to generate something that future employers will value (such as customer service skills or team-work).

It is true to say that employers place great value on those graduates with experience. However, gaining this can be difficult, especially at times when the market is sluggish. Nevertheless, it is worth the effort since one or two weeks of experience can help to enhance your attractiveness and can prove invaluable in helping to identify where you might want to pursue your career. Experiences can be sought with public, private and voluntary-sector organisations and can take place during your university holidays or concurrently with your studies. It may be necessary to speak to your course tutor if you intend to pursue the latter to ensure that any additional work you take on is compatible with your academic studies.

Applying for work

Once you are clear as to the type of work you want to get, have identified some good examples to document the skills and attributes you currently have, and see appropriate opportunities come forward, then you can begin to work on your application. Applying for jobs can take a variety of forms but it is likely that you will need to do one or more of the following:

- Provide an up-to-date curriculum vitae (CV), with covering letter, to the appointing employer.
- Complete an application form, which is then returned to the employer by post or by submitting online.
- Attend an interview or assessment centre, which often follows the submission of a CV or application form.

Preparing a curriculum vitae

A curriculum vitae (CV) is the standard tool for communicating basic information about you and what you have to offer potential employers. It is probable that you will have a CV already but it is always good to ensure that it is up-to-date as once you start job-hunting it may be necessary for you to send it out to interested parties at short notice.

Making the most of your CV is particularly important since most employers will only look at it briefly; your CV therefore has to stand out from the many others that are likely to be received. There are no particular rules as to what a CV should contain or how it needs to be structured but there are two broad types:

- the chronological CV where your education and employment is set out in reverse chronological order. Relevant skills are extracted in relation to each entry; and
- the skills-based CV where greater emphasis is given to documenting your skills and attributes. Entries concerning your education and work experience are kept brief but more detailed descriptions are given under a number of skill-based headings such as communication, leadership, team-work and so on.

Whatever your chosen structure, your CV should seek to include the following information:

- Personal details, including your name, address and contact details. An email address is useful but ensure that your username is a sensible one.
- Details of your education, with information about the qualifications you have achieved to date or those that are pending. You will need to identify the institution that you attended, the subject areas studied, key dates, and the level of award that you achieved. Greater attention should be given to your most recent study. Employers are often keen to understand what you achieved at A-level but you may be able to provide a general summary by identifying your overall UCAS points score (if applicable). For GCSEs, employers are generally interested in your attainment in English and Mathematics. It is obviously important to say

more about your degree. You should certainly outline the type of award that you are pursuing or have been awarded and state whether your course has been accredited by the Royal Town Planning Institute as a spatial, specialist or combined programme; will you satisfy the RTPI's educational requirements for becoming a professional planner on graduation? Employers are keen to gain an understanding of the topics you have covered but try to make your descriptions as clear as possible. Citing the name of a particular module will be unhelpful if the title is vague. You may want to focus on a particular project, especially if this fits with the general area of work the employer is engaged with.

- Information about past work experience. Again be selective and ensure that you pull out the key skills and attributes that were developed or tested.
- Personal interests and hobbies. This is self-explanatory and is a section where you can begin to introduce some of your own character and personality into the CV. Entries here can help to reinforce some of your job-related qualities too. For example, being a member of the university's hockey team is likely to have helped with your teamwork and leadership skills while the need to train on a regular basis may be useful in demonstrating drive and motivation. You may also be involved with the team's organising committee which could help develop expertise in such things as chairing a meeting or managing a financial account.
- Details of your referees. Most CVs typically require two referees. One may be required to comment on your academic performance and could be one of your lecturers. The other may be your current, or most recent, boss who can provide a view on your general employability. It is courteous to tell your referees that an application is due to be made and who they might be contacted by. It is often useful to provide them with a copy of your CV and covering letter.

There are also some general rules which you should try and follow:

- Do not pack too much information onto your CV. Text should be kept short and punchy with bullet points being used where appropriate. Your CV should be approximately two sides of A4 in length.
- Try and be original and develop your own look. Using a common template will do little for demonstrating that you are both innovative and creative.
- Be wary of choosing an unconventional font and ensure that all of your text is clear and readable. Avoid over-emphasising too much text; keep bold, underlined or italic text to a minimum in order that it retains its intended purpose.
- Introducing some colour into your work might be useful but too much might be off-putting. Remember that your CV may be photocopied for distributing around the interview panel; will it look as good as a black and white document?
- Headings should be used throughout to help provide a structure. Employers will become frustrated if information is illogically set out.
- Ensure that you print your CV on good quality paper.
- Take the time to proof-read your CV since errors will discourage employers at the first opportunity.
- Invite a range of people to comment on your CV. They may not be able to say anything too substantive but even the slightest comment may be useful to you.

Covering letters

Your CV should be accompanied by a short and well-written covering letter. This should state the job you are applying for, where you saw the post being advertised, and why you are the best candidate for the job. It should be tailored to the particular vacancy and employer and provide links to the enclosed CV. Ideally the letter should be kept to a single side of A4 paper.

It always best to write your letter to a named contact. The details might be provided to you as part of the application process but, if not, contact the organisation concerned to get a name of somebody in human resources or a senior director or manager.

Application forms

Completing an application form is relatively simple to begin with since the initial questions simply ask for details about you, your education and your employment to date. It is important for you to read these questions carefully and provide accurate answers in response. As with a CV, it is important that you use an application form to demonstrate how you have the skills and attributes that the employer is looking for. Ensure that your answers are appropriately focused; short responses will be better than those that waffle. Later sections tend to be more challenging and often require you to complete a personal statement which allows you to offer a view, in some detail, as to why you feel you are appropriate for the post.

Most forms tend to include a number of questions towards the end which require you to provide examples of how a particular skill or attribute has been applied or demonstrated. Again your answers must be clearly laid out. One way to do this is by using the so-called STAR approach which many recruitment sites refer to. This requires you to build an answer around four key areas, namely:

- The **S**ituation you found yourself in, and the timescales at which the event occurred.
- The **T**ask you were asked to complete to help resolve the situation, with detail being provided on the goals that were intended to be met.
- The **A**ction that you took to achieve the task.
- The **R**esults that arose from your actions.

It is likely that you will have a number of examples to give. However, it is best to choose the one that is most related to the vacancy; is recent; refers to something that you did; and one that had a positive outcome.

The questions that form the basis to the activity below focus around teamwork, project management and personal motivation.

Activity

Application forms tend to require you to recall situations when certain skills or attributes needed to be applied. Have a look the following questions and provide answers (of approximately 250 words) in your notebook.

- We are seeking to recruit people with initiative and drive. Can you describe a situation where you have demonstrated these skills?
- Can you tell us about a time when you had to adapt your own style in order to work effectively with others to help achieve a goal? How did you approach this? What was the outcome? How did you ensure that the team worked effectively together?
- Tell us about a time when you needed to organise time and resources to complete a project? How did you identify the necessary resources? What did you do to organise the time for those involved to complete the project? How did you monitor the progress of the project?
- Give an example of a situation where you dealt effectively with a complex organisational problem.
- What has motivated you to apply to this organisation and why have you chosen this particular role?

Interviews

An interview is often the final part of the process and may follow your submission of either a CV or application form. Interviews can vary in their length. Sometimes the session will involve you being questioned by senior staff but in others you might have a short task to complete, such as delivering a presentation or producing a briefing note for a particular site or policy. You may also be required to undertake short tests which can appraise basic competencies in numeracy and literacy. Interviews may also form part of a much larger assessment centre which may require you, and other shortlisted candidates, to engage with an intensive series of activities over one or two days.

Some demonstration of your technical knowledge may also be necessary and could include, for example, a summary of the steps by which a planning application is submitted, registered and determined, or the procedures that underpin Environmental Impact Assessment.

Interviews are often feared but if you are prepared there is nothing to worry about. The following tips may be useful:

- Ensure you know the basic details concerning the interview, such as where it is to be held and how long it might last for. It may also be possible to find out who will be on the interview panel.

- It is important that you remain engaged throughout the process. Although your formal interview may represent a small part of your overall visit, it is likely that the appointing team will speak to everyone you came into contact with and ask for their opinion of you.
- Undertake some research on both the job and the employer and take care to read through the original particulars of the job and the CV or application form you sent in to register your interest.

It is always useful to anticipate the type of questions you may be asked and to develop some model answers in response. Example questions could include:

- How would you describe yourself?
- How would others describe you?
- Do you have a hobby?
- What are your strengths and weaknesses?
- Can you work under pressure?
- How do you handle criticism?
- What has been your biggest failure?
- Are you accepted into a team quickly?
- What management style gets the best results out of you?
- Why did you choose a career in planning/geography etc?
- How long have you been looking for a new job?
- What attracted you to the post?
- What qualities do you think will be required for the position?
- Do you prefer to work in a small, medium or large company/organisation?
- Why do you want this job?
- Why are you the right person for the job?
- How does your degree/work experience equip you for the role?
- You have not done this sort of job before. How will you cope/succeed?
- How many hours are you prepared to work?
- What salary are you looking for?
- Are you over qualified for this position?
- How do you see your career evolving?
- Would you compete for my job?
- Would you accept the position if we offered it to you?
- When can you take up the post?

Don't forget that at university there will be support available. This might include workshops, seminars or presentations about employability and careers. Taking advantage of these can be hugely beneficial, especially when opportunities to discuss your 'model answers' exist.

Conclusions

In this chapter we have turned our attention to the time after university. Some of you may have thought about this already in depth and made steps to help achieve your ideal job. For others, life after university may seem daunting. The chapter identified the measures that you can use to look for opportunities and the type of approaches you can take to help sell yourself.

Review points

When reflecting on this chapter you might consider the following:

- that a variety of jobs exist across the planning sector
- opportunities are communicated both formally and informally
- networking forms an important part to finding out about possible opportunities
- employers will need reassurance that you are a 'safe bet' to employ – evidence about your skills and attributes will help to minimise this risk
- application forms and CVs are quickly reviewed by employers – errors will be immediately off-putting
- support of some form will be available at your university to help you improve your employ-ability and talk about careers.

Further reading

As you would expect, a wide range of resources exist in this area. Some of these will be made available to you by your university but the provision will vary. We have already mentioned where jobs might be advertised and have identified the importance of trying to understand the range of employers that exist. A good place to start for researching local planning authorities is via this website: www.gov.uk/find-your-local-council. An online directory of planning consultants and consultancies is available via this link: www.rtpiconsultants.co.uk.

A range of websites offer advice about writing an effective CV or excelling at interview. Typing some key words into your search engine will highlight a variety of resources, although the quality of these will vary. This is also the same for books but a useful series of books is provided by Pearson Education. The author of these, James Innes, is the founder of the

CV Centre which proclaims to be the UK's leading CV consultancy. Sample texts include:

- Innes, J. (2012a) *The cover letter book: Your definitive guide to writing the perfect cover letter.* Second ed. Harlow: Pearson Education.
- Innes, J. (2012b) *The CV book: Your definitive guide to writing the perfect CV.* Second ed. Harlow: Pearson Education.
- Innes, J. (2012c) *The interview book: Your definitive guide to the perfect interview.* Second ed. Harlow: Pearson Education.

If you are interested in undertaking further study, and specifically a PhD, then the following texts may be of use:

- Dunleavy, P. (2003) *Authoring a PhD: How to plan, draft, write and finish a doctoral thesis or dissertation.* Basingstoke: Palgrave Macmillan.
- Phillips, E. And Pugh, D. (2010) *How to get a PhD: A handbook for students and their supervisors.* Fifth ed. Maidenhead: Open University Press.

14

The Next Steps: Continuing Professional Development

Aims

To explore the process for becoming a professional and chartered planner, with particular emphasis on the need to develop as a reflective practitioner.

Learning outcomes

After reading this chapter you will:

- appreciate the steps that you will need to take to become a professional planner
- be able to differentiate between the terms 'student' and 'licentiate' planner
- recognise the broad steps that are aligned with the Assessment of Professional Competence (and be clear where the latest information on this process can be found)
- identify the importance of becoming a reflective practitioner
- appreciate what is meant by lifelong learning and how you will need to commit to a programme of continuing professional development that will help you develop.

Having read the last chapter you may be surprised to see a further one appear here. Such a view is perhaps logical given that the previous chapter was about helping to find your ideal job and enabling you to demonstrate the personal skills and competencies that are likely to be required for securing such a position. However, if your career path aligns itself to becoming a professional planner then further learning is necessary, not just in the immediate years after your degree but beyond. This concluding chapter will outline the broad steps for becoming a professional and 'chartered' town planner and will emphasise the importance of lifelong learning. This leads to a discussion about continuing professional development (CPD) and the need to keep up-to-date professional development plans (PDP).

Engaging with your profession

It is likely, when you chose your course, that you would have seen the words 'professionally accredited' appear somewhere in the literature. At the time you may have been slightly unsure about what this actually meant but we hope that our second chapter has shed some light on this by examining the role that the Royal Town Planning Institute (RTPI) has in accrediting planning courses. Indeed, you may remember some of the so-called learning objectives that planning schools are expected to adhere to and how, on the basis of these, the institute makes a distinction between spatial, specialist and combined degrees. It was noted that in order to satisfy the RTPI's educational requirements you will need to complete both the spatial and specialist elements in sequence or take them together in the form of a single combined degree.

Once these educational requirements are met you are able to progress towards becoming a chartered member of the RTPI, a designation that allows you to use the words MRTPI after your name. While these chartered planners form the basis of the institute's 23,000 members (at March 2012), two other categories of membership also exist before this point and these will be discussed below.

Student membership of the RTPI

You will probably have been told about this during the opening weeks of your programme and many of you reading this book may already be a student member (particularly given the prompt set out in Box 3.4). In essence, student membership is a useful way to start engaging with the profession and provides a clear statement of intent that you are interested in planning and its associated profession. The category is open to students who, at the time of their application, are enrolled for either full or part-time study, or are involved in distance learning, at any educational establishment (and not just accredited planning schools). Full details of the benefits associated with this class can be accessed via the RTPI's website, but in broad terms it offers access to *Planning*, the institute's journal, and to a variety of low-cost events and networking opportunities that are arranged throughout the year. Some events are organised nationally but others are convened through a regional network of offices that extend across the UK. Membership also enables you to access a host of web-based resources and a series of online networks which you can join and take part in helping to shape the wide ranging debate and discussions that are supported. These networks are often useful for identifying the type of job or placement opportunities that we spoke about in the last chapter. Current networks focus on:

- development management
- development planning
- The European Spatial Planning Observation Network
- independent consultants
- international development
- planning education and research
- planning enforcement
- planning for housing
- politicians in planning
- regeneration
- transport planning
- urban design
- young planners.

Becoming a student member also requires you to adhere to certain standards. These are set out in Box 14.1.

Box 14.1   Code of professional conduct for members of the Royal Town Planning Institute (RTPI)

Once you become a member of the RTPI you are bound by a code of professional conduct. This code states how members:

a) shall act with competence, honesty and integrity

b) shall fearlessly and impartially exercise their independent professional judgement to the best of their skill and understanding

c) shall discharge their duty to their employers, clients, colleagues and others with due care and diligence in accordance with the provisions of this Code

e) shall not discriminate on the grounds of race, sex, sexual orientation, creed, religion, disability or age and shall seek to eliminate such discrimination by others and to promote equality of opportunity

h) shall not bring the profession or the Royal Town Planning Institute into disrepute.

Source: Royal Town Planning Institute (2012f)

Licentiate membership

This category is open to those students who have satisfied the institute's educational requirements and hold a fully accredited qualification. Although it provides the same tangible benefits to student membership, becoming a licentiate is an essential first step in the Assessment of Professional Competence (APC). This is the route that the institute sets for becoming a chartered member. It requires you to undertake a period of practical experience, which needs to be structured, mentored and sufficiently monitored, and to continuously reflect on how your learning and personal development can continue (RTPI, 2013). Before we say some more about the APC process it is worth stepping back to think about what we mean when we refer to being 'reflective'.

Becoming a reflective learner

While the concluding sentence of the previous paragraph may have got you thinking, the need for you to be reflective should actually be quite familiar to you. It is something that your course will inevitably touch upon, and it is something that we have tried to do through the discussion and activities of this book. For example, the activity set out in Table 2.1 required you to *reflect* upon perceived confidence in relation to a range of study skills, such as your ability to meet deadlines or to lead a team. A similar assessment was also required implicitly through the activity set out in Table 13.1, although the emphasis here was very much on logging your achievements and demonstrating where particular skills and activities had been tested. Finally, in turning back to the activity included in Table 2.1, we also encouraged you to reflect upon the conclusions you had made to generate some kind of action. You will remember that we asked you to identify four areas where you thought action was needed and to consider the type of things you could proactively do to strengthen your capabilities and your general level of confidence.

In planning these future steps you might have discussed possible actions with family or friends, or possibly asked your programme team for help. Equally, you may have gone to the library to follow up on some of our suggested reading or perhaps taken advantage of another opportunity that has come your way (such as your university arranging a seminar on report writing).

Taking part in this type of reflection is not easy in that you often have to return to an experience or an event that you would rather forget. For example, you might have to think back to the report that was failed by one of your lecturers, or to the presentation in which you were unable to speak for more than half of the allotted time. However, it is these types of experience that are most useful in helping you to learn and to avoid the same things happening again. So, in relation to the disastrous presentation you could ask yourself:

- Did I stop because I ran out of time? If so, why was that? Did I misunderstand the brief, did I cover material too quickly, or did I not do enough reading? Did other students do better and, if so, why?
- Did I stop because of feeling panicked in speaking publically? Would further practice have helped? Should I have used some better prompts to keep me on track? Was I distracted in some way and, if so, how could these be limited in the future?
- Did I stop because of some other reason? Was I feeling unwell? If that is the case then perhaps the issue was a one-off and I do not need to worry to any great extent?

A number of authors have written about this process of reflection, with Kolb's learning cycle being a commonly cited model (Kolb, 1984). While the model is not without its critics, it is useful for introducing the relationship between how we might think and learn. The model has four phases:

- A 'concrete' experience, such as the presentation that we spoke about above.
- Reflective observation, in terms of the type of questions we posed above in relation to why the presentation did not go to plan.
- Abstract conceptualisation, where you are attempting to make some kind of generalisation by distilling and assimilating your observations and reflections of the experience (e.g. I just do not like speaking in public).
- Active experimentation, where you are developing plans and actions for the future to ensure that your next experience is repeated with greater success.

Becoming a reflective practitioner

While the ability to reflect is recognised as a key educational skill, it is also seen as an important tool for professional development (Bolton, 2010). Schön (1987) identifies the importance of becoming a 'reflective practitioner' which Kitchen (2006) interprets it as someone who:

> seeks constantly to think about and try to learn from his or her own experiences and those of colleagues so that personal and contextual understanding develop continuously. (2006: 153)

Kitchen (2006) identifies reflection as an important tool for helping a professional adapt and to positively embrace change. This type of change is likely to be wide-ranging in one's career but could require reflections on starting a new job, changing your employer, or responding to some kind of new policy or initiative. Equally the need to reflect may also relate to some of the skills or attributes that we have introduced through this book. The reality is that nobody is perfect; even the most successful practitioner would have to acknowledge certain scenarios where they could have performed better in some way. For example, perhaps they could have phrased a certain point slightly clearer, or kept to budget a little closer, or managed junior staff rather more effectively. Consequently, Kitchen explains how:

> developing the skills and habits of a reflective practitioner is not just about being a good professional; it is also about being a better-performing professional, and about achieving better outcomes for our customers [of planning]. (2006: 155)

The process of learning is therefore never-ending. Although the quote could be construed as representing some kind of thought process that the practitioner undertakes alone, it is clear that some external support is needed as well. Consequently, in a similar vein to what you might have done (or be doing) as a student, the practitioner will probably choose to speak with colleagues, engage with external support networks, refer to relevant literature and resources, or undertake some kind of training or education. These actions can be planned fairly informally but it is clearly better, as we have explained through this book, to develop a fuller plan that sets clear and measurable goals and objectives.

tip

Referring to best-practice advice is clearly useful in highlighting scenarios or examples that have worked well. Many of these guides include useful sections on 'lessons learnt' or toolkits for identifying how a process could be better managed. The Planning Advisory Service (PAS) is a particularly useful source which provides a variety of information on a range of topics. Have a look at their website: www.pas.gov.uk.

The Assessment of Professional Competence (APC)

These reflective principles are embedded in the Assessment of Professional Competence which is a structured programme of work-based learning that concludes with a competence-based assessment (RTPI, 2012c). The APC process essentially seeks to test the extent to which you, as a graduate of a planning degree, have been able to build upon your time at university. Essentially the process requires you to reflect, and make a record of the knowledge, understanding, skills and competences that you have been able to acquire through your practical experiences in 'spatial planning'. In explaining what is meant by the term competence, the institute explains how this is achieved through the improvement of an individual's skills and knowledge. The guidance defines knowledge as learning about 'concepts, principles and information', and a skill as the ability to use that information and apply it in a context (RTPI, 2012c). Although we have already set out a number of skills intrinsic to planning, the guidance for APC presents a list that candidates are encouraged to refer to during the recording process. Broad headings include:

- Creative vision
- Project management
- Problem-solving
- Leadership
- Collaborative and multi-disciplinary working
- Communication
- Stakeholder management and conflict resolution
  (RTPI, 2012c: 10)

Overall, the APC process seeks to:

- foster independent learning and career direction
- raise standards of professional competence
- empower graduates to drive their own development
- encourage networking and participation
- instil a habit of lifelong learning and continuing professional development
  (RTPI, 2012c)

While you should check the RTPI's website for information on the APC process, the current guidance (January 2013) outlines four key elements (RTPI, 2013). These will be considered in turn below.

1. Experience. To be eligible for APC you must undertake a minimum amount of professional experience. This is currently set at two full-time years of employment (440 working days). Of this, at least one year must have been achieved following graduation from an RTPI-accredited course. The current guidance stipulates how this experience must be achieved in spatial planning but this is defined quite broadly in terms of encompassing:

   o the preparation of plans, policies and related tasks: you might be involved in helping to outline and compose the evidence base of a plan, or consulting the community about initial ideas

   o plan implementation: you might be required to assess a planning application if you work in a local planning authority, or be asked to prepare a planning submission on behalf of a client if you are working in the private sector

- monitoring and research: you may be involved in monitoring the discharge of planning conditions or legal obligations
- teaching: you may have some kind of teaching experience post university.

It is probably likely that you will need to be a licentiate for at least two years while you acquire the experience required. However, if you were able to gain relevant employment in advance of satisfying the institute's educational requirements then you can be a licentiate for a shorter period of time by using this experience towards your APC. This means that you can use experience gained whilst on a sandwich or vacation placement but the job should have lasted for a minimum of three months. Experience can be gained in either the UK or overseas.

2. A mentor, who can provide support and advice as you progress with the APC. You do not have to have a mentor but if you do have one then they must be a chartered member of the institute. A mentor could be someone you work with (such as your line-manager), or possibly someone quite separate from your current position in work (e.g. you could approach one of your former lecturers).

3. A log book, which needs to comprise a written record of the work you have completed and the skills you have been able to develop over the course of the experience period. The log book therefore forms an important and fundamental part of the learning and reflection that will develop your competences as a professional planner. The document should provide an accurate record of the experience you have gained, starting from your election as a licentiate up to the point of submission. The log book underpins your final submission (see below) in that it must cover any projects and competencies that are referred to in the final submission. Significantly, your log book might be used by the assessors of your final submission if they are keen to learn more about the examples or projects you are referring to.

   The institute offers a downloadable template via its website to help create this log book. This includes space for giving details of:

- the nature of the professional activity, which should be factual and not too generic
- the skills that this activity allowed to be developed
- the knowledge and understanding gained from the activity
- the type of development you feel you need in the future to further enhance these skills and your knowledge and understanding.

Importantly your log book needs to be corroborated by the person or persons who have employed or supervised you during the entire period of the experience. Further detail on this process is set out in the RTPI's guidance but essentially one or a number of corroborating statements must be supplied with your final APC submission.

It is important to keep your log book regularly updated and safely stored for two reasons. The first part is essential for encouraging the type of critical reflection you need for undertaking the professional development planning that we will discuss below. The second aspect is equally important – remember to regularly back up your work. Just imagine the task you would need to complete if the file containing your log book became corrupted during the latter stages of your professional experience.

4. A professional development plan (PDP), which should be created as soon as you become a licentiate. A PDP is a common tool which is used throughout education and employment. As the Quality Assurance Agency for Higher Education (QAA) explains:

> The primary objectives of PDP are to enhance the capacity of learners to reflect, plan and take responsibility for their own learning and to understand what and how they learn. PDP is based on the skills of reflection and planning which are integral to knowing how to learn in different contexts and to transfer that learning throughout life. (QAA, 2009: 5)

PDP is more about the process than the final product but a physical record is useful for setting milestones for what needs to be achieved, and for discussing these requirements with others. With regards to APC, the institute explains how your plan should be individual to you; be kept under review; and be regularly updated to provide a framework for your development. The guidance explains how your PDP must cover three essential elements:

i. What have I learnt in my career to date?
ii. What direction do I want my career to take?
iii. How will I get there?

Again the RTPI provides a template that can be used to develop this plan but whatever you create the output must be clearly presented, understandable, and thorough (RTPI, 2013: 19). The plan must also consist of:

o a SWOT analysis, i.e. you must outline your strengths and weaknesses and the opportunities and threats that might affect your future development. This SWOT analysis should lead to a current PDP for the forthcoming two-year period
o your goals and objectives for the next two years. A goal is defined as a broad statement of what you want to achieve. It should specify the end result. Your objectives are the type of outcomes that will help you achieve your goals
o an action plan on how you intend to achieve these objectives. Questions you need to ask yourself to do this include: What will be done? Who will do it? How will it be done? When will it happen? (RTPI, 2013).

When you are preparing your PDP it is important that you use the SMART model to ensure that your objectives are Specific, Measurable, Achievable, Relevant and Time-based.

Preparing your APC application

Once you have accumulated the necessary experience you will be in a position to submit your APC. Submissions are currently invited at four points across the year with specific deadlines being provided via the institute's website. Again you will need to consult the RTPI's guidance for making a submission, not only in advance of making the submission but as you commence as a licentiate. However, with that caveat set, the latest guidance requires each submission to comprise:

- A completed application form and APC application cover sheet, both of which are available to be downloaded from the institute's website.
- A written submission of 5,000 words (+/– 10%) which comprises:
  - a Practical Experience Statement (PES) summarising your experiences by drawing from your log book;
  - a Professional Competence Statement (PCS), which builds upon the above and requires you to take a critical and analytical approach in setting out your professional competencies. The guidance explains how including a couple of case studies is a useful way for outlining this information;
  - a Professional Development Plan (PDP) which should respond to your PCS and set a strategy for supporting your continuing development. This element has been considered above;
  - a log book, which, as explained above, should detail the practical experience undertaken;
  - a sponsor declaration, to endorse your application; and
  - corroboration statements relating to your work experience.

Each submission is assessed by two chartered planners with a decision coming after eight weeks. If your application is successful, and you are adjudged to have passed the APC, then you will be allowed to call yourself a chartered town planner and use the letters 'MRTPI' after your name.

A lifetime of learning

As we have noted already, learning is a lifelong activity; this is certainly the case when you become a professional planner (see RTPI, 2011). All members of the RTPI (except for students and those who have retired) make a commitment to maintain and develop their expertise through Continuing Professional Development (CPD). We have touched upon this term already but it is defined by the RTPI as the:

> systematic maintenance, improvement and broadening of knowledge and skill and the development of personal qualities necessary for the execution of professional and technical duties throughout the practitioners working life. (RTPI, 2012d)

The institute's current regulations state how members must:

- annually spend at least an hour preparing a PDP plan, to help define development needs for the next two years
- undertake and record a minimum of 50 hours of CPD activity in any two-year period

- record the type of CPD and the number of hours for each activity
- reflect on, and explain, the value of each CPD activity and the relationship between this and the member's PDP
- submit their records when required to do so by the RTPI (specifically, a copy of the DPD covering the previous two years, a copy of their current DPD, a written record of their CPD activity and, where necessary, a written explanation detailing the reasons for why they have not been able to meet certain CPD requirements).
  (RTPI, 2012e)

The role of the PDP is once again a fundamental element to this since the objectives and needs you set out in your plan have a bearing as to what constitutes CPD. For instance, attending an all day conference on a subject upon which you are already an expert may not constitute CPD; you are likely to be restricted to recording the time that you spent listening and reflecting upon an item or session that was new to you which you purposefully went out to seek.

The RTPI provides a template by which CPD can be recorded. This can be downloaded but steps are being taken to provide an opportunity for information to be entered and stored online. The existing template is fairly simple in that it requires you to make a note of:

- the CPD event, with appropriate details of its title and general content
- when and where the CPD was undertaken
- the benefit that accrued from the event, in terms of CPD and its relationship to your PDP
- an indication of the number of hours spent.

With respect to recording details about the type of CPD undertaken, the RTPI provides some coded categories which members are expected to look at. These categories include:

- home-based learning
- action-based learning (where a work-based issue is identified with subsequent action taken to help find a solution)
- the preparation of material for courses, technical meetings or publications in the technical press
- supervised and academic research
- background reading, research or preparation required in order to approach a new area of work
- RTPI activities of a technical or professional nature
- conferences, seminars, workshops and other technical and professional events and meetings
- courses leading to a qualification
- other forms of CPD (this needs to be explained on a case-by-case basis)
  (RTPI, 2012f: 5–6)

Conclusions

In this chapter we have begun to focus on the stages of professional development that you will need to complete if you are to become a professional member of the Royal Town Planning Institute. It has offered a summary of the broad steps that you will need to take as a 'licentiate' member and has identified the importance of continuing professional development in the context of a wider strategy for education and lifelong learning.

Review points

When reflecting on this chapter you might consider the following:

- the opportunities for engaging with your profession as a student, by becoming a member of the Royal Town Planning Institute (together with the other groups and associations outlined in Box 3.4)
- the importance of lifelong learning to your development as a professional planner
- the need to take a reflective approach to your experiences in planning
- the role for professional development planning and the association that this has with continuing professional development.

Further reading

You should visit the website of the RTPI for the latest details about the process for completing the Assessment of Professional Competence. This same website also outlines the expectations that exist for continuing professional development. At the time of press, detailed information on the APC process is set out in two very useful documents:

- Royal Town Planning Institute (RTPI) (2012c) *Becoming a chartered town planner: A guide for licentiates*. London: RTPI.
- Royal Town Planning Institute (RTPI) (2013) *Preparing your APC submission: 2013 guidelines*. London: RTPI.

The following document outlines the expectations concerning continuing professional development:

- Royal Town Planning Institute (RTPI) (2012f) *Professional conduct advice note one: Continuing professional development*. London: RTPI.

A number of more general texts focus on the need to become a reflective practitioner. Some good examples include:

- Bolton, G. (2010) *Reflective practice: writing and professional development.* London: Sage.
- Schön, D. (1991) *The reflective practitioner: How professionals think in action.* Farnham: Ashgate Publishing Limited.
- Thompson, S. and Thompson, N. (2008) *The critically reflective practitioner.* Basingstoke: Palgrave Macmillan.

Appendix One

Key books on town and country planning

Allmendinger, P. (2009) *Planning theory*. Second ed. Basingstoke: Palgrave Macmillan.

Barton, H., Grant, M. and Guise, R. (2010) *Shaping neighbourhoods: For local health and global sustainability*. London: Routledge.

Booth, P (2003) *Planning by consent: The origins and nature of British development control*. London: Routledge.

Carmona, M., Heath, T., Oc, T. and Tiesdell, S. (2010) *Public places urban spaces: The dimensions of urban design*. London: Architectural Press.

Clifford, B. and Tewdwr-Jones, M. (2013) *The collaborating planner? Practitioners in the neoliberal age*. Bristol: Policy Press.

Cullingworth, B. and Nadin, V. (2006) *Town and country planning in the UK*. Fourteenth ed. London: Routledge.

Dimitrou, H. and Thompson, R. (2007) *Strategic planning for regional development in the UK*. London: Routledge.

Dühr, S., Colomb, C. and Nadin, V. (2010) *European spatial planning and territorial cooperation*. London: Routledge.

Fainstein, S. (2011) *Readings in urban theory*. Third ed. Chichester: Wiley-Blackwell.

Gallent, N. and Tewdwr-Jones, M. (2006) *Decent homes for all: Reviewing planning's role in housing provision*. London: Routledge.

Gallent, N., Juntti, M., Kidd, S. and Shaw, D., eds (2008) *Introduction to rural planning (the natural and built environment series)*. London: Routledge.

Gehl, J. (2010) *Cities for people*. Washington: Island Press.

Gibbs, R. (2011) *Principles of urban retail planning and development*. London: John Wiley and Sons.

Gilg, A. (2005) *Planning in Britain: Understanding and evaluating the post-war system*. London: Sage.

Glasson, J, Therivel, R. and Chadwick, A. (2011) *Introduction to environmental impact assessment (natural and built environment series)*. London: Routledge.

Hall, P. (2002) *Cities of tomorrow: An intellectual history of urban planning and design in the twentieth century*. Third ed. Chichester: Wiley-Blackwell.

Hall, P. and Tewdwr-Jones, M. (2010) *Urban and regional planning*. Fifth ed. London: Routledge.

Headicar, P. (2009) *Transport policy and planning in Great Britain*. London: Routledge.

Healey, P. (2010) *Making better places: the planning project in the twenty-first century*. Basingstoke: Palgrave Macmillan.

Hull, A. (2010) *Transport matters: Integrated approaches to planning city-regions*. London: Routledge.

Isaac, D., O'Leary, J., and Daley, M. (2010) *Property development: Appraisal and finance (building and surveying series)*. Basingstoke: Palgrave Macmillan.

LeGates, R. (ed.) (2011) *The city reader*. Fifth ed. London: Routledge.

Marshall, T. (2012) *Planning major infrastructure: A critical analysis*. London: Routledge.

Moor, N. (2011) *The look and shape of England*. London: The Book Guild.

Moore, V and Purdue, M. (2012) *A practical approach to planning law*. Twelfth ed. Oxford: Oxford University Press.

Morphet, J. (2010) *Effective practice in spatial planning*. London: Routledge.

Morphet, J. (2013) *How Europe shapes British public policy*. Bristol: Policy Press.

Morris, A. (1994) *A history of urban form: Before the industrial revolutions*. London: Longman.

Pacione, M. (2009) *Urban geography: A global perspective*. Third ed. London: Routledge.

Parker, G. and Doak, J. (2012) *Key concepts in planning (key concepts in human geography)*. London: Sage.

Ratcliffe, J., Stubbs M. and Shepherd, M. (2009) *Urban planning and real estate development*. Third ed. London: Routledge Press.

Rudlin, D. and Falk, N. (2009) *Sustainable urban neighbourhood: Building the 21st century home*. London: Architectural Press.

Rydin, Y. (2011) *The purpose of planning: Creating sustainable towns and cities*. Bristol: The Policy Press.

Squires, G. (2012) *Urban and environmental economics*. London: Routledge.

Tallon, A. (2013) *Urban regeneration in the UK*. Second ed. London: Routledge.

Taylor, N. (1998) *Urban planning theory since 1945*. London: Sage.

Tewdwr-Jones, M. (2012) *Spatial planning and governance*. Basingstoke: Palgrave Macmillan.

Ward, C. (2004) *Planning and urban change*. Second ed. London: Sage.

Wates, N. and Thompson, J. (2008) *The community planning event manual: How to use collaborative planning and urban design events to improve your environment (tools for community planning)*. London: Routledge.

Williams, J. (2011) *Zero-carbon homes: A road map*. London: Routledge.

Wilson, E. and Piper, J. (eds.) (2010) *Spatial planning and climate change (natural and built environment series)*. London: Routledge.

Appendix Two

Key journals associated with town and country planning

Annals of the Association of American Geographers (Routledge)
Applied Geography (Elsevier)
Area (Wiley)
Cities (Elsevier)
City, Culture and Society (Elsevier)
Coastal Management (Taylor & Francis)
Conservation and Sustainability in Historic Cities (Wiley)
Cultural Geographies (Sage)
Environment and Planning A (Pion)
Environment and Planning B: Planning and Design (Pion)
Environment and Planning C: Government and Policy (Pion)
Environment and Planning D: Society and Space (Pion)
European Planning Studies (Routledge)
European Urban and Regional Studies (Sage)
Gender, Place and Culture (Routledge)
Geoforum (Elsevier)
Geopolitics (Routledge)
Housing Studies (Routledge)
International Journal of Urban Sustainable Development (Taylor & Francis)
International Planning Studies (Routledge)
Irish Geography (Routledge)
Journal of Cultural Geography (Routledge)
Journal of Developing Studies (Sage)
Journal of Environment Planning and Management (Routledge)
Journal of Environmental Policy and Planning (Routledge)
Journal of Historical Geography (Elsevier)
Journal of Planning Education and Research (Sage)
Journal of Planning History (Sage)
Journal of Rural Studies (Elsevier)

Journal of the American Planning Association (Routledge)
Journal of Town and City Management (Henry Stewart Publications)
Journal of Urban Affairs (Wiley)
Journal of Urban Design (Routledge)
Journal of Urbanism (Routledge)
Journal of Urban Regeneration and Renewal (Henry Stewart)
Land Use Policy (Elsevier)
Local Environment (Routledge)
Planning Perspectives (Routledge)
Planning Practice and Research (Routledge)
Planning Theory and Practice (Routledge)
Population Studies (Routledge)
Progress in Human Geography (Sage)
Progress in Planning (Elsevier)
Regional Studies (Routledge)
Social and Cultural Geography (Routledge)
Sociologia Ruralis (Wiley)
Sustainable Cities and Society (Elsevier)
The Geographical Journal (Wiley)
The Journal of Environment and Development (Sage)
The Professional Geographer (Routledge)
Tourism Geographies (Routledge)
Town Planning Review (Liverpool University Press)
Transactions of the Institute of British Geographers (Wiley)
Transport Reviews (Routledge)
Transportation Planning and Technology (Routledge)
Urban Affairs Review (Sage)
Urban Policy and Research (Routledge)
Urban Studies (Sage)

Appendix Three

Useful websites relating to town and country planning

A general A to Z

- ATLAS (planning for large scale development): http://www.atlasplanning.com/page/index.cfm
- Association of National Park Authorities: http://www.nationalparks.gov.uk
- Building Research Establishment: http://www.bre.co.uk/
- Campaign for Better Transport: http://www.bettertransport.org.uk/
- Chartered Institute of Logistics and Transport in the UK – CILT(UK): http://www.ciltuk.org.uk/pages/home
- Community Planning: http://communityplanning.net/
- Design Council CABE: http://www.designcouncil.org.uk/our-work/CABE/
- GOV.UK: https://www.gov.uk
- European Parliament: http://www.europarl.europa.eu
- European Union: http://europa.eu/
- Institute of Environmental Management and Assessment: http://www.iema.net/
- Local Transport Planning Network: http://www.ltpnetwork.gov.uk/
- Office for National Statistics Authority: http://ons.gov.uk/ons/index.html
- Planning Advisory Service: http://www.pas.gov.uk/pas/core/page.do?pageId=1
- Planning Aid: http://www.rtpi.org.uk/planning-aid/
- Planning Portal: http://www.planningportal.gov.uk
- Planning Resource: http://www.planningresource.co.uk/home/
- Planning for Sustainable Travel: http://www.plan4sustainabletravel.org/
- Regeneration and Renewal: http://www.regen.net/
- Resource for Urban Design Information: http://www.rudi.net/
- Royal Geographical Association: http://www.rgs.org/HomePage.htm
- Royal Institution of Chartered Surveyors: http://rics.org/
- Royal Town Planning Institute: www.rtpi.org.uk
- Town and Country Planning Association: www.tcpa.org.uk
- Transport Planning Society: http://www.tps.org.uk/
- United Nations Statistical Division: http://unstats.un.org/unsd/default.htm
- Urban Design Group: http://www.udg.org.uk/

UK government departments

(The jurisdiction of each of these departments and bodies varies in response to the devolution of UK policy. Coverage often varies with the specific policy being covered. You should check the coverage of relevant policy by referring to the websites listed here.)

- (Department for) Business, Innovation and Skills: http://www.bis.gov.uk/ (United Kingdom)
- Cabinet Office: http://www.cabinetoffice.gov.uk (United Kingdom)
- (Department for) Communities and Local Government: http://www.communities.gov.uk (England)
- (Department for) Culture, Media and Sport: http://www.culture.gov.uk/ (England)
- (Department for) Energy and Climate Change: http://www.decc.gov.uk/ (United Kingdom)
- English Heritage: http://www.english-heritage.org.uk/ (England)
- Environment Agency: http://www.environment-agency.gov.uk/ (England and Wales)
- (Department for) Environment, Food and Rural Affairs: http://www.defra.gov.uk/ (United Kingdom)
- Forestry Commission: http://www.forestry.gov.uk (Great Britain)
- (Department of) Health: http://www.dh.gov.uk/en/ (United Kingdom)
- The Highways Agency: http://www.highways.gov.uk/ (England)
- Historic Scotland: http://www.historic-scotland.gov.uk/index.htm (Scotland)
- Homes and Communities Agency: http://www.homesandcommunities.co.uk (England)
- (Department for) International Development: http://www.dfid.gov.uk (United Kingdom)
- (Her Majesty's) Land Registry: http://www1.landregistry.gov.uk/genq/ (England and Wales)
- Ordnance Survey: http://www.ordnancesurvey.co.uk (Great Britain)
- The National Archives: http://www.nationalarchives.gov.uk (United Kingdom)
- National Assembly for Wales: http://www.assemblywales.org (Wales)
- Natural England: http://www.naturalengland.org.uk (England)
- Northern Ireland Assembly: http://www.niassembly.gov.uk/
- Northern Ireland Planning Portal: http://www.planningni.gov.uk/ (Northern Ireland)
- Planning Inspectorate: http://www.planning-inspectorate.gov.uk (England); http://planninginspectorate.wales.gov.uk (Wales)
- Scottish Environment Protection Agency: http://sepa.org.uk/ (Scotland)
- Scottish Government (Planning): http://www.scotland.gov.uk/Topics/Built-Environment/planning (Scotland)
- The Scottish Parliament: http://www.scottish.parliament.uk/index.aspx (Scotland)
- Statistics Authority, UK: http://www.statisticsauthority.gov.uk (United Kingdom)
- (Department for) Transport: http://www.dft.gov.uk (England and Wales)
- Transport Scotland: www.transportscotland.gov.uk (Scotland)
- Welsh Government: http://wales.gov.uk (Wales)
- Welsh Government (Heritage): http://cadw.wales.gov.uk/?lang=en (Wales)
- Welsh Government (Planning): http://wales.gov.uk/topics/planning/?lang=en (Wales)

Appendix Four

How do I reference...

An Act of Parliament (Statutes)

Great Britain. *Name of Act. Chapter number.* (Year of publication) Place of publication: Publisher.

E.g.:

Great Britain. *Local Democracy, Economic Development and Construction Act. Chapter 20.* (2009) London: The Stationary Office.

A book

Author's surname, Author's initial. (Year of publication) *Title.* Edition (if it is not the first). Place of publication: Publisher.

E.g.:

Rydin, Y. (2011) *The Purpose of planning: Creating sustainable towns and cities.* Bristol: Policy Press.

An electronic book

Author's surname, Author's initial. (Year of publication) *Title* [online]. Edition (if it is not the first). Place of publication: Publisher. [Accessed DD Month YYYY]

E.g.:

Hall, P. and Tewdwr-Jones, M. (2010) *Urban and regional planning* [online]. Fifth ed. London: Routledge. [Accessed 10 August 2012]

A book chapter

Author's surname, Author's initial. (Year of publication) 'Book chapter title'. In Author's surname, Author's initial., *Title of Book.* Place of publication: Publisher, page numbers.

E.g.:

Shaftoe, H. and Tallon, A. (2009) 'Bristol: not a design-led renaissance'. In Punter, J., *Urban design and the British urban renaissance*. London: Routledge, pp. 115–131.

An official command paper ('white' and 'green' publications issued by the UK Government) or departmental paper

Country. Name of Committee, Department or Royal Commission (Year of publication) *Title*. Place of publication: Publisher. (Paper number)

E.g.:

Great Britain. Department of Communities and Local Government (2012) *Re-imagining urban spaces to help revitalise our high streets*. Department for Communities and Local Government.

Great Britain. Secretary of State for Foreign and Commonwealth Affairs (2012) *Review of the balance of competences between the United Kingdom and the European Union* [online]. London: The Stationary Office. (Cm 8415)

A House of Commons/House of Lords paper

Country. Parliament. Name of House. Name of Committee (if applies) (Year of publication) *Title*. Place of publication: Publisher. (HC/HL paper number YYYY/YYYY)

E.g.:

Great Britain. Parliament. House of Commons (2012) *Olympic Delivery Authority Annual Report and Accounts 2011–12*. London: The Stationary Office. (HC 0321 2012–13)

A conference paper

Author's surname, Author's initial. (Year of publication) 'Title of conference paper/contribution'. In Editor Surname, initials., ed. *Title of Conference Proceedings*. Place of conference, date of conference. Place of publication (if known): Publisher, page numbers.

E.g.:

Gehl, Y. (2010) 'People cities = sustainable cities'. In Naidu, D. ed. *Liveable and Sustainable Cities for the Future: World Cities Summit*. Singapore, 28 June to 1 July. Singapore: Centre for Liveable Cities, pp. 81–2.

Discussion Group

Listname/Groupname/Board [online] (Year of latest update). Available from: URL. [Accessed DD Month YYYY]

E.g.:

Royal Town Planning Institute LinkedIn (2012). Available from: http://www.linkedin.com/ groups?gid=3036245&trk=myg_ugrp_ovr. [Accessed 10 August 2012]

A (student) dissertation

Author's surname, initials. (Year of publication) *Title of Thesis, Dissertation or Project*. Level of qualification, Name of University.

E.g.:

Crellen, J. (2012) *Do the principles underpinning Sharp's 1946 reconstruction plan have relevance to the future of Exeter?* BA (Hons) Town and Country Planning, University of the West of England.

A film or one-off TV programme

Title of programme (Year of first broadcast) [TV]. Directed by Directors name. Channel of first broadcast, Day and Month of first broadcast.

E.g.:

The Truth about Climate Change (2008) [TV]. Directed by Sir David Attenborough. BBC1, 11 November.

A journal article

In print:

Author's surname, Author's initial. (Year of publication) 'Title of the article'. *Journal Title*. Volume no.(Part no.): page numbers.

E.g.:

Vigar, G. and Healey, P. (2010) 'Territorial integration and plan-led planning'. *Planning Practice and Research*. 14(2): 153–69.

Electronic format:

Author's surname, Author's initial (Year) Title of the article. *Journal Title* [online]. Volume no.(Part no.): page numbers if available. [Accessed DD Month YYYY]

E.g.:

Pendlebury, J. and Strange, I. (2011) 'Urban conservation and the shaping of the English city'. *Town Planning Review* [online]. 82(4): 361–92. [Accessed 10 August 2012]

A map

Corporate author or publisher (Year of publication) *Title,* sheet number, scale. Place of publication: Publisher. (Series).

E.g.:

Ordnance Survey (2007) *Bristol and Bath (OS Explorer Map Series): Keynsham and Marshfield*, sheet 155, 1:25,000. Southampton: Ordnance Survey.

Minutes of a meeting

Author's surname, Author's initial. (Individual or group if identified) (Year of meeting) 'Item being referenced'. *Title and DD Month of Meeting*, Organisation, Location of Meeting.

E.g.:

Alexander, L. (2012) 'Provision of gypsy and traveller sites'. *Minutes of Full Council Meeting 17 June*, Bristol City Council, Bristol.

A newspaper article

Where the author is known:

Author's surname, Author's initial. (Year of publication) 'Title of the article'. *Title of Newspaper*. Day and Month of publication, page number of article (if given).

E.g.:

Harvey, F. (2012) 'Europe looking for a shortcut in race for resources'. The *Guardian*. 1 August, p. 18.

In an electronic format:

Author's surname, Author's initial. (Year of publication) 'Title of article'. Title of Newspaper [online]. Day and Month of publication, page number of article (if given). Available from: URL. [Accessed DD Month YYYY]

E.g.:

Goldenberg, S. (2012) 'Climate change the cause of summer's extreme weather, Congress told'. The Guardian [online]. 1 August. Available from: http://www.guardian.co.uk/environment/2012/aug/01/climate-change-extreme-weather-congress. [Accessed 02 August 2012]

Podcast

Author's surname, Author's initial. (Year of posting) 'Title of the podcast'. Title of the website [podcast]. Available from: URL. [Accessed DD Month YYYY]

E.g.:

Blyth, R. (2012) 'Why we need a map for England'. Recent podcasts from the RTPI [podcast]. Available from: http://www.rtpi.org.uk/briefing-room/podcasts/#2031. [Accessed 02 August 2012]

Reports

Author's surname, Author's initial. / Organisation (Year of publication) *Report title.* Place of Publication: Publisher.E.g.:

Savills (2012) *UK shopping centre and high street bulletin: quarter three.* London: Savills.

Websites

Author's surname, Author's initial. / Organisation (Year of publication or last update) 'Title of website'. Available from: URL. [Accessed DD Month YYYY]

E.g.:

Town and Country Planning Association (2012) 'Planning and climate change coalition'. Available from: http://www.tcpa.org.uk/pages/climate-coalition.html. [Accessed 02 August 2012]

References

Academy for Sustainable Communities (2007) *Mind the skills gap: The skills we need for sustainable communities*. Leeds: ASC.

Adair, John (2003) in N. Thomas (ed.) *'Concise Adair on communication and presentation skills'*. London: Thorogood.

Adair, J (2009) *Effective teambuilding: How to make a winning team*. London: Pan Macmillan.

Aldridge, A. and Levine, K. (2001) *Surveying the social world: Principles and practice in survey research*. Maidenhead: Open University Press.

Arnstein, S. (1969) 'A ladder of citizen participation'. *JAIP*, 35(4) July: 216–24.

Belbin, M. (2010) *Team roles at work*. Oxford: Butterworth-Heinmann.

Bell, J. (2010) *Doing your research project: A guide for first-time researchers in education, health and the social sciences*. Fifth ed. Maidenhead: Open University Press.

Bolton, G. (2010) *Reflective practice: Writing and professional development*. London: Sage.

Booth, P. (2003) *Planning by consent: The origins and nature of British development control*. London: Routledge.

Burns, T. and Sinfield, S. (2012) *Essential study skills: The complete guide to success at university*. Third ed. London: Sage.

Collins, J. and More, P. (2009) *Negotiating the planning maze*. London: Royal Institute of British Architects.

Cottrell, S. (2008) *The study skills handbook*. Third ed. Basingstoke: Palgrave Macmillan.

DCLG (2011) *'Neighbourhood planning – frequently asked questions'* [online]. Available from: http://www.communities.gov.uk/documents/planningandbuilding/pdf/2099152.pdf. [Accessed 27 August 2012]

Hargie, O (2011) *Skilled interpersonal communication: Research, theory and practice*. Fifth ed. Hove: Routledge.

Hargie, O. Dickson, D and Toursih, D. (2004) *Communication skills for effective management*. Basingstoke: Palgrave Macmillan.

Innes, J. (2012a) *The cover letter book: Your definitive guide to writing the perfect cover letter*. Second ed. Harlow: Pearson Education.

Innes, J. (2012b) *The CV book: Your definitive guide to writing the perfect CV*. Second ed. Harlow: Pearson Education.

Innes, J. (2012c) *The interview book: Your definitive guide to the perfect interview*. Second ed. Harlow: Pearson Education.

Kalay, Y. (2004) *Architecture's new media*. Cambridge, MA: The MIT Press.

Kitchen, T. (2006) *Skills for planning practice*. London: Palgrave Macmillan.

Kolb, D. (1984) *Experiential learning experience as a source of learning and development*. Englewood Cliffs, NJ: Prentice Hall.

Library of Congress, The (2012a) *'Library of Congress classification outline'* [online]. Available from: http://www.loc.gov/catdir/cpso/lcco/ [Accessed 27 August 2012]

Library of Congress, The (2012b) *'Library of Congress classification outline – Subclass HT'* [online]. Available from: http://www.loc.gov/aba/cataloging/classification/lcco/lcco_h.pdf [Accessed 27 August 2012].

Marsen, S. (2007) *Professional writing*. Second ed. Basingstoke: Palgrave Macmillan.

Morley, I.E. (2006) 'Negotiating and bargaining' In: Hargie O. (eds) *The handbook of communication skills*. Third ed. London: Routledge.pp.403–26

OCLC (2011) *'Introduction to the Dewey Decimal Classification'* [online]. Available from: http://www.oclc.org/content/dam/oclc/dewey/versions/print/intro.pdf [Accessed 23 March 2013].

Ordnance Survey (2013) *Our history* [online]. Available from: http://www.ordnancesurvey.co.uk/oswebsite/about-us/our-history/index.html. [Accessed 23rd March 2013].

The Quality Assurance Agency (QAA) for Higher Education (2008) *Subject benchmark standards: Town and country planning*. Mansfield: QAA.

The Quality Assurance Agency (QAA) for Higher Education (2009) *Personal development planning: Guidance for institutional policy and practice in higher education*. Mansfield: QAA.

Redman, P. (2001) *Good essay writing: A social sciences guide*, Second ed. London: The Open University and Sage.

Robson, C. (2007) *How to do a research project: A guide for undergraduate students*. Oxford: Blackwell Publishing.

Rogers, C. (1962) 'The interpersonal relationship: the core of guidance'. *Harvard Educational Review*, 32(4) Fall: 416–29.

Royal Town Planning Institute (RTPI) (2001) *A new vision for planning: Delivering sustainable communities*. London: RTPI

Royal Town Planning Institute (RTPI) (2011) *The RTPI lifelong learning strategy 2011– 2014* [online]. Available from: http://www.rtpi.org.uk/media/1136707/The-RTPI-Lifelong-Learning-Strategy-2011-14.pdf. [Accessed 10 August 2012]

Royal Town Planning Institute (RTPI) (2012a) *What planning does* [online]. Available from: http://www.rtpi.org.uk/education-and-careers/learning-about-planning/what-planning-does/. [Accessed 10 August 2012]

Royal Town Planning Institute (RTPI) (2012b) *Policy statement on initial planning education*. London: RTPI.

Royal Town Planning Institute (RTPI) (2012c) *Becoming a chartered town planner: A guide for licentiates*. London: RTPI.

Royal Town Planning Institute (RTPI) (2012d) *CPD* [online]. Available from: http://www.rtpi.org.uk/education-and-careers/cpd/cpd/. [Accessed 10 August 2012]

Royal Town Planning Institute (RTPI) (2012e) *Requirements for CPD* [online]. Available from: http://www.rtpi.org.uk/education-and-careers/cpd/cpd/requirements-for-cpd/. [Accessed 10 August 2012]

Royal Town Planning Institute (RTPI) (2012f) *Professional conduct advice note one: Continuing professional development*. London: RTPI.

Royal Town Planning Institute (RTPI) (2013) *Preparing your APC submission: 2013 guidelines*. London: RTPI.

Schön, D. (1987) *Educating the reflective practitioner: Toward a new design for teaching and learning in the professions*. San Francisco: Jossey-Bass.

Yin, R. (2008) *Case study research: Design and methods*. Fourth ed. Thousand Oaks, CA: Sage Publications Inc.

Index